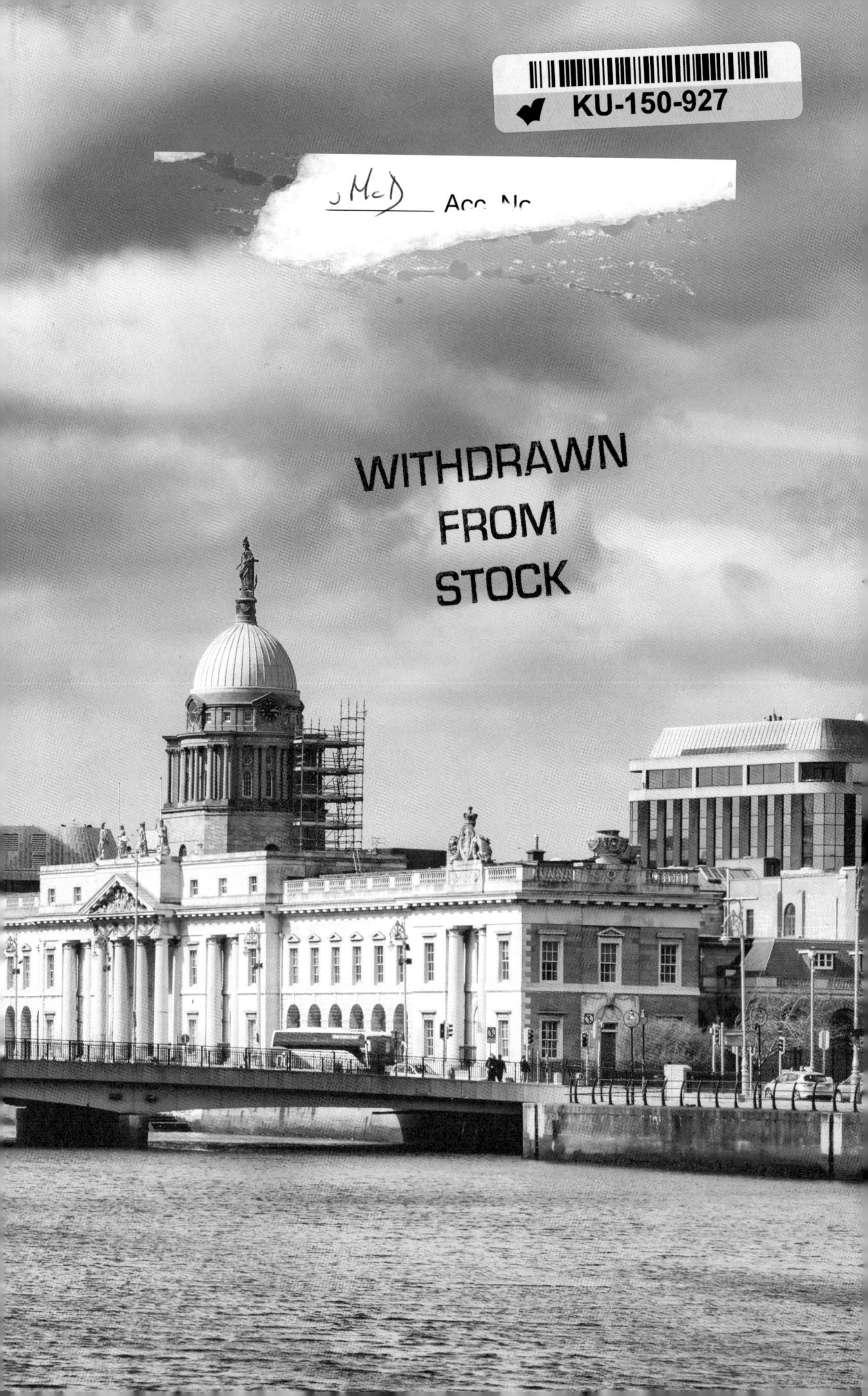

KU-150-927

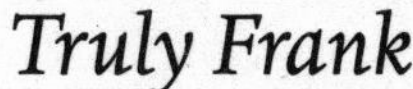

Truly Frank

Truly Frank

A Dublin Memoir

FRANK McDONALD

PENGUIN
IRELAND

PENGUIN IRELAND

UK | USA | Canada | Ireland | Australia
India | New Zealand | South Africa

Penguin Ireland is part of the Penguin Random House group of companies whose addresses can be found at global.penguinrandomhouse.com.

First published 2018
001

Set in 12/14.75 pt Dante MT Std
Typeset by Jouve (UK), Milton Keynes
Printed and bound in Great Britain by Clays Ltd, Elcograf S.p.A.

A CIP catalogue record for this book is available from the British Library

ISBN: 978–1–844–88380–6

To Eamon with love,
and in fond memory of my parents,
Maura and William McDonald

On Saturday 23 May 2015, I was sitting out on the roof terrace of our apartment building in Temple Bar, overlooked only by the Central Bank of Ireland. The sun was shining and, from a few hundred metres away, I could hear waves of clapping and cheering from a large and delighted crowd in the courtyard of Dublin Castle. Later on, after it was announced that the Irish people had voted overwhelmingly in a referendum to give same-sex couples the right to marry, there was the almost constant honking of car horns as the city centre turned delirious in celebrating a momentous event that provided extraordinary evidence of just how profoundly Ireland had changed.

It was only a few miles, but a much longer cultural journey, from where I had grown up in Dublin 7, in a devoutly Catholic home, with a holy-water font in the hall, a framed papal blessing above the mantelpiece, a small statue of the Child of Prague in the breakfast room, and a picture of the Sacred Heart in our parents' bedroom.

Of course, the influence of the Catholic Church was in every bedroom in Ireland in an even more powerful way. The State had prohibited the sale of contraceptives for many years, because the Church said it was wrong. There was no divorce in Ireland until 1996, because that was contrary to Catholic teaching too. And as for homosexual acts, until 1993 they remained crimes punishable by imprisonment, because they were seen by the Church as deeply sinful and – in Victorian language matching the era from which the law dated – an abomination. For people of my generation, it was clear from a young age that when it came to sex, who did what to whom, and how they did it, were matters of deep concern to the

Church and, if you got it wrong, you could end up in jail, and ultimately in Hell.

With me on that glorious May day, listening to the sound of change, was my life partner Eamon Slater. When we first met nearly four decades earlier, we had carefully concealed our attachment to each other in public. Friends of ours recently remarked on something I had never noticed – that old photos of us as a young couple, looking happy, were mostly taken on holidays abroad or within the four walls of our previous home in Harold's Cross. If you were gay in Ireland during the 1960s, '70s and '80s, you ducked and dived, you lied and covered up. (No more! Eamon and I got married a year after the referendum and had a large and joyful reception in the National Botanic Gardens.)

The popular vote for marriage equality in Ireland was one of the most personally significant and important signals of change in my lifetime – a huge milestone in a journey towards a very different, more secular society. By then, Ireland had changed in other dramatic ways. We grew out of an acceptance that economic stagnation and failure were natural states for us. Political corruption, deeply embedded in public life – and obvious to me from when I started working as a journalist – had been exposed and its occurrence reduced substantially. And on an issue close to my heart, Dublin's architectural heritage, particularly its stock of Georgian and Victorian buildings, a post-colonial contempt had been replaced by some respect and appreciation. (What's now in danger, as never before, is the city's modernist legacy, epitomized by the iconic – now former – Central Bank.) I firmly believe that all this change – sometimes imperceptible, sometimes radical – has made Ireland a much better country for all of us.

This is my story. I have tried to tell the truth in so far as I can. Doing so involves a degree of exposure – perhaps an indecent degree. Although, as a journalist, I have never shied away from revealing what I believe to be true, revisiting my life and times has been as challenging as it has been therapeutic and even enjoyable.

But in this context, I recall what John Butler, director of the gay 'coming-of-age' film *Handsome Devil*, told the *Irish Times*: 'I think for any art to be good you have to feel extraordinarily vulnerable having made it. If . . . you're not incredibly nervous about what you're exposing to the world, then you haven't done anything of value.'

I

One of the useful lessons I've learned in life is that not everything you are told is true, and that many things that happen to be true are not told.

Children were much more credulous when I was growing up, and I still believed in Santa Claus at the age of eleven – until I found hard evidence to the contrary in a friend's house not far from where we lived. It happened one mid-December day after school. When my pal Tom Hensey and I got to his place on Cabra Drive, there was nobody at home, so we did a bit of exploring upstairs. In his parents' bedroom we found bulging bags on top of the big wardrobe. Standing on chairs, we took the bags down and looked inside – to find all the toys and other Christmas presents that the Hensey kids had requested in their letters to Santa at the North Pole. We were devastated. It wasn't just that there was no Santa; it was that our parents had been lying to us about him for years. So I went home to confront my mother: 'There is no Santa Claus – and I can prove it!' She scolded me for having the cheek to go into Tom Hensey's parents' bedroom, but she was also dismayed by my discovery – perhaps even as much as I was – because she probably knew it signalled the end of childhood and the beginning of something else.

We lived at 9 Glenmore Road, a little cul-de-sac between Old Cabra Road and Blackhorse Avenue in what came to be known as Dublin 7. The house had been built in 1948, the year of my parents' wedding. They got married in Corpus Christi Church on Griffith Avenue, because my mother was living with an aunt on Home Farm Road at the time. A framed watercolour of that fine low-domed church, which they received as a wedding present, hung for decades in our living room over the sideboard where all the good china cups, saucers and plates were kept. After having their wedding breakfast (as it used to be called) in the Central Hotel on Exchequer Street, they took the train to Killarney and onwards to Waterville by bus to spend their honeymoon at the Butler Arms Hotel, using bicycles to explore the Ring of Kerry.

The house in Glenmore Road was too small for what became a family of four children. A terraced bungalow, it only had two bedrooms; there was no easy way to extend it, and no money to do that either. I was born in 1950; my brother Liam, with curly red hair, followed in 1952; our sister Edel (called after the Irish Legion of Mary missionary, Edel Quinn) in 1954; and our youngest brother Denis came along in 1959 as a welcome 'afterthought'.

I entered this world in the comfortable confines of Stella Maris Nursing Home at 17 Earlsfort Terrace on 24 January 1950. Mam, who had herself been born at Stella Maris thirty years earlier, laboured for three days and nights. Her small pocket diary, densely written in pencil, recorded it as a 'Red Letter Day', noting, 'Baby born at 8.30. What a relief after a terrible night . . . I was delighted.' She had to rest after that ordeal, so it was a week before they brought me to University Church on St Stephen's Green to be baptized. Also in attendance were my godparents; my mother Maura's best friend, Bridie O'Mara; and my uncle Denis, who was known as Din, a carpenter with the Office of Public Works. The priest gave out yards to Dad for 'leaving this baby a heathen for so long'. It was in honour of my two grandfathers that I was named Thomas Francis. And since my dad's father, Thomas McDonald, was long dead and my mother's father, Francis Xavier Coghlan, was still very much alive, I came to be called Frank, after him.

The Church was everywhere then, of course, and my parents were devout Catholics. Above the fireplace in our living room there was a gilt-framed scroll with a picture of Pope Pius XII above a Latin inscription, '*Anno Jubilari 1950*', and then (in English), rendered in outsize Gothic calligraphy, 'Most Holy Father', going on, in smaller script:

> William and Maura McDonald and family humbly prostrate at the feet of Your Holiness, beg the Apostolic Blessing and a Plenary

> Indulgence to be gained at the hour of death on condition that, being truly sorry for their sins but being unable to confess them or to receive the Holy Viaticum, they shall at least invoke with their lips or heart the Holy Name of Jesus.

There was something in Latin to indicate that it had been issued at the Vatican on 25 November 1950, and it's stamped with the papal seal. It was a bit terrifying for us kids to read that scroll, since we knew nothing of death then. But there was also something comforting about it; even if we were unconscious, 'out for the count', we could still go straight to Heaven. We also had a holy-water font in the hall, a picture of the Sacred Heart in my parents' bedroom and, in the breakfast room, a statue of the Child of Prague with a glowing red light in front of it that never went out. We all had brown scapulars and blue miraculous medals, and we said the Family Rosary every night, kneeling on the hard art-deco linoleum of the living-room floor (or the hearthrug, if we were lucky), and prayed for God's blessings on each and every one. Miraculously, that same lino was still on the floor more than sixty years later.

Mam used to enjoy telling a story about how, when I was just three years old, she took me into Lynch's grocery shop on Blackhorse Avenue – opposite the City Abattoir – and old Mrs Lynch asked me how long I'd been living on Glenmore Road.

'Since before my mother and father were married,' I replied, in all innocence.

My mother would break out laughing at the memory of this faux pas and everyone else would laugh too. Eventually I came to understand that the very idea that a child could be born to unmarried parents was impossible to imagine. Little did we know then that the Irish Sisters of Charity were running a 'mother and baby home' – St Patrick's – for unmarried mothers and their children on the Navan Road, not too far from where we lived.

Even though our parents found it hard going financially, the first two of us were enrolled in Mrs Kelly's Private School on Cabra Road until we were aged seven and old enough to go to national school. Mam had her standards; she had been educated, to Leaving Cert level, by the Loreto nuns in Rathfarnham. Mrs Kelly's didn't look much like the Loreto, being almost indistinguishable from any of the other large 1930s semi-detached houses on this stretch of Cabra Road. But that's where we were taught the rudiments of reading and writing in English and Irish (in the old Gaelic script), arithmetic and religion, by nice teachers in small classes, in the dining room, the sitting room or the converted garage. What I remember most about the three years I spent there was the penny Catechism. Laid out in Q&A format, it started at the beginning with a big question, 'Who made the world?' to which the answer (inevitably) was, 'God made the world.' Years would pass before we heard about Charles Darwin and evolution.

We were told that we all had individual guardian angels who watched over us night and day; I called mine Gabriel. We learned the Apostles' Creed by rote and could recite it flawlessly, and we believed in the Immaculate Conception, the Resurrection of Jesus Christ, the Assumption of Our Lady into Heaven, the Holy Catholic Church, the forgiveness of sins and life everlasting. And, of course, the Devil. We were also taught that St Patrick had lit a fire on the Hill of Slane, opposite the ancient royal site of Tara, where he converted the 'pagan' High King to Christianity and then drove the snakes out of Ireland – and we lapped it all up without question. We knew that Our Lady had appeared in Lourdes and later in Fatima, and that there was something so important about the messages she delivered to those who saw her there that it had to be kept secret. There had also been a vision of the Blessed Virgin in Knock, Co. Mayo; it was said that a magic lantern waved by members of the RIC might have been involved, but we didn't believe that.

When the time came, I was well prepared to make my First Communion in the Dominican Convent chapel on Ratoath Road, not far from Cabra Cross. There is charming colour film footage from the day showing me in my Communion suit and white rosette, with Dad holding my hand; it was made by Mr Devlin, from Glencar Road, who was the only person in our area with a cine camera. The only neighbour with a television set was old Mr Murphy, father of Terry Murphy, then director of Dublin Zoo and the first Protestant we ever met. He used to invite Liam and myself over to watch the Bertram Mills circus on his black-and-white BBC-only television, and we had fun trying to identify acrobats and animals in the fuzzy images flickering on the small screen. We could hear lions roaring in the Lion House at the Zoo, and I distinctly remember being woken up by the IRA bomb in 1957 that finally toppled sculptor John Henry Foley's superb equestrian statue of Field Marshal Viscount Gough, which stood on the main avenue of the Phoenix Park. Gough was an easy target. At least they couldn't blow up the massive Wellington Monument that perfectly terminates the vista on North Circular Road, framed by lines of London plane trees.

At the time of my birth, my father, William McDonald (always known as Bill), was working for John McGrotty, who owned a motor factors' firm off Talbot Street, supplying spare parts for cars. It was taken over later by Welsh firm Quinton Hazell, and my dad then ran its Irish business. He had a fully equipped carpentry workshop in the garage at the bottom of the garden. There he made our bunk beds with solid mahogany uprights, which he French-polished himself, and head and tail boards from mahogany-veneered plywood with solid-wood capping. He made cabinets for the kitchen and breakfast room (we called it that because it was so small, but it was where we had nearly all our family meals). He made a four-level rack over the draining board beside our Belfast sink for plates to drip-dry, although we always took turns to dry them with a tea towel. Whatever went wrong in the house, Mam would always say, 'Dad will fix it.'

He had one secret project that happened at night-time after we had gone to bed. For months one year, he worked on making a huge railway set for Liam and me, including a mountain tunnel made from battered papier mâché painted in charcoal grey streaked with silver. The whole thing was brought to life by Hornby passenger and goods trains chugging along the spindly tracks. Dad used to blow smoke from his pipe into the tunnel so that it would come billowing out when one of the model steam trains went through. We also collected Dinky cars, from Paddy Barrett's toy shop in Mary Street; my favourite was a shocking pink Chevrolet Impala. But my enthusiasm for cars was short-lived and I never learned how to drive, even after reaching the age when it would have been legal. (Liam and I did learn how to cycle, thanks to our father, with a lot of wobbly trial-and-error on our back lane, and we're both still cycling more than sixty years later.)

Dad loved the model railway set at least as much as we did. But then, he had been a railway child, who grew up in station houses. Both his father and grandfather were stationmasters on the Dublin South Eastern Railway that ran from Harcourt Street Station to Rosslare Harbour. One of Dad's earliest memories was of a 'British Tommy' putting his soldier's cap on his four-year-old head at Rathgarogue Station, near New Ross, in 1920 (during the War of Independence). He also remembered his eldest brother Paddy, who ended up as a commandant in the Irish Army, raising the Tricolour over the railway bridge at Rathgarogue.

The family had a milking cow and two goats in the garden as well as drills for potatoes and vegetables, and a terrier called Captain after my uncle Paddy. During the Civil War, when the railway lines were under attack from republican irregulars, the family were moved to Rathnew, Co. Wicklow, for their safety. Paddy had been elected lieutenant by his colleagues in Wexford (they did that kind of thing then) and later moved to Dublin, where he was second-in-command of the troops that accepted the handover of Beggar's Bush Barracks from British forces to the fledgling Irish Free State in 1922. When Uncle Paddy got a car, he took his youngest brother on a day trip north just to see the border at Carrickarnon; having had a look at it, my father recalled, 'We turned around and drove back.'

In 1930, when Dad was fourteen, his own father died suddenly from an aneurysm, and he moved with his mother to Dublin, to a Victorian terraced house at the Fairview end of Malahide Road. Decades later, he could still remember being woken up by a huge explosion in May 1941 caused by a Luftwaffe bomb that hit the North Strand, less than a mile away from their house, killing twenty-eight people and leaving many others homeless. Granny McDonald, as we called her, was still alive and living on her own when I was little. She always dressed in 'widow's weeds', even though her husband had died more than twenty years earlier. I was six when she died.

We went to Mass every Sunday in the Church of the Holy Family on Aughrim Street and to Confession every other Saturday, along with novenas, sodalities, 'first Fridays' and God knows what else. The most conspicuous communal religious devotion in the parish centred on the Feast of Corpus Christi, with an annual, and very solemn, procession in Aughrim Street and environs. Every house in the area seemed to have a papal flag, which was hung out of a window or even flown from flagpoles, to demonstrate fidelity to the Catholic Church. There was a steel pole in our lower garden, which had been put up to hold a long washing line; Dad extended it, to turn it into a flagpole. And the first flag we flew, naturally, was the papal flag. It never occurred to us that it was the emblem of another country, the Vatican city-state.

For us, Home Rule really was Rome Rule. It was pervasive and overwhelming at Corpus Christi, the sense that the entire community was united in a higher cause. The parish priest would be dressed in ceremonial regalia, carrying a glittering monstrance under a white canopy with golden tassels while the army provided a guard of honour; after all, Aughrim Street was the parish church of the President of Ireland, Seán T. Ó Ceallaigh, and also had McKee Barracks within its boundary. Out in front were altar boys in their white-and-black vestments, walking two by two, supervised by head altar boy Aodhán Madden, who went on to become a troubled writer of some renown. Then came the Catholic Boy Scouts and Girl Guides, the Knights of Malta, nuns from Stanhope Street Convent and the much more exotic French Sisters of Charity, with their distinctive starched white cornettes, followed by the St Vincent de Paul Society, the Legion of Mary and St John's Ambulance Brigade. The streets were festooned with yellow-and-white bunting and the footpaths lined with people who would all bless themselves when the Host was carried aloft in front of them, a scent of incense in the air.

Holy Week was another high point. Statues in the church would be shrouded from top to bottom in mourning purple and, on Good Friday itself, the tabernacle doors would be thrown open, as if the bird had flown. Later on, in our early teens, we would endure annual retreats in Aughrim Street given by fire-breathing Redemptorists, who were just as scary as the one depicted by James Joyce in *A Portrait of the Artist as a Young Man*. A whole congregation of men and boys could be held in the palm of their hands, as they sketched the prospect of Hellfire or at least a long spell in Purgatory if we didn't mend our ways and strictly observe each and every one of the Ten Commandments. At the head of it all was the authoritarian figure of John Charles McQuaid, effective ruler of Catholic Ireland for more than thirty years, with his mitre and crozier, Hudson limousine, palatial private home in Killiney and rustling princely vestments that sometimes required a team of altar boys to carry the train. But even McQuaid was temporarily eclipsed by Cardinal Agagianian, broad-smiling Papal Legate for the Patrician Congress in 1961, whose arrival in Ireland was marked by elaborate pomp and circumstance, including an escort of four Air Corps Vampire jets and a twenty-one-gun salute at Dublin Airport, bedecked in Irish and papal flags. I was so agog at Agagianian that I took to making 'vestments' in different colours from crêpe paper, dressing up as a priest and 'saying Mass' in our back garden, with a mock-silver chalice, paten and all. Religious devotion takes many forms, I suppose. No wonder I felt cheated when I made my Confirmation (taking the name Patrick), because it was done by one of Dublin's auxiliary bishops and not by the Archbishop himself.

Even though he seemed very old, everyone liked the new Pope, John XXIII. His warm smile and lack of pomp were welcome after years of austerity under Pius XII. He seemed jolly, even human. His inauguration of the Second Vatican Council looked very promising – adults were talking about it a lot – and there was some excitement about the novel prospect of Mass said in 'the vernacular' rather than in Latin. Although we might miss the priest saying, *'Dominus vobiscum,'* and responding with, *'Et cum spiritu tuo,'* people would understand more fully what was going on at the altar and even participate in it. As kids, we listened without much comprehension as the inimitable Seán Mac Réamoinn, with his raspy voice, reported the twists and turns of the council from Rome for Raidió Éireann, and there was no doubt that change was in the air. When the council was finally brought to a conclusion by Pope Paul VI in December 1965, John Charles McQuaid assured us on his return to Dublin that 'no change will worry the tranquillity of your Christian lives'. He was quite wrong about that, as he was about many things.

Mam was a great baker, and every day she would put on an apron over her blouse, cardigan and skirt, and get to work. She made brown and white soda bread, as well as buns, biscuits, sponge cakes filled with cream and raspberry jam (the classic Victoria sponge, but we didn't call it that) and all sorts of other goodies. We couldn't have asked for more. In the run-up to Christmas, our kitchen in Glenmore Road was turned into a virtual industrial zone for the production of plum puddings and cakes, mostly for distribution as presents to close relatives. Some of them just wanted a plain rich fruitcake, while others preferred theirs plastered with royal icing, with or without the marzipan layer. Either way, there were lots of opportunities for us as kids to get 'the lick' – a taste of the batter straight from the bowl, before it was all put into greaseproof paper-lined baking tins and then into the oven of our electric Moffat cooker.

In the week before Christmas, we would 'do the rounds' in our first family car – a Ford Anglia, instantly recognizable by its backward-slanting rear window – delivering all the cakes and puddings. (Liam can still remember the car's registration, EZC 774; there were no 'D' plates then.) Dad was a careful driver, which reflected his moderation in all things, especially alcohol; he might drink a couple of pints of Smithwick's when he would meet his brothers Paddy and Din in a pub, and have the odd glass of whiskey on occasion, but that was it. I never once saw him drunk – merry, yes, but never 'scuttered'. Dad's version of an expletive was, 'Suffering ducks!'

Our small illuminated Christmas crib had been made by Dad on his carpentry bench, and we loved filling it with straw and figurines representing Mary, Joseph, baby Jesus, sheep, goats, shepherds and a donkey. We also had figurines of the Three Wise Men, but only put them in later, on 6 January, the Feast of the Epiphany. On Christmas Eve, we would carefully place a flickering red candle in the living-room window and leave out long socks at the ends of our beds for Santa Claus, waking up in the morning to find them filled with bars of Cadbury's Dairy Milk chocolate, a Toblerone and other treats. All delightful, and it never once occurred to us that our parents might be struggling financially because we never felt it.

My mother was a teetotaller, so the closest she ever got to alcohol was brandy butter or sherry trifle at Christmas time. She had too much to do and, in any case, was in no mind to break the 'pledge' she made at her Confirmation. There was a Singer sewing machine in a corner of the living room, beneath our three flying ducks where she made short grey pants for us and pleated skirts for Edel. She was also an expert at knitting and turned out any number of pullovers for us all, never missing a stitch while chatting away amiably to us or to her guests on 'First Tuesdays' – monthly social gatherings of women relatives or friends in different houses, including ours. We always knew when it was coming up because the kitchen would go into overdrive to produce sandwiches, buns and cakes – and we would get to eat some of this glorious feast.

Provisions usually came from an old-fashioned general store at 52 Manor Street, opposite the former Dublin Metropolitan Police Barracks, with its high window overlooking the city. Flour and oatmeal were shovelled out of sacks on the floor, put onto weighing scales, bagged to order and paid for at a brass cash register on a large oak desk in the middle of the shop. Ironically, the first 'self-service' store in the area opened just opposite in about 1960, and it was such a novelty then to pick up a basket inside the door of this tiny premises and choose from the limited range of stuff they had on open shelves. Mam had a bike and she would often cycle into town, usually to go shopping in Dunnes Stores off Henry Street, as she was suspicious of the 'Maggies' in Moore Street and their sharp trading practices.

One Christmas Eve, realizing that we had no Brussels sprouts, she went to Moore Street *in extremis*. Knowing that most of us hated the vile 'little cabbages', she approached one of the traders who had a mountainous pile of sprouts on a bakery tray sitting on top of a pram.

'I'll take six of them,' Mam said.

The woman was aghast and, holding up the little paper bag of sprouts, called out to a colleague, 'Hey, Mary, here's the last of the big spenders.' (Of course, any potential customer who rooted through their vegetables looking for the best got the curt response: 'If you don't want them, don't maul them!')

Every 8 December, without fail, our mother would take us into town to go shopping, watch *Tom and Jerry* cartoons in the Grafton Cinema, feed the ducks in St Stephen's Green and then have tea and buns in Bewley's, with its aromatic coffee roaster in the window. It was all waitress service then, and the staff included twins Bridie and Kathleen 'Tattens' Toomey, who gave as good as they got. We also queued up to visit every department store's Santa, including the one who landed by helicopter on the roof of Pim's, on South Great George's Street, as we watched in awe at this dramatic event that was obviously designed to outdo Brown Thomas, Switzers, Arnotts, McBirney's and Clerys. We would rate them all on the basis of price, presents, friendliness and the fit-out of each shop's 'grotto'.

We were fascinated by the pneumatic tube system Clerys had to transport dockets and cash from every sales counter to the accounts department, or the spring-loaded pulley contraption Lee's department store on the corner of Mary Street used for the same purpose. After Roches Stores on Henry Street installed Ireland's first set of escalators in 1963, we couldn't wait to try them out – with some trepidation. We were also mesmerized by the neon lights outside McDowell's Happy Ring House on O'Connell Street and the dazzling Donnelly's Sausages display above the Regent Hotel in D'Olier

Street featuring two kids ('Don' and 'Nelly') endlessly tossing sausages from frying pan to fork. Other treats we looked forward to were the annual Spring Show and Horse Show at the RDS in Ballsbridge – one featuring tractors and combine harvesters, the other devoted to horses, ponies, dressage and showjumping. The Horse Show was our favourite, because our day out among all the toffs would end with strawberries and cream in a huge tent serenaded by Miss Bay Jellett and Her Orchestra or the Army No. 1 Band.

Mam had worked for Brown Thomas, in the hosiery department, but she had to give up her job when she got married; that was the rule then. She never earned another penny for the rest of her life, but whenever she had housekeeping money left over she would put it into Post Office savings certs or bonds and, by the time of her death in January 2009 at the age of eighty-eight, we were astonished to discover that she had accumulated nearly €200,000 in cash. We shouldn't have been so surprised, really. After all, we had been reared in an era of thrift, of make-do and mend, of waste not, want not. And our parents had such a horror of debt that they had paid off their mortgage in just five years. God knows how they did that in the early 1950s when there was so little money around, but they did.

Dublin was a different place, another world really, when we were growing up. Nobody seemed to have any money and, if they did, they were very discreet about it. There were no flash cars, indeed not many cars at all. In the 1950s, on our little cul-de-sac, there were only one or two cars between fifteen houses, and we were able to play on the road; even football games were feasible because there was so much space. At least in our day, cars were quite distinctive; you could easily tell the difference between one marque and another – between a Morris Minor and a Volkswagen, or even between an Austin Seven and a Ford Prefect.

My uncle Paddy, who looked every inch the retired army officer, with his clipped grey moustache and ramrod-straight bearing, had an Austin Seven that he used only as a summer touring car; in the winter, it was kept in his garage on Cremore Road in Glasnevin. He and his wife Rose were renting their house, which had been beautifully built by Alexander Strain in the early 1930s. It was only later I discovered that all the houses on the Cremore Estate were for sale to Protestants only; with their characteristic red-tiled roofs, it became known for a time as the 'Orange Free State'. (Coincidentally, my youngest brother Denis, who went on to become a very busy senior counsel and more recently a High Court judge, bought and renovated a house directly opposite Uncle Paddy's in the late 1990s. At his housewarming party, when the cherry trees on the road were at their best, one of the legal guests from Dalkey or Killiney remarked, 'I never thought the Northside was so pretty!')

Our neighbours on Glenmore Road were a mixed bunch. Apart from Mr Murphy, they included the widowed Mrs Halliday, one of the most elegant women I've ever seen, who had a different rig-out for every day of the week and even dressed her front door with a striped canvas cover in summertime to protect its scumbled surface from the sun. She lived in the house directly opposite ours with her older sister, Miss Kennedy, who had a hump and was very kind to us as kids. Mr Conroy was a Garda sergeant who, on occasion, put on long white gloves to direct traffic at the junction of D'Olier Street, Westmoreland Street and the Liffey quays from a black-and-white striped booth at the southern end of O'Connell Bridge, with an enormous concrete flower bed – popularly known as the 'Tomb of the Unknown Gurrier' – behind him.

Mr Donoghue, who was from Cavan, lived at the end of the road; one of his daughters, Olive, surprised us all by becoming a priest in the Church of Ireland and, later, Rector of Mountmellick in Co. Laois. Mr Fitzpatrick, who lived three doors down from us, had a small vegetable shop on Aughrim Street, next door to Kavanagh's turreted pub, where he eked out a living to support quite a large family; they had eight children, as did the Devoys, who lived right across from us behind a tall thick privet hedge. And when Mrs Maher's husband died suddenly, leaving her with five children under eight years old, Dad organized a whip-round among all the neighbours and raised enough money to pay off her mortgage. On Glencar Road, the last house was occupied by the curmudgeonly

Mr Wheatley and his rather more benign wife. Kids in the area would taunt him as he cycled past in his 'National Health' glasses, calling him by his nickname 'Piggles'. For sheer eccentricity, Mrs Bolster took the biscuit. She had a pair of houses on Aughrim Street that seemed to be full of cats and old newspapers, and she could be seen cycling up and down between there and her huckster shop on North King Street, which had an aspidistra in the window and very few customers.

Once we got the Ford Anglia, there was no stopping us. Every Sunday night, we would go 'visiting' – often to Grandad's house on Taylor's Lane in Whitechurch, above Rathfarnham. F. X. Coghlan was a kindly old man who would slip each of us half-a-crown every time we went there, and a green pound note at Christmas, although we'd have to do our 'party piece' to earn it; ours was that tedious old ditty 'There's a Hole in My Bucket', which I used to dread having to perform as I couldn't really sing for my supper, or at all. St Roch, as the house was called, had a long garden to the side that was full of drills for onions, potatoes and other vegetables, as well as apple and pear trees and, most intriguingly of all, three beehives. I can still remember Grandad in his beekeeper's hat and veil, carefully harvesting the honey one sunny evening while we stood back just in case there was a swarm.

You'd never think, to look at him, that he had fathered ten children with two wives in succession. He had first married Brigid McCourt, the daughter of a coach-builder from Co. Tyrone in 1914, and she bore him five – Pádraig, Éamon, my mother Maura, Dónal and Proinsías (or Frank). After my grandmother had died prematurely of tuberculosis in 1927, when my mother was only seven, he married again and had another set of five children – Peig, Éilís, twins Micheál and Peadar, who were wild boys in their day, and Dermot, the youngest of his seven sons. St Roch was rented, probably because my grandfather was a socialist at heart and didn't share the strong Irish obsession with property ownership. With a few whiskeys on board, he would fulminate about the new class of 'chancers' who had enriched themselves under the Free State – men like Joe McGrath, who got a licence to operate the Irish Hospitals' Sweepstake and built his family fortune on the back of this scam.

We knew that Grandad had been 'out' in 1916, although we didn't know any details because he never talked about it – not even around the fiftieth anniversary of the Rising in 1966. But we could see that he was highly valued by his former comrades because there was a 'smoking cabinet' for his crooked pipes in the sitting room, with a silver plaque that read, 'Presented to Commdt. F. X. Coghlan by the Association of Old Dublin Brigade, Óglaiġ na h-Éireann, 21st February 1939.' The presentation was made at a 'smoking concert' in the association's clubhouse on Dorset Street Upper. A charming photograph showed him as a fifteen-year-old student at Rockwell College, in Co. Tipperary, where he was on the school rugby team and had one of the 1916 leaders, Thomas MacDonagh, as a teacher. (How his own father, a national school teacher on the Sheep's Head peninsula in West Cork, could have afforded to send him to Rockwell is anyone's guess, but the family home in Kilcrohane, a three-bay mid-nineteenth-century house with an impressive front door, would suggest that they were relatively comfortable.) He went on from Rockwell to the Civil Service College in Cork, and then got a job at the General Post Office in Manchester, where he worked for a few years before returning to Ireland to take up the post of clerical officer in the Land Commission and indulge his passion for handball, for which he won a Dublin championship in 1912.

It was not until the Bureau of Military History released a vast wealth of witness statements from Old IRA veterans that we found out what Grandad had done in 1916. A five-page typewritten statement, signed by him, detailed how he had joined the Irish Volunteers at its inaugural meeting in the Rotunda (later the Ambassador Cinema) in November 1913. Under the command of Ned Daly in the Rising, he was involved in a group that built barricades in the Church Street area, fired at British Lancers on their horses and 'took Linenhall Barracks, by burning it'. Later, they were told to prepare an escape route for the beleaguered GPO garrison, but this line of retreat for the Rising's leaders was cut off 'as the British advanced into Capel Street in force'. On Saturday evening, he recalled, 'We were withdrawn to the Four Courts and addressed by Daly, who told us that we were about to surrender . . . Some of the men started breaking up their guns, others just threw them away, and the "beaten team" feeling came over us.' They were taken prisoner and held overnight in front of the Rotunda, then conveyed to Richmond Barracks in Inchicore and, from there, to the boat for England and Stafford Gaol. Grandad was lucky to be released after an outbreak of measles there, so he didn't move on to the internment camp at Frongoch in North Wales; others would languish there until December 1916. He lost his Civil Service post for being a rebel, but became chief clerk to Michael Collins at the Irish National Aid and Volunteer Dependants' Fund, which raised a then staggering sum of £100,000 in donations to help the families of those who took part in the Rising.

Further evidence of my grandfather's role has emerged from the Military Service Pensions Collection, which shows that he was assiduous in making representations for former colleagues, and from a huge trunk full of his personal papers, photographs and other artefacts, in the 'lumber room' at St Roch, as his youngest grandson, Gareth Coghlan, called it. After some two hundred republican irregulars led by Rory O'Connor and Liam Mellows seized the Four Courts in April 1922, my grandfather enlisted in the National Army under the command of Collins who had 'borrowed' four 18-pounder artillery pieces from the withdrawing British and started shelling the Four Courts mercilessly. Grandad was not directly involved in this assault, but he was in command of the Free State troops gathered to the west of the Four Courts, waiting to move in after the artillery barrage was over. By then, the building was on fire. Worst of all, the Public Records Office, which the irregulars had been using as a munitions store, blew up – causing the irreplaceable loss of Ireland's official records, including chancery rolls dating back to the fourteenth century. O'Connor and Mellows were among the first of seventy-seven irregulars to be executed by firing squad after being 'tried' by ruthless Free State military tribunals.

While moonlighting as captain of the IRA's Rathfarnham Company during the War of Independence, Grandad had become an agent for New Ireland Assurance, the first wholly Irish-owned life insurance company, which was set up to challenge the dominance of British insurers. Later he returned to the Civil Service, working in the Land Commission until his retirement. Four of his sons would follow him into the insurance business, working as agents for Liverpool-based Royal Liver Assurance.

Grandad's eldest son, Pádraig Pearse Coghlan, lived in one of the grander houses on Brighton Square, in Rathgar, with his wife Bridie; they had no children. Then one day in July 1959, aged forty-two, he disappeared. Some time later, his car was found at the edge of a flooded quarry in Crumlin and his body recovered from the depths. It was obviously a case of suicide – and Bridie was blamed, with allegations that she had involved her husband in some sort of 'cult' and he had lost his mind as a result. I doubt there was any truth in that; perhaps it was a typically misogynist attempt to blame the woman for a man taking his life. At Uncle Pádraig's funeral at Glasnevin Cemetery, she found herself isolated and unwelcome. 'The Coghlans kept her away from the grave,' as one family member recalled. But Bridie got her own back by commissioning Uncle Pádraig's gravestone, 'In loving memory of my dear husband.' There was an inquest, at which she gave evidence that he had been attending psychoanalysts for four years, going four days a week at times, but he wouldn't tell her anything about what went on because it was 'all secret'. Such was the strong taboo associated with suicide at the time, and for long afterwards, that the sad fate of Uncle Pádraig was never spoken of again in our family.

Grandad died in 1970 at the age of eighty-four, when I was twenty. He had gone out to assist someone whose car wouldn't start by helping to push it, went back into the house to have his tea, had a massive heart attack and was found dead at the table. A traditional Irish wake followed, with his waxen-looking body laid out in an open coffin in the living room of St Roch. At his own request, there was no army firing party at his graveside in Glasnevin Cemetery, but his coffin was draped in the Tricolour.

Others on our visiting list included 'Auntie' on Home Farm Road, a sister-in-law of Grandad's whose name was Moira, with whom my mother had lived in the 1940s, having moved out of St Roch because she felt that her stepmother was treating her as little more than a skivvy to look after her own growing family. Then there were the Blacks on Palmerston Road, who were first cousins of Dad. His Uncle William had died, leaving fearsome Aunt Nell to dominate the lives of her son and three daughters, all of whom were adults by then. None of them ever married, it was said, because Aunt Nell thought nobody they might have set their hearts on would be good enough for them. So Sheila, Nancy and Tess remained 'spinsters' to the end of their days in Shankill, while Aunt Nell's son Billy died prematurely, having 'taken to the drink'.

More enjoyable were our regular visits to the Kavanaghs, on Belton Park Road, in Donnycarney. Dad's elder sister, who was always known as Nana, had married Tom Kavanagh, a dyed-in-the-wool republican and Fianna Fáil supporter from Cork Street, and they had three children who were slightly older than us – Irene, Tony and Mary. Charlie Haughey's mother, we knew, lived just down the road. But what really made the visits enjoyable was that Auntie Nana would give us tea, sandwiches and biscuits before we headed back home. The Kavanaghs didn't have a television, but our first cousins in Ballyroan Road did – five boys, all younger than us, the sons of Mam's younger brother Dónal and his wife Mary; before getting married, the pair of them used to travel around on his Lambretta scooter. It was there that we watched *Sunday Night at the London Palladium*, presented by a youngish Bruce Forsyth.

After three years at Mrs Kelly's Private School, we were dispatched to St Vincent's in Glasnevin, as Mam thought the CBS in Brunswick Street, much closer to home, was 'too rough'. Not even the fact that Paddy Crosbie – famous for his *School Around the Corner* radio show – was one of the teachers there would sway her in favour of 'Brunner'. St Vincent's had started as a boarding school in 1860, began taking 'day boys' in 1927, and opened a new primary school off Finglas Road twelve years later. Going there was like being thrown to the wolves. It was a brutal regime, under the control of sadistic Brother Cahill, who would produce his leather strap and slap our outstretched palms with it for even minor infringements of the rules. There was sexual abuse, too. An elderly teacher, Brother McAteer, used to like sitting beside his 'pets' in fourth class, putting his hand up our short pants and fiddling with our private parts. He went no further than that with me, at least, but I did see something very disturbing one day. The school storeroom was locked, and I could hear somebody inside. So I looked through the keyhole and saw Brother McAteer, wearing his black soutane, going down on one of my classmates, whose pants were around his ankles. I knew that what he was doing was wrong, but it never occurred to me to report him, or even mention what I saw to close friends, or to my parents. I suppose I was afraid to say anything, such was the atmosphere of raw terror in the school.

Like most families then, we had our dinner in the middle of the day, sitting at the breakfast-room table that came from the DSER railway station in Killurin, Co. Wexford. Dad would power-cycle home from work on his VéloSoleX, Liam and I would scramble home on our bikes from St Vincent's, and Edel would walk up from Stanhope Street. It would always be 'meat and two veg', or shepherd's pie, except on Fridays when we had fish, usually whiting, herring or mackerel bought from Muldoon's in Stoneybatter. While having our dinner, we'd listen to the latest episode of the Raidió Éireann series, *The Kennedys of Castleross*, on our old Zenith radio set that had London, Luxembourg, Hilversum, Moscow, Prague, Stockholm, Athlone and God knows where else on its dial. We were tuned into Athlone, which used to crackle into life in the morning with its station signal and rendering of 'Donnell Abú', followed by the 'pips' and an announcement of what saint's day it was.

Mam made porridge for breakfast, served up with brown bread and marmalade. We usually drank tea, or Irel Coffee, which wasn't really coffee at all but a concoction made largely from chicory; you just added a spoonful to a cup of boiling water and – hey presto! – you had 'coffee'. For our tea in the evening, we'd usually have baked beans on toast, macaroni and cheese, scrambled eggs or potato cakes fried on the Moffat's oblong hotplate and then spread with lashings of Mam's handmade mix of 'fifty/fifty' butter and margarine – her own invention, in an effort to save money. If we were sick, the remedy nearly always involved taking a horrible-tasting spoonful of cod liver oil. For skin cuts, Mam would take out a little bottle of Mercurochrome and dab the red liquid on a bloody wound. We were all inoculated against polio, which had crippled so many kids, by old Dr Plaisted at his surgery in Manor Street, but we still got mumps and measles because there was no vaccine available to ward off these diseases until the mid-1960s. I succumbed to both and still remember being alarmed by the swollen face mumps gave me and all the red spots that came with measles. My skin also turned pale yellow from jaundice, but at least this had the bonus that I could never become a blood donor; the very idea of having a needle stuck in my arm to extract a pint of blood would have made me faint.

Our pantry was full of baking material and equipment, including several cardboard trays of eggs that Mam used to preserve with lard, as well as home-made jam and marmalade in jars with cellophane tops held in place by elastic bands. There was a dairy at 29 Prussia Street where we would be sent to get unpasteurized buttermilk for the brown bread; it was ladled out of galvanized steel milk churns into the empty bottles we brought with us. Arbour Hill still had its piggeries then, and you could often hear the pigs squealing as you walked past. There was even an open-topped lorry that used to trundle around the area collecting organic waste for pigswill.

Before Mr Whippy arrived on the scene, ice cream came from Hughes Bros in Rathfarnham – better known as HB. We wouldn't have known that even our favourite Raspberry Ripple was largely made from hydrogenated palm oil, with very little actual cream in it. There was also a small factory in Monck Place, Phibsboro, that used to produce Cleeve's toffee, and we'd occasionally help ourselves to some of it while they weren't looking, on our way home from school. And every once in a while Mr Devlin would take out his camera and make a little 'movie'; some amazing footage still survives, showing our back lane (shared by Glenmore and Glencar roads) before it was irrevocably altered by breeze-block walls and barbed wire. The trellis (we called it 'the rustic') that Dad had made to divide our back garden into two sections was laden with scented pink roses in the summertime; it was also where we posed for family photographs on special occasions, such as First Communion and Confirmation. Our parents were keen gardeners, and the lower half of the garden, beyond 'the rustic', was given over to a bed of rhubarb and rows of vegetables, so we had our own supply of potatoes, cabbage, onions, green beans and lettuce.

We had a view of the remarkable Raj-scape of McKee Barracks from our breakfast-room window, with the Dublin Mountains (Kippure and Montpelier, topped by the Hell Fire Club) on the horizon. Every morning, we could tell what kind of a day it was going to be by the size of the Tricolour that the army ran up its flagpole. If the forecast was windy, a small flag was used, but if it was likely to be a calm day they would hoist a huge, flapping *drapeau*. We knew that the barracks had been built as Marlborough Barracks, headquarters of the British cavalry regiment in Ireland; at one stage, it housed more than eight hundred horses. It was from here that the Lancers set out in an effort to crush the 1916 Rising. We knew a family who lived in the barracks, the Treacys – their dad was the quartermaster – and it was a real treat to visit them in their house just behind the long brick wall on Blackhorse Avenue, having been waved through an army checkpoint at the entrance gates. It was said that the Brits had got plans for the barracks mixed up, and this red-brick Hindu-Gothic extravaganza dating from 1891 was meant to have been built in the Punjab or somewhere in India. But that's all nonsense according to Maurice Craig, whose magisterial *Dublin 1660–1860* I didn't read until years later; it was simply the British Empire style of the time.

We went to Turner's Newsagents, a candy-striped single-storey shop tacked onto the front of an old house on Manor Street, to get our *Beano*, *Dandy* and *Billy Bunter* comics, and we looked forward to the next issue of *Our Boys*, a monthly magazine for children produced by the Christian Brothers. Packed with puzzles and stories, it had a comic strip featuring Labhrás Leprechaun and some scary stuff about banshees and haunted houses written under the pseudonym 'Kitty the Hare'. Or maybe that was in *Ireland's Own*, which Dad used to get every month.

We had our hair cut regularly (short back and sides) in an old barber's shop on Prussia Street. Much more excruciating were our six-monthly visits to the dentist on North Frederick Street, not least because Kevin Harrington didn't seem to believe in pain relief. (His son Barry also became a dentist, married our cousin Laura and ended up as dean of the Dental Hospital at Trinity College.) Uncle Din would call to our house every week on his High Nelly bike and give us a bag of bull's-eye sweets. We also went through a lot of Taylor Keith red lemonade and loved bringing back empty bottles to a shop beside the railway bridge on Blackhorse Avenue, where we'd get a few pennies for the returns and buy a bar of chocolate with this windfall.

The railway line was still very much in use, with steam engines pulling goods trains. As a train came along, we would lean over the parapet on one side of the bridge to get a blast of smoke and then run over to the other side – it was perfectly safe to do that – to get another blast. The railway embankments were productive allotments then, probably a holdover from 'the Emergency', but have since reverted to a wilderness of sycamore and scrub that's hacked down periodically by Iarnród Éireann for fear of autumn leaves sticking to the tracks.

2

There were always books in our house, some borrowed for a couple of weeks from Phibsboro Library, where we were regulars. Our permanent collection included a very useful set of books with titles like *How to Write, Think and Speak Correctly* and *The Wonderful Story of the Human Body* ('by a well-known physician'), which had a chapter at the end dealing with 'Reproduction and Sex'; that's how we must have learned about the mechanics of it all, since our parents never really talked to us about it.

Another book that made an indelible impression on me was a biography of Blessed Oliver Plunkett, who became Ireland's first saint for nearly seven hundred years when he was canonized in 1975. Archbishop of Armagh and Primate of All Ireland, he was implicated in a 'popish plot' by the despicable perjurer Titus Oates, found guilty of treason in 1681 and sentenced to death at Tyburn. And this terrible thing had happened despite the fact that King Charles II, reputedly a closet Catholic himself, knew that Plunkett was innocent but felt it would be politically dangerous to intervene on his behalf. Most chilling of all was the sentence, pronounced by England's Lord Chief Justice, Sir Francis Pemberton, who told our Archbishop, 'You shall be drawn through the City of London to Tyburn, there you shall be hanged by the neck but cut down before you are dead, your bowels shall be taken out and burnt before your face, your head shall be cut off and your body be divided into four quarters, to be disposed of as his majesty pleases.' The sheer barbarity of it all gave me nightmares, as did the first sight of Plunkett's severed head in St Peter's Church, Drogheda, which we went to see on a school trip.

Catholics were, we were often told, still being persecuted for their faith. Cardinal József Mindszenty, the anti-communist Primate of

Hungary, had to seek refuge in the US embassy in Budapest after the Soviet invasion of 1956. We used to pray for his early release, but our prayers didn't do much good because he was holed up there for fifteen years. We also learned about Matt Talbot, the Dublin labourer whose devotion to the Blessed Virgin was so extreme that he wrapped chains tightly around his body as a symbol of his spiritual slavery.

We cheered ourselves up with cream buns from the White Spot, a tuck shop at Hart's Corner that backed onto the school grounds and is now (surprise, surprise) a Spar. The middle-aged woman who ran it had no problem selling single cigarettes to schoolboys. People smoked everywhere then – in theatres and cinemas, buses (upstairs only) and trains (every second carriage). Department stores even had ashtrays on their counters to accommodate customers and staff who smoked. We would get Woodbines in the White Spot because they were the cheapest, and we'd head for the Sixth Lock of the Royal Canal, near Shandon Mills, to smoke them – or rather, to cough uncontrollably as we 'dragged' on the fags until we got used to it. One day, a whole matchbox flared up and singed my eyebrows, so I had to rub them hard to get rid of the evidence.

Liam and I would usually cycle to and from school, often through droves of cattle or sheep being herded to the vast market on North Circular Road, between Aughrim Street and Prussia Street. The poor animals left their droppings all over the place, and it took a bit of skill on the bike to avoid them. I once gave out to a cattle drover who was beating a heifer down the shitty gangplank of a trailer outside the abattoir, telling him to 'stop being so cruel'; he told me to 'fuck off!' The market attracted lots of burly men up from the country, many of them drinking in Hanlon's pub or having a square meal in the City Arms Hotel on Prussia Street. But then, we ourselves felt quite close to the country. For years before McKee Park was built, initially for army housing but later turned into a sink estate by Dublin Corporation, there were fields just beyond where we lived, with cattle grazing in them behind a big, unruly hedgerow.

Further along Blackhorse Avenue there was a lovely old thatched cottage, with the high wall of the Phoenix Park looming up behind it and a beautifully busy garden in front – all tragically destroyed by fire some years later. The Phoenix Park was the big thing for us, almost like having a huge back garden. Our favourite trees were the great horse chestnuts because of their prodigious yield of 'conkers' every year. We went to the People's Gardens regularly as well as the Polo Grounds, the Tea Rooms and the Zoo. Through Edel's best friend at school – Anne-Marie Kenny, younger sister of the broadcaster Pat Kenny – we knew her dad, the elephant keeper, and he used to give us free rides on one or other of these enormous beasts, strapped to their backs in bench seats. Out beyond the city limits were Castleknock, Blanchardstown and Clonsilla, all villages then, and the vast 'market garden' of north County Dublin, dotted with glasshouses full of tomato plants.

Our parents brought us to see the best that Dublin had to offer. We went out to the airport at Collinstown to watch Dakota, Viscount and Super-Constellation planes taking off and landing – all much, much noisier than today's fleet. When Uncle Dónal married his wife Mary, they had their wedding reception in the original terminal building's dining room, with net curtains flapping in the French windows and planes pulling up on the apron just outside. We also went to Weston Aerodrome for air shows, and we were up and down Nelson's Pillar – then usually known simply as 'the Pillar', except on the destination scrolls of buses – numerous times; it only cost threepence for kids to get in and climb the winding stair to the top. We went to Dublin Castle, marvelling at the Bermingham Tower from which Red Hugh O'Donnell escaped in 1590, when he was not yet twenty, and at the Chapel Royal, with its crests of every viceroy from Strongbow onwards.

Another favourite was St Michan's, in Church Street, with leathery cadavers in the crypt preserved by its ultra-dry atmosphere, where you could 'shake hands with the Crusader'. Or St Patrick's Cathedral, with its bust of Jonathan Swift, decaying Union Jacks and the old oak door with a slot in the middle that gave rise to the phrase 'to chance your arm'. Or Christ Church Cathedral, which had Strongbow's tomb and a crypt containing the mummified remains of a cat and a mouse. It seemed a bit unfair to us that the Protestants had two cathedrals in Dublin, while we only had St Mary's Pro-Cathedral. They should give us back one of theirs, because they were really *ours* anyway, we thought. On our way back home by car from Rathfarnham, we would pass them by with a degree of resentment, ducking under the bridge linking Christ Church with the Synod Hall, then down Winetavern Street to Wood Quay. We'd always be entranced by the Irish House pub on the corner, with its colourful patriotic woodcut tableaux topped by timber round towers – a surreal sight on a snowy winter night.

Prior to buying the Anglia in 1961, Dad used to rent a Ford Prefect and later a Standard Ten for our annual two-week holiday in Wexford, where we stayed with our cousins in The Faythe, that ancient route leading south out of the town. Bill and Maura Hendrick had two sons, Paddy and Tom, who were roughly the same age as Liam and I, and we became the best of friends during our school years. We would cheer as we crossed the county boundary between Wicklow and Wexford, travelling south through Ballycanew, Ballyedmond and Castlebridge to arrive in Wexford town on what's still called the 'New Bridge'. And from miles out, we'd have a competition in the back of the car to see who would be the first to spot the twin spires of Bride Street and Rowe Street churches. Every day, we went to a different beach – Curracloe, Ballinesker, Carne, Kilmore, and all the way down to the Hook Head with its totemic lighthouse fashioned from a Norman lookout tower. And Bannow Bay, where they landed in 1169.

Mam taught us all how to swim, with varying degrees of success, me not managing much more than a dog-paddle; I took after Dad, who never ventured beyond rolling up his trousers and paddling his feet at the water's edge. Who could blame him? The Irish Sea was always cold, even in August, and we'd be shivering and turning blue after getting out, desperate to wrap up in a beach towel. A good range of sandwiches would have been prepared in advance and packed for a picnic in the sand dunes. Dad always brought along a volcano kettle that looked like a miniature milk churn to boil water for tea; it was activated by feeding tightly rolled newspaper into its concave fire chamber and simply lighting the lot. Smoke would billow from the top of this contraption and, within a short time, the water in a 'jacket' around the chamber would boil and be poured into a catering teapot big enough for a platoon. We still have lots of black-and-white photographs from those days, all taken with Dad's Kodak Brownie box camera, which was old even then but didn't give up the ghost until 1973. The finished rolls of film were dropped into McGrath's Chemists on Oxmantown Road to be sent off for developing and printing; we'd get prints a week later, always opening up the neat little folder with great excitement.

Wexford town itself had a lot going for it. Mainline trains trundled slowly along the quay to and from Rosslare Harbour, separated from fishing boats by 'the Woodenworks' (since replaced by a broader concrete structure). The Staffords, local merchant princes, owned numerous buildings on the quay, and these were all painted light blue as if to delineate a property empire. Their family home in Wexford was called Cromwell's Fort, and it was said that one of their ancestors had opened the gates of Wexford in 1649 to his Roundhead 'model army'. We went to the pilgrimage site on Our Lady's Island, and to Mass every Sunday in the Church of the Assumption, on Bride Street. Not far from the town was Johnstown Castle, which had been turned over to an agricultural college, and we'd walk around the grounds, feeling tiny among the tall trees and thinking how old they were compared to us. But we shivered in the coldness of Loftus Hall, on the Hook Head, on being told the tale of a mysterious stranger who called in one night to play cards and turned out to have a cloven hoof; the idea that the Devil himself had been there quite terrified us.

There was a theatre called Dún Mhuire on Wexford's South Main Street, nearly opposite the Capitol Cinema, that staged safe drama from time to time. But our favourite place was the old Cinema Palace, in a laneway off North Main Street; it specialized in Westerns and horror films like *The Pit and the Pendulum*, starring

Vincent Price, or *The Hound of the Baskervilles*, with Peter Cushing and Christopher Lee. And for afters, we would call in to a steamy old chipper on Barrack Street, on our way back to 53 The Faythe. I liked the Hendricks' house for the one good room it had, the front parlour, with its comfortable chairs, antimacassars and semicircular china cabinet, and for Uncle Bill's amazing carpentry workshop out the back. (It's all gone now, demolished to release the development potential of a long rear garden.)

There was no shortage of cinemas in Dublin, either. Phibsboro had two – the Bohemian and the State – and we used to go to one or other of them on a regular basis on the way home from school, frequently for what were known as 'follier-uppers' – Westerns that were serialized to make us come back again and again. Cabra had its Grand, on Quarry Road, long since turned into a bingo hall. O'Connell Street had the Savoy, Carlton, Ambassador, Metropole and Capitol cinemas; Caffola's and Palm Grove ice-cream parlours, where you could pig out on a Knickerbocker Glory; and the Gresham Hotel, then run by the legendary Toddy O'Sullivan, where Princess Grace of Monaco used to stay (and where my uncle Dónal, Mam's younger brother, worked as a chef).

Couples going out on a date would meet at the Pillar or under Clerys clock and the demand for cinema seats on a Sunday night was so high that the street would be crawling with touts trying to sell overpriced tickets. Clerys had a ballroom then, and so did the Metropole, as well as a bar, restaurant and cinema with a ruched stage curtain hinting at the Folies Bergère. (Dating from the 1920s, when O'Connell Street was rebuilt in grand neoclassical style under the direction of then City Architect Horace Tennyson O'Rourke, the Metropole was pulled down in 1970 to make way for the blandness of British Home Stores, called 'BHS' here for obvious reasons, and now occupied by Penneys.)

The Capitol, originally built as La Scala Opera House, was around the corner in Prince's Street, with beckoning neon lights. Whenever we went to see a film there, we could only afford cheap seats in 'the gods' – an upper circle so steeply raked that you felt you might fall off it. Epics like *Ben Hur* usually landed at the Ambassador, although I distinctly remember being enthralled by *Lawrence of Arabia* in the Metropole. Later on, after Cinerama with its 180-degree screen opened on Talbot Street, right beside the Loop Line, we all trooped off to see *The Sound of Music*, which ran for a record-breaking ninety-one weeks from May 1966 to February 1968.

Across the river, in Hawkins Street, was the incomparable Theatre Royal, which had been inspired by Radio City Music Hall in New York and could accommodate an audience of 3,700 – much larger than the Grand Canal Theatre. And like Radio City, it staged a variety show featuring dancing girls (the Royalettes, modelled on the Rockettes in New York's version) followed by a film. Regular entertainers in the Royal included Jack Cruise, who later moved to the Olympia Theatre, and the duo of Jimmy O'Dea and Maureen Potter, who became the Gaiety Theatre's anchors. (Along with the Regal Cinema next door, the Royal was demolished in 1962 by the Rank Organization and replaced with the unspeakable horror of Hawkins House.) Christmas was our main theatre-going time and we went to *all* the pantomimes – not just the Gaiety and Olympia, but also St Anthony's Hall on Merchant's Quay, St Francis Xavier Hall off Gardiner Street, and the Father Matthew Hall on Church Street. The Queen's on Pearse Street, temporary home of the Abbey while its new theatre was being built, always put on something in Irish during the Christmas season.

Dad would also regularly bring us to Croke Park to cheer for Wexford's hurling team, with the legendary Rackard brothers, against Kilkenny, Tipperary or Cork. Christy Ring was the most lethal Cork hurler then and I used to have nightmares about him, usually involving me defending the Wexford goal with a savage-looking Ring coming at me brandishing his hurley. We were very much aware that Croke Park's collection of shed-like stands around the pitch constituted hallowed ground, because of the Bloody Sunday massacre perpetrated by British forces in November 1920, as a reprisal for the assassination of fourteen agents by IRA hit squads, organized by Michael Collins.

The most shocking thing that happened when we were kids was the Niemba Ambush, in faraway Katanga. A platoon of Irish soldiers serving with a UN peacekeeping force in the newly independent Congo was attacked in November 1960 by Baluba tribesmen armed with bows and poison-tipped arrows as well as clubs, spears and guns. Commanding officer Lieutenant Kevin Gleeson, from Carlow, was beaten to death and eight of his eleven men were killed. The Baluba were believed to indulge in cannibalism, and there were grisly tales in the tabloids that the Irish soldiers' bodies had been mutilated and even that their hearts had been eaten. After years of contributing to collections for 'black babies', many Irish people were outraged at the thought that some of them were killing and perhaps even eating our boys. For a while afterwards, 'Baluba' became a term of abuse, as in, 'Get away from me, ya feckin' Baluba.' But at least we got a half-day off school to attend a military funeral for the Niemba Nine. Their bodies had been flown into Casement Aerodrome, Baldonnel, where they lay in state, before being drawn through the city – Lieutenant Gleeson's coffin on a gun carriage, and his men's on army lorries. Even in death, the defence forces maintained a rigid pecking order.

We rented a caravan in Salthill in summer 1961, calling in to see Phila Carroll, one of Mam's best friends, who had a lovely house near Oughterard, overlooking Lough Corrib, with a deck near the water's edge – one of relatively few houses around the lake then. We also toured around Connemara, where we witnessed a man and his son selling bottles of *poitín* from the boot of their old car, visited Pádraig Pearse's yet-to-be-restored cottage in Rosmuc, and went to Carraroe, where we met a woman in her nineties, dressed in a traditional shawl and smoking an old clay pipe. Speaking to me in Irish, she asked where I was from.

'*Baile Átha Cliath*,' I replied.

'*Ah, an chathair mhór!*' she exclaimed: the big city. I asked her *as Gaeilge* if she had been to Dublin and was amazed when she told me that she hadn't.

In the summer of 1962, we went to North Wales to visit Aunt

Éilís in Ruthin, travelling for the first time outside Ireland. We had previously seen a red telephone box in Warrenpoint, Co. Down, after taking a small boat there from Omeath, Co. Louth. It was, we thought at the time, a very visible and unwelcome evidence of Partition, but we were all unquestioning republicans then, reared on '800 years of oppression'. We had also gone on a school day trip to Belfast, where we stole packets of Spangles – boiled sweets that were then unavailable in the Republic – from Woolworths on Royal Avenue.

But going to Wales was different. For a start, it was the first time we had been on a ship – the B&I Line's old *Leinster*, which seemed to have been designed for emigrants. And there were a lot of them, bound for Liverpool. At the quayside on the North Wall, middle-aged men with battered suitcases or even just big bags tied with twine were taking leave of their wives, and younger men their girlfriends or mothers, as they reluctantly returned to jobs and digs in Britain: McAlpine's Fusiliers. The bars on the ship stayed open late, judging by the spilled Guinness still sloshing on its staircases in the morning. We all slept in second-class bunks, until we were woken by a commotion before 5 a.m. as the *Leinster* docked in Birkenhead to let off the cattle – hundreds of them, all steaming and bellowing as they were herded off onto the dock. Then the ship crossed the Mersey, heading for the twin towers of the Royal Liver building, and made its way through a system of locks to tie up at Prince's Dock. We all walked down the gangplank and into England.

We had no time to linger in Liverpool, as we had to catch a train to Ruthin, via the historic city of Chester where we stopped to have sandwiches and did a walkabout. I was amazed by all its timber-framed Tudor buildings, with their upper floors hanging over the streets, especially as we had nothing like these in Dublin, because they had all been demolished. The other real surprise of our trip was to find that Catholics were a tiny minority in North Wales, and the place we went to Mass on Sunday was a small tin church, no different from what Baptists might have had at home. The shoe was on the other foot now. But we loved the long sweep of strand at

Colwyn Bay and were thrilled to travel there along the hair-raising Horseshoe Pass, through some of the most magnificent mountain scenery in these islands. We were also charmed by the country cottage that Éilís was sharing with a Welsh friend called Joan, who was also a nurse; it even had a name, *Pen-y-Waen*. I had a funny feeling even then that there was more to their friendship than met the eye. We also had to visit Uncle Frank, by then a well-established vet in St Helen's, and he brought us to lunch at a fish restaurant in Blackpool, with its poor man's answer to the Tour Eiffel and double-decker trams clanging along the seafront. Horrified to hear that we had travelled 'steerage' on the boat to Liverpool, our ever *flaith-iúlach* uncle upgraded us to first-class cabins on the way home, which was a real treat.

Nearly everyone was transfixed by television in the 1960s. Raidió Éireann had branched into TV on New Year's Eve 1961, and things would never be the same again. As Éamon de Valera himself famously said in the opening broadcast, 'Never before was there in the hands of men an instrument so powerful to influence the thoughts and actions of the multitude.' Not that we as kids were thinking about that then; all we knew was that we wanted a television set. So we kept campaigning for it until our parents relented and bought a fourteen-inch Philips model with a 'rabbit's ears' aerial that sat on top of the box and regularly had to be tweaked. When it was turned off, a bright white dot appeared in the middle of the screen, and we would even watch that until it faded away. If you wanted anything other than Teilifís Éireann, you had to put up a steel aerial on the roof to capture BBC and ITV signals from the North or from Wales.

Our little TV was part of the furniture in November 1963, when the moment came that everyone who was alive then remembers: regular programming was interrupted for what we would now call a 'newsflash' and legendary newsreader Charles Mitchel appeared on the screen to announce, gravely, that President Kennedy had been shot in Dallas. Our next-door neighbour, young Mrs McMenamin, was so upset that she came to our door in tears and had to be comforted with cups of tea. Within hours, it was confirmed that Kennedy was dead. It was almost unbelievable, especially after we had taken such delight in his visit to Ireland five months earlier. Then, it seemed as if this golden-boy President would live forever, and we were glued to the TV coverage of his tour, especially the Wexford bit when he dropped in for tea with his cousins in Dunganstown, not far from my father's birthplace in Rathgarogue. We were also intensely proud of the extraordinary role of Irish Army cadets in providing a superbly well-drilled guard of honour – personally requested by Jacqueline Kennedy – at her husband's graveside in Arlington Cemetery.

For good or ill, the McDonald family stuck with Teilifís Éireann and got hooked on reruns of *The Honeymooners*, an American TV sitcom featuring Jackie Gleason and Art Carney, set in an otherwise gloomy apartment block in Brooklyn. We became avid followers of *The Fugitive*, starring David Janssen as Richard Kimble, a doctor wrongfully convicted of murder, and Barry Morse as Lieutenant Philip Gerard, the vindictive policeman who doggedly pursues him, with the shadowy figure of a one-armed man lurking in the background. And *The Man from U.N.C.L.E.*, with Robert Vaughn as the suave Napoleon Solo and David McCallum as his cute Ukrainian sidekick, Illya Kuryakin; I had a crush on Illya. RTÉ also gave us home-produced drama when *Tolka Row* started in 1964, followed by *The Riordans* a year later.

Mam was a fan of Monica Sheridan, Ireland's first TV chef, who used to lick her fingers while cooking, just as we did. She also had a soft spot for Waterford-born crooner Val Doonican, possibly because of his hand-knitted jumpers. And who could forget *Quicksilver*, the quiz show compered by Bunny Carr? Its catchphrase, 'Stop the Lights!' entered the language as an expression of mock-shock. We were also bursting with national pride when Butch Moore sang 'Walking the Streets in the Rain' at Naples in 1965, representing Ireland for the first time in a *Eurovision Song Contest* and ending up a respectable sixth; if anyone had told me then that

Ireland would go on to win it seven times I would have said, 'Stop the lights!'

And then there was *The Late Late Show*, presented by this cheeky chap called Gay Byrne whose voice we already knew from sponsored programmes on Raidió Éireann. I can clearly remember the regular rows between the writer Ulick O'Connor, a one-time pugilist, and Dennis Franks, a rather camp old actor of Polish-Jewish descent with an upper-crust English accent; how they didn't beat each other up backstage we'll never know. We also blanched over Brian Trevaskis. A left-wing Trinity student, he turned up on *The Late Late* in March 1966 to launch an unprecedented attack on the Bishop of Galway, Dr Michael Browne, for spending a vast sum of money on his new cathedral (with its 'shrine' to JFK) when it could have been used to help the poor. Trevaskis branded the cathedral a 'monstrosity' and described the Bishop himself as a 'moron'.

Given the kind of society we had grown up in, his outburst was truly shocking, and a grovelling apology was broadcast by RTÉ. (This drama followed hot on the heels of the 'Bishop and the Nightie' affair, in which another bishop – Dr Tom Ryan, of Clonfert – condemned *The Late Late* for purveying 'filth' after a woman from Terenure, responding to a question from Gaybo, implied that she had worn nothing in bed on her wedding night.) A red-hot rumour spread around the school that Trevaskis had been a boarder at St Vincent's – and it turned out to be true. Apparently, he went on to renounce Catholicism and become an Anglican, before being fatally injured when he was hit by a train near Cabra in 1980.

Having lived through the terror of the Cuban Missile Crisis in 1962, we were intrigued when the Cold War came to Dublin in 1964. Smithfield was kitted out as Berlin's Checkpoint Charlie for *The Spy Who Came in from the Cold*, a film based on the John le Carré novel starring Richard Burton and Claire Bloom. Burton arrived with his glamorous new wife Elizabeth Taylor (Cleopatra to us), and they stayed at the Gresham for ten weeks with an entourage that included her little bushbaby. We thought it was very strange for anyone, even a Hollywood star, to have such an exotic pet, because all we ever had was a budgie. The film's producers probably chose Smithfield as a suitable location as the area was quite bleak then. We visited the set one Sunday evening on our way home from Rathfarnham and found it weirdly vacant, like the *Mary Celeste.* There were tall street lights, unusually bright for Dublin, and a replica of the hut at Checkpoint Charlie with its famous sign – in English, Russian and French – saying, 'You are leaving the American Sector', as if anyone in West Berlin would have had any doubt about that. The hut was made from timber, but so was nearly everything else. Even the footpaths were wooden, but skimmed with a thin layer of cement to make them look real, at least for the cameras; some of it was already breaking up. A year later, when the film came out, we felt a certain pride in the fact that much of it had been shot in Dublin.

In secondary school, we had some great teachers. Two of them were brothers – the very patient Dónal Ó Laoire, nicknamed Goofy, who taught us Irish; and Frank, who had a hot temper, so we called him Fury; he taught us geography. (Dónal's son, Seán Ó Laoire, went on to become a leading architect and president of the Royal Institute of the Architects of Ireland.) Brother Beere, the Latin master, was also good. But our favourite was Bob Eagar, who taught us French and English. Whatever his faults as a non-native speaker in communicating French, we thought he was the best teacher ever. He gave us a love of the English language, because he clearly loved it himself. Dressed in a beige tweed jacket, light waistcoat and cavalry twill trousers, with a moth-eaten black gown casually draped over the lot, he encouraged us in writing essays, discussed the hidden meanings of poems by Yeats and led us through the works of Shakespeare, or at least *As You Like It* for the Inter Cert and *Hamlet* for the Leaving. At the time we were at school, *Hamlet* rotated with *King Lear* and *Macbeth* on the Leaving Cert syllabus. Bob Eagar lived in Dartmouth Square and would usually either walk or cycle to work in Glasnevin, as there was no direct bus route. It's almost entirely due to him that I developed the confidence to write and, ultimately, become a journalist.

Maths with Mr Buckley was rather more challenging, so I had to go for grinds to an elderly retired maths teacher in a decrepit Georgian house beside the former Plaza Cinema on Granby Row. Up the bare wooden staircase in the first-floor back room, there'd usually be ten boys sitting around an enormous oak table, with foolscap notebooks in front of them, doing exercises in calculus or whatever. The old teacher would be hovering in the background, leaning over our shoulders every so often to check that we were getting our sums right. We'd all have to slip him five shillings (I think) on the way out of each gruelling two-hour grind, week after week, so it was a handy little earner for him. I can't remember his name, but he was a dead ringer for Mr Squeers in Dickens's third novel, *Nicholas Nickleby*.

I was still so Catholic then that I joined the Legion of Mary, going to meetings of a praesidium in North Great George's Street headed by Brendan Shortall. At weekends, we would clean windows at the Morning Star Hostel, behind Richmond Hospital, and butter batch-loaf bread for the homeless men looked after by the Legion, or deliver copies of the *Irish Catholic*, the *Universe* and the *Catholic Herald* to subscribers in and around the leafy roads of Glasnevin. Just after I had turned fifteen, Brendan Shortall left to work as a missionary in Tanzania, following in the footsteps of Edel Quinn, and we all went out to Dublin Airport to say goodbye to him. '[His] sisters were crying and mother also,' I recorded in my diary. As the plane was taking off, we all recited the catena, a chain of prayers that supposedly bound together all members of the Legion. A few days later, there was a 'Curia Reunion' in St Lawrence's Hotel in Howth, as my diary notes, recording what in retrospect was a bizarre sequence of events:

> Had four-course tea – Fruit juice, Plate of Cold Roast Turkey, Ham salad & mayonnaise; tea & bread, éclairs & trifle. After tea, said Rosary and room was cleared for dancing. I was a bit reluctant at first. Won spot prize on Ladies Choice. Packet of biscuits. Girlfriend retired after a while to look at TV.

Teenagers had more freedom in those days than they do now. When Paddy and Tom Hendrick came up from Wexford in the summertime to visit Liam and me, we'd get Runabout tickets from CIÉ's Dublin bus headquarters in O'Connell Street and go to the beaches and dunes at Donabate or Portmarnock on the Northside, and Blackrock and Dún Laoghaire on the Southside, where the old sea baths were real draws, or Bray, where we spent our pocket money on candyfloss and dodgems. One madcap adventure involved renting a paddle-boat off the stony strand. As soon as we had got out to sea, I went into Captain Ahab mode and decided we should aim to round Bray Head and land in Greystones; but a rebellion among the 'crew' and a rescue by the paddle-boat owner put an end to this crackpot idea. We'd also visit Jacob's biscuit factory to see how they put the figs into fig rolls, the Guinness Brewery for the free pints at the end of it, and the Player's and Wills's cigarette factories, where we'd get a free packet each. Two summers in succession, when we were still in our mid-teens, the four of us took the *St David* from Rosslare to Fishguard and then the train to Neath, in Glamorgan, where a widowed cousin of the Hendricks, matronly Mary Power, had a small terraced house in Briton Ferry.

In 1965, when St Vincent's moved to a new building on Finglas Road, right opposite one of Glasnevin Cemetery's watchtowers, we all lined up in our school uniforms for the arrival of Archbishop John Charles McQuaid to bless the place, followed by a sung Mass in Iona Road Church. As I noted in my diary, 'Five of the previous superiors attended. Also Minister for Education [George] Colley.' I was involved in setting up the school's first debating society, and we had a lot of fun holding competitions with other schools, such as the Dominican College and Scoil Caitríona, both in Eccles Street, which were bought up and demolished by the Mater Hospital to make way for a car park. One of our most formidable opponents was Eithne Ingoldsby, who came from a fearsomely bright family on Botanic Road. She went on to marry John FitzGerald, economist son of Garret, and served as a Labour TD for Dublin South and Minister of State until she lost her Dáil seat in 1997. An entry in my 1967 diary for Friday 27 January says, 'School today. Went to Irish debate afterwards in Muckross Park, Donnybrook. We won.' There were disagreements in our little group and, during one heated exchange, my brother Liam recalls me declaring, 'But I *am* the debating society!' I was clearly an arrogant pup then.

Some of us slathered our hair in Brylcreem to look cool at 'teenage hops' in Charleville Lawn Tennis Club at Cross Guns Bridge, or the Teachers Club on Parnell Square. On one occasion, an attractive girl declined my invitation to dance, and it took me ages to recover from that feeling of rejection. She ended up marrying one of my best friends, Kevin Fox, who was once told by Brother Burke, superior of the secondary school, to go back to the barber and get his hair cut again because it was still 'far too long'. The last thing Brother Burke wanted was that Vincent's students would go around looking like unkempt 'corner boys'; he had plans (never realized) to re-brand the school as a 'college' and, indeed, it was the first CBS on the Northside to get its own swimming pool.

We could also do solemn. On a cold, rainy day in March 1965, we all got off school to turn out along Prospect Road, shoulder to shoulder, for the State funeral of Roger Casement, hanged for treason against the British Crown in 1916, on the final stretch of its route to the Republican Plot in Glasnevin Cemetery. The Tricolour-draped coffin containing his remains, exhumed from the graveyard at Pentonville Prison in London, was transported through the streets on a gun carriage, drawn by a military jeep and flanked by an honour guard of army officers. An estimated half a million people had filed past the coffin while it lay in state for five days at Arbour Hill, and hundreds of thousands lined the streets for the funeral itself. Of course, we had heard about the 'Black Diaries' suggesting that Casement had a secret life as a homosexual while he was championing human rights for indigenous people in Africa and Latin America. But like almost everyone else in Ireland, we assumed that the diaries had been forged by the Brits. There was also a lot of excitement over the 1965 General Election, which was the first to be televised, and we stayed up to watch the results programme presented by a youthful John O'Donoghue. Fianna Fáil won with their slogan 'Let Lemass Lead On' and plummy-voiced James Dillon immediately resigned as leader of Fine Gael. We liked Seán Lemass because he was a Dubliner who seemed to have a handle on the country's economy and wasn't afraid of trying to make peace with those Orangemen in the 'Six Counties'.

The country was consumed by nationalist fervour as the fiftieth anniversary of the 1916 Rising approached, and Seán Ó Riada's *Mise Éire* became its national soundtrack. Something 'dramatic' was bound to happen and, in the early hours of 8 February 1966, it did: Nelson's Pillar was blown up. The statue of Admiral Nelson, its pedestal, caged viewing gallery and the top half of the Doric column that supported it all came crashing down – so 'cleanly' that it was suspected to be the work of a French explosives expert, commissioned by the IRA. Certainly, the army made more of a mess when its engineers blew up the rest of it. On Easter Monday my grandfather, as a veteran of the Rising, was a guest at the official opening of the Garden of Remembrance on Parnell Square. He could have used this as an opportunity to tell us all about what he did then, but he remained silent on the subject. Maybe we should have just asked him, especially as the whole thing was being re-enacted in *Insurrection*, a gritty Teilifís Éireann series that gripped the nation.

I took to compiling large-format scrapbooks, full of pictures of pop stars and television personalities culled from magazines and newspapers. The Beatles featured heavily, including a handwritten spreadsheet detailing the age, height, weight, hair and eye colour, chest and waist dimensions, and even shoe size for each of them. About Paul McCartney, I wrote that black was his favourite colour, noting that he 'loathes shaving, washes hair every two days, likes casual gear, soft leather and Kraft cheese, and wears Cuban heels'. Black was also John Lennon's favourite colour and he 'likes suede and leather, high-heeled boots, polo-neck sweaters, and wears glasses off stage. Created the haircut while in Paris.' I noted that all four of the Beatles 'prefer Italian-styled suits and clothes. Shirts bought at Stevens of Wardour Street. Anello and Davide are their shoemakers. Tailor: Dougie Millings of London. Barber: Mr James Cannon of Liverpool.'

Cliff Richard was also in several of my scrapbooks, as well as Elvis Presley, Pat Boone, Cilla Black, Joe Brown, Adam Faith, Helen Shapiro, Dusty Springfield, the Dave Clark Five and of course The Bachelors, our own three lovely lads from Inchicore. One entire scrapbook of thirty pages was 'in memory of President Kennedy', with lots of pictures of his utterly captivating visit to Ireland in June 1963, including the tea and buns in Dunganstown, as well as Senator Ted Kennedy's visit in May 1964, and numerous photographs of this gilded Irish-American Catholic family in Hyannisport and elsewhere over the years.

There were the inevitable rows at home about being allowed out and coming in late, but that's a cross all eldest children must bear as they try to push out the boundaries. Sometimes, I think my parents despaired of me. I made my mother cry more than once, which is an awful thing to admit. On 12 January 1965 I recorded in my (otherwise anodyne) diary, 'Had a row with family and was nearly going to run away.' It might have been the time that Dad threatened to sell the television unless I ate my carrots. I stormed out of the house and walked around for a bit before returning home, rather sheepishly, after an hour or so. Two days later, according to my diary, 'I had a row with Mam again and I was not allowed to watch *The Fugitive*.' She saw me as a difficult, stubborn teenager, and I thought it was probably her fault that I was gay, that she had made me that way. This was nonsense, of course.

As a child, I had always imagined following the conventional route of getting married and having children of my own. But even as young as ten, I was getting crushes on other boys in my class, one of them in particular; his name was David, and I wanted to be with him all the time. The magnet pulling me towards him and other boys was something innate, buried deep in my psyche, and I had no control over it. I also noticed that I didn't have much of an

Adam's apple but did have knocking knees, like girls, and I assumed that something had gone wrong, as most boys were bow-legged; maybe I was meant to be a girl after all. Around the same time, I started biting my fingernails, which was probably a sign of my underlying anxiety about who or what I was; the only treatment available was a bitter-tasting liquid 'polish' that had to be applied every day. Later on, when I was fourteen, I 'messed around' with a school friend. We shared a desk and used to play with each other during class and regularly in cinemas, usually the Carlton. But it was a furtive thing that the two of us didn't really acknowledge to each other.

By then, I knew that I was taking the road less travelled, and still remember the first time it occurred to me, reading Robert Frost's poem 'The Road Not Taken' in the library in Phibsboro. But as this realization dawned, I didn't like it one bit because I feared that mine was going to be a lonely journey. There was a norm, and I was deviating from it. And with no role models at the time, I was navigating through uncharted territory, or so it seemed to me. None of it was easy. Gripped by Catholic guilt, I hated the idea of being 'queer' and wondered if there was a cure. It was my dark secret, something that could never be admitted to my family or friends. Regularly, I would have to listen to boys at school telling jokes about 'queers' without letting on that I was one of them; my face would flush with embarrassment as I feigned joining in the laughter. It was awful. I began to imagine my brain as a series of compartments – rooms off a central corridor, as it were. So I would put the 'homo thing' in one of these rooms and open the door to it every so often, but otherwise pretended that it didn't exist.

Liam and I eventually shook off devotion to Catholicism in our late teens, giving up going to Mass on Sundays. But there was no way we could tell our parents then. So we would leave the house and cycle up to the Botanic Gardens in Glasnevin, armed with a packet of cigarettes, some lemonade and a copy of the *Sunday Times*, which became an absolute must-read after Harold Evans took over as editor in 1967 and started publishing crusading investigative journalism. It was quite a while before our parents twigged that we were mitching from Mass. I had stopped going to Confession, of course, because I found it increasingly strange to have to kneel in a dark box and tell my sins to some (perhaps pervy) priest. The Catholic Church's attitude to homosexuality was toxic anyway, holding that it was 'as much a sickness as measles, and needs proper treatment'. It would take years for inquiries and commissions to document the number of priests and others in Holy Orders who had sexually abused minors on a recidivist basis. And all this was covered up for decades, even as the Catholic hierarchy continued to insist that homosexual acts were an 'abomination' in the sight of God. In all her years as an agony aunt on radio, from 1963 to 1985, I don't believe that Frankie Byrne ever read out a letter from a guy saying he was having problems with his boyfriend; it was all strictly heterosexual. Had there been one, I like to think I would have used that opportunity to talk to my mother about it. But there wasn't, and I didn't.

Just as there were no tapas bars or sushi counters in Dublin then, there were no gay discos either, which was a problem for those of us who were tentatively exploring alternatives. Homosexual acts were criminalized by the 1861 Offences Against the Person Act, and so the gay scene was largely underground, focused on parks and public toilets. I discovered this netherworld after going into the 'gents' on Infirmary Road, right beside the People's Gardens, and a guy in the next cubicle inched his foot under the partition until it touched mine; we ended up having it off. It seems quite sordid in retrospect, but lots of gay guys were doing that sort of thing; 'cottaging' was the Grindr of the era. The gents on Burgh Quay and the underground facility on College Street were very busy, as was the last remaining Parisian-style *pissoir* at Capel Street Bridge, erected for all the pious men going to the Eucharistic Congress in 1932. All are long since gone. When the cottage-style loo in St Stephen's Green closed down, one of its older habitués reputedly placed a bouquet of flowers outside it, on the railings.

There were risks, of course. One guy I met early on plied me with gin, vodka and whiskey at the Mullingar House in Chapelizod, before taking me, almost comatose from all the hard liquor, to a relatively remote part of the Phoenix Park and having his way with me. He was what we called a 'chicken butcher', with a predilection for firm young flesh. They weren't all like that. The more civilized 'tricks' included a middle-aged Dutch guy called Willem van Heerden, who had a fabulous flat on the west side of St Stephen's Green in a building long since demolished; a gorgeous Swedish airline pilot called Jahn Wennerholm, who had a mews in Lad Lane and a strong weakness for younger guys; a student from Ghana doing medicine at the Royal College of Surgeons who lived in Leinster Road; and an elderly man who had a bedsit on Holles Street. That was one of the good things about the 'gay scene', I suppose – it was both ageless and classless; you could meet guys from any walk of life.

The trick I remember most was a well-spoken academic in his mid-thirties who called himself 'Martin' and was otherwise known as 'Minty' because of his practice of giving Polo mints to the boys he picked up on Burgh Quay and other places, to freshen their mouths for French kissing. When I had just turned seventeen, I met him in the toilets on College Street, and he whisked me off in his car to the TCD Botanic Gardens on Lansdowne Road, where the Berkeley Court Hotel was later built. For some reason, he had the keys to this little kingdom and used it regularly for trysts in one of the glasshouses, lying down with boys on a car rug between the potting racks. He took me there at least twice, and to one of the more private bathrooms in Trinity College on another occasion. 'Martin' passed me on to 'Alan', a blond-haired English postgraduate student in Trinity, who was also kind and gentle. The names were all phoney – I didn't use my real name either, calling myself 'Tom' – such was the fear of being blackmailed by someone or simply exposed as a 'queer'.

Fast-forward nearly thirty years, and there I was watching a current-affairs programme on RTÉ when a strangely familiar figure appeared on the screen, being interrogated about his role in relation to a matter of serious public controversy. Although he was wearing thick-framed glasses, probably as a partial disguise, I thought I knew him from somewhere. Suddenly, it hit me like a bolt from the blue: it was the man I had known as 'Martin' who had keys to the long-lost botanic gardens in Ballsbridge. 'Jesus, that's Minty!' I remember saying out loud, even though I was alone at the time.

There were girls, too, but not for sex. The one I was closest to was Jean Anne Berry, who lived in St David's Terrace, on Blackhorse Avenue. She was quite prim and proper (as most girls were then), but still sent me a Valentine's card in February 1967. She appears quite frequently in my diary as 'JAB' and I took her to my first dress dance in Jury's Hotel, but never did more than kiss her goodnight. With a group of friends, we'd take hikes up the Dublin Mountains, even in poor weather. Our craziest trip was to Connemara, where the tents we pitched near Carraroe were nearly washed away in a flood; that experience put me off camping for life.

At school, I knuckled down to swot for the Leaving Cert. In the end, I got enough honours to enroll for Arts in UCD (fees were a snip at £65), even though I had no idea at that stage what I really wanted to do with my life. I was among the few who went to college; most of my classmates opted for jobs in the Civil Service or a bank.

I was only seventeen and a half in mid-1967, too young to work in a pea factory in England for the summer because you had to be eighteen to get a national insurance card there; all I had done work-wise was to help out Dad from time to time in Quinton Hazell or take a temporary job in the Sheriff Street sorting office before Christmas, dealing with bulging sacks of post and putting it all in pigeonholes. So, just like Dick Whittington, I went to London (by boat to Holyhead and train to Euston) to seek my fortune, or at least to earn some money to keep me going during the academic year.

I remember staying first in a crowded hostel beside the solid and imposing Freemasons' Hall, off Drury Lane, not far from the then still-thriving Covent Garden market; you could almost hear Eliza Doolittle singing her heart out in a grating cockney accent. The phallic Post Office Tower had just been completed and I nearly got a crick in my neck from looking up at it. Miniskirts were all the rage – Carnaby Street was lined with shops selling them – Mary Quant was riding high, and the Beatles had just released *Sgt. Pepper's Lonely Hearts Club Band*, although the BBC banned 'A Day in the Life' because of 'drug references' in the lyrics, which we all thought was silly.

In red telephone boxes around seedy Soho, you'd often see handwritten messages, saying things like, 'French lessons. 2nd Floor,' and then giving the street address; it was one of the informal ways prostitutes made contact with potential clients then. The smash-hit record in London that summer was 'Up, Up and Away' by the 5th Dimension; you could hear it everywhere, even in your head. While I was there, the Westminster Parliament decriminalized homosexual acts (something it was impossible to imagine Dáil Éireann doing); the 'Fifth Beatle', their manager Brian Epstein, who was quite discreet about being gay himself, died after taking an overdose of sleeping pills; and playwright Joe Orton was battered to death by his lover Kenneth Halliwell, who then committed suicide, at their home in Islington.

One of the guidebooks I bought was *The Good Loo Guide: Where to Go in London*, compiled by Jonathan Routh with the aim of 'bringing to your notice loos which you may not have realised existed . . . to make your day in town a more comfortable one'. It gave star ratings to loos like the gents in Sloane Square where, as the attendant used to say, 'We always have a welcome for our regular gentlemen.' I imagined him as Charles Hawtrey playing that role in one of the *Carry On* films. At Marble Arch, I was picked up in an underground loo 'approached through long, Kafka-type tunnels' by a balding middle-aged man who had a flat in Edgware Road, and ended up going back there a few times. Victoria Station was also good, and it was there I met a young English chap called Tom, who took me to a restaurant in Pimlico where we had a 'very nice evening', as my diary records; it was so good to be treated as a human being, rather than merely a 'trick'.

Another was Mark, who was staying at the Avalon Hotel in Bloomsbury. 'Talked until 1 o'c, then went to bed with Mark,' as I noted shamelessly in my diary. There was also a Jamaican, who picked me up at Piccadilly Circus and whisked me off to his flat in Bayswater, and an Australian guy with a flat that was way out in Arnos Grove, near the Piccadilly Line's salaciously named Cockfosters terminus; I think I met him while hanging around outside the Bolton pub in Earl's Court, then the busiest of London's gay bars. My favourite, though, was a beautiful boy of my own age called Gordon, who I took to the Regent Palace Hotel, where there was open access to communal bathrooms on the upper floors. All you needed to do was to walk into the hotel as if you owned the place, and it was so busy that nobody even noticed.

I had managed to find a bedsit in West Hampstead – a cut above Cricklewood – sharing it with my old school friend Dermot Meleady, who was a year older than me and thus had no trouble getting a factory job. The flat didn't even have a fridge, so milk and other perishables went off quickly, leaving an acrid smell in the air. By then I was training to be a salesman for Collier's – an American competitor for long-established *Encylopædia Britannica* – at St Cuthbert's Parish Hall in Earl's Court, to which I got the Bakerloo and Piccadilly lines every day. The operation was run by a tall English spiv with an Aston Martin, Brylcreem-slicked hair and a big office in a much swankier building off Park Lane. He gave American-style motivational talks, telling us that he had started out as a door-to-door salesman before rising up through the ranks to the very top, with the clear implication that we could do the same if we were good enough. So after we were all given our sales material, we'd be driven out to one or other of London's suburbs and left there for the evening knocking on doors.

It was not easy. My diary includes lots of entries like, 'Worked an area in Isleworth and Twickenham. No luck.' Council flats in

Battersea were also a 'dead loss', as was Cobham, a 'dreadful area'. But I still managed to sell ten sets of encyclopedias that summer, and the commission I received from Collier's kept me going. One sale I was sure I had clinched fell through at the last minute when the couple told me they couldn't go ahead because the deal included a free volume every year for ten years, updating the wealth of information in the main set of twenty volumes. I was perplexed, but they explained that they were Jehovah's Witnesses who believed the world was going to end in 1975, and they couldn't sign up for anything that went beyond that fateful year. I'm sorry I didn't keep their address, to write and ask whether their faith had been sorely tested when the predicted Armageddon didn't happen.

We'd be collected from the suburbs late at night and dropped off in central London, usually in the vicinity of Trafalgar Square. Feeling thirsty at 1 a.m. on 27 July, after 'blanking' in Basildon, I helped myself to a carton of milk from a crate that had just been delivered to a J. Lyons Corner House café on William IV Street when two policeman apprehended me with a, 'Hallo, hallo, wot have we got here then?' I was arrested and taken to Leicester Square, where I was put in a Paddy wagon full of prostitutes and drunks, and conveyed to Bow Street Police Station, where three sets of my fingerprints were taken – for Bow Street, Scotland Yard and Dublin Castle. I spent the rest of the night in a cell, sleeping fitfully on a hard bed with a thin grey blanket before being woken in the morning, served some breakfast and then told to wait with other defendants in the anteroom of Bow Street Magistrates Court until our cases were called.

Fortunately, I was wearing my best suit with a white shirt and tie, so at least I looked respectable compared to most of the others. Eventually, I was escorted into the courtroom to take my place in the same dock where Roger Casement had once stood, although this time the public gallery was thronged with tourists eager to see British justice being dispensed. The magistrate on his dais looked at the charge sheet and then at me, with scarcely concealed contempt, saying, 'You're Irish, are you?' To which I replied, 'Yes, your honour,' and he said, 'Ah, I see,' as if that explained my crime. Having been caught red-handed, I pleaded guilty. All that remained to be decided was what the sentence should be for my transgression. I could barely believe my ears when the magistrate gave me a month in Brixton Prison – and then added, after a pregnant pause – 'suspended on payment of a three-pound fine'. Fortunately, I had the money on me, paid it into the court clerk's office, and walked out into the summer sunshine on Bow Street a free man. Well, a free teenager anyway.

3

There wasn't a crucifix over every blackboard in Earlsfort Terrace, but it felt as if there ought to be. Those who ran UCD saw it as direct-line successor of the Catholic University of Ireland, founded by John Henry Cardinal Newman, and they zealously held on to the big house named after him on St Stephen's Green, beside University Church. The Catholicism of the place was thinly disguised. Catholic chaplains were euphemistically called 'deans of residence', Opus Dei and other religious organizations ran halls of residence, our days off coincided with Catholic holy days, and nuns in their habits would always take the front row in lecture theatres.

The metaphysics department was headed by Monsignor John Horgan, a classic Thomist who believed that Heidegger and Kierkegaard should be taught only for the purpose of demonstrating that they were 'in error'. The English-born philosopher and Oxford graduate Denys Turner – one of the few lecturers that I had a crush on at college – boldly challenged this thesis and earned kudos from us lefties for his first book, *On the Philosophy of Karl Marx*. Another remarkable teacher was Paddy Masterson, who tried to steer a middle course between orthodoxy and free-thinking, and subsequently became President of UCD and head of the European University Institute in Florence. Horgan's understudy was the Reverend Desmond Connell, who had done his doctoral thesis on the insubstantiality of angels – how many you could fit on the head of a pin, we thought – and went on to become Cardinal Archbishop of Dublin. UCD was that kind of place.

It took me a while to adjust to college life. Suddenly, the constraints of secondary school, where you had to do as you were told, were gone, and you could do as you pleased – including not bothering to go to 9 a.m. lectures if you were feeling tired or hungover. Not that we had much money to spend on drink. Frequently we were so short of cash that we'd each nurse a single pint for a couple of hours in O'Dwyer's or Kirwan's on Lower Leeson Street until it became too warm and sickly to drink. For some reason, we avoided Hartigan's, leaving it to the medical students. We also knew that Robin Dudley Edwards, one of our history professors, had been 'barred' from Hartigan's. With wild white hair that made him look as if he had just been electrocuted, he had a fondness for the drink. One night, quite forgetting about the prohibition order against him, he lurched in and ordered a pint of Guinness.

'But, Professor, you're barred,' the barman said.

'Well,' replied Dudley Edwards, drawing himself up to his full height, 'if you won't give me a pint of your piss, I'll give you a pint of mine!'

Whereupon, he whipped out his willy and urinated over the bar counter.

He was a true eccentric academically, too. The preposterous title of one of his seminar series was 'Irish Nationalism from St Patrick to Pearse', as if Ireland had seen itself as a 'nation' since the fifth century AD. Lazy as an old dog, he would turn up twenty minutes late and leave after half an hour, declaring himself bored by the lot of us and our collective ignorance.

But then, the entire history department was full of 'characters' – chain-smoking Desmond Williams; stickler-for-detail Maureen Wall; the wonderful Sister Benvenuta (aka Margaret MacCurtain); the Reverend Professor F. X. Martin, who went on to lead the Wood Quay campaign; the theatrical Hilary Jenkins, who had fled from Ian Smith's Rhodesia (now Zimbabwe); and jovial Art Cosgrove, who subsequently became President of UCD. We couldn't have had a more amazing bunch of teachers. In the then relatively new Politics Department, we had Brian Farrell, Maurice Manning and Philip Pettit. Manchester-born Farrell was already famous as a bow-tied broadcaster on RTÉ television, modelling himself on the BBC's Richard Dimbleby, and pranced about the place as a self-conscious celebrity; he would later be parodied as 'Farrell O'Brien' on *Hall's Pictorial Weekly*.

Every Saturday night, there was the ritual of attending a Literary & Historical (L&H) Society debate in the Physics Theatre, to watch and listen to fruity-accented future barristers and other scions of the south Dublin middle class scoring points against each other. Star performers included Dermot Gleeson, future SC, Attorney General and chairman of AIB; Gerald Barry, whose high-pitched voice later became known to the nation from his *This Week* broadcasts on RTÉ; and golden boy Henry Kelly, who took up journalism before moving to London, where he reappeared later as a co-presenter of *Game for a Laugh* on ITV. George D. Hodnett, jazz correspondent of the *Irish Times* and author of the bawdy ballad 'Monto', was a regular at the L&H, looking for all the world like a reincarnation of legendary Dublin tramp Johnny Fortycoats; he was often homeless and sometimes even slept overnight in the paper's newsroom or wireroom, as I later found out. Afterwards, we'd adjourn to the pub and then head for the Olympic Ballroom, off Camden Street, where the 'Ags' – the college's Agricultural Society – ran a dance featuring some showband or other, with chattering girls lined up on one side and half-cut fellows on the other, just like in Glenamaddy, or anywhere in rural Ireland.

I made at least one good move early on by joining the staff of *Campus*, one of the college newspapers; its rival was called *Awake*. Tullamore-born Conor Brady was the editor; ably assisted by Jim Lockhart, who went on to join Irish rock band Horslips and ended up as a radio producer with RTÉ; and Maurice Sweeney, who became a lifelong journalist. Even though I was only a junior reporter, I had found something that I really enjoyed doing, so I quickly became immersed in it – alongside my old school pals Dermot Meleady and Ronnie Storrs, who had encouraged me to get involved. Although Brady was only a year older than me, he seemed much more mature and appeared to enjoy his role as editor until he was replaced by the more left-wing Maurice Sweeney, after a palace coup. *Campus* used traditional hot-metal letterpress printing, which made it very expensive to produce, but it had a generous patron in John Crimmins, an independently wealthy Corkonian, who kept the whole thing afloat.

(Much to my dismay, Dermot Meleady turned to Maoism, and I'll never forget him talking in slogans and waving his *Little Red Book* at me after returning from a trip to Tullamore, where he had set up a soapbox to preach Mao's gospel to the townsfolk. After graduating from UCD, he became a secondary school teacher; joined the British and Irish Communist Organisation, whose main *shtick* was supporting 'self-determination' for Ulster Protestants; and emerged years later as an unapologetic press spokesman for the Israeli Embassy in Dublin and biographer of Irish nationalist leader John Redmond.)

Having thrown myself so enthusiastically into extracurricular activities, I neglected my studies and failed the first-year exams. So I went off to England yet again for the summer to earn some money, knowing that I'd have to repeat the entire year on my return. This time, I was eligible for a national insurance card and could therefore work in a factory. I got a job on the night shift at Bird's Eye, in Grimsby, where I stood on a platform and stirred newly frozen peas as they poured out of a chute into a gargantuan vat. I was billeted in digs with an elderly couple who lived above a shop not far from the town centre. They were so mean that they wouldn't even put enough water in the saucepan to boil an egg for my supper, before I headed off to stir more peas. My time at the factory was short, as the pea crop was devastated by unseasonably heavy rain, and all the temporary staff – including me – were laid off. I was lucky enough to get a job as a barman in a busy pub where I developed a taste for Advocaat, that sickly-sweet Dutch tipple made from eggs, sugar and brandy; I would swig it from the bottle when nobody was looking. My 'black diary' list also records a few conquests in Grimsby and nearby Cleethorpes, usually of the 'fast love' variety.

Back at UCD, I got elected to the Students' Representative Council for the Arts faculty without much difficulty. At that time, the

SRC was run by 'the Machine', an outfit that had been founded some years earlier by Gerry Collins, who later became Minister for Foreign Affairs under Charlie Haughey. The Machine was an extension of Fianna Fáil's Kevin Barry Cumann in UCD and served as a training ground for young, ambitious FF-inclined students on how to play politics: very rough. Usually 'up from the country', they were alienated by the Dublin set that controlled the L&H, so they took over the SRC instead. I used to have long, circular discussions with Gerry Collins's nephew, Bob Collins, about the meaning of it all, or whether it even had any meaning. A philosophy student, he was the most civilized member of the Machine and always wore a three-piece suit, shirt and tie, when we were all going around in jeans, jumpers and anoraks. It was only after leaving UCD that Bob Collins had a Pauline conversion, taking a decidedly left turn; and he went on to become director-general of RTÉ.

The Machine was opposed by a loose coalition of Fine Gael, Labour and left-wing students who called themselves, with great originality, the Anti-Machine. Its leading strategist was P. J. Carty, from Roscommon, who was more than a match for Bob Collins. I joined the Anti-Machine, naturally. SRC meetings in Newman House could get very fractious. George Williams, the head porter there, was in league with the Machine. At one particular meeting, before a crucial vote could be called, he rang the bell to clear us out when it looked as if the Fianna Fáil gang would lose. So it was a great triumph when we got our inspirational leader, engineering student Eddie O'Connor, elected as president of the SRC. He lived on St Helen's Road in Booterstown, where we used to meet and plot his campaign, next door to Seán Finlay, who became a good friend and a geologist at Tara Mines.

The SRC had its own travel office on the hall floor of Newman House, with Janet Matthews as the sole staff member. I was travel officer, and also became a director of the Union of Students of Ireland Travel Service, aka USIT, representing UCD. This involved going to regular board meetings in USI's offices on Harcourt Street, where its charismatic president, Howard Kinlay, was based along with his attractive young secretary, Doreen Foley, who wore skimpy miniskirts and had a Twiggy-style hair-do. The legendary Gordon Colleary had set up USIT and continued running it for decades, helping to open up the wider world for Irish students. Kitted out in his emblematic bow-tie, he was a brilliant lateral thinker who was well able to run rings around USIT's generally left-wing student directors. When Mickey Joe Walsh from UCG and myself sought to block flights to Athens in protest against the military junta in Greece, he listened to the fiery speeches before announcing that the planes had already been chartered. Game, set and match to Gordon.

It was quite an experience to be a company director at the age of nineteen or twenty. I only abused my position once, after missing a train from Victoria Station in London to catch the last USIT flight back to Dublin from Gatwick. I went to a public telephone box and rang the airline, British Midland, telling them I was a director of the chartering company and asking if they could hold the plane for half an hour. Incredibly, they did.

Gordon Colleary also invested heavily in the multiple journalistic enterprises of his long-time friend Vincent Browne. As co-founder of *Magill* magazine and chairman for many years of the loss-making *Sunday Tribune*, he contributed enormously to Ireland's political and cultural life. USIT subsequently went global and, at one point, had a turnover of over €600 million per annum, employing 1,500 people. Colleary ('Gordie' to his family and close friends) met then US President Jimmy Carter to secure student visas, and even danced with Imelda Marcos in Manila. But he took a step too far in mid-2001 by engineering USIT's reverse takeover of the US Student Travel Service. After the 9/11 catastrophe, Americans stopped travelling and the business empire that Colleary had built up so assiduously collapsed like a house of cards – at great personal cost to himself and many others.

In 1968 I joined a new organization, Students for Democratic Action (SDA). This was very much in the spirit of left-wing student activism in Paris and elsewhere that year, but we had a very particular focus: the college's plan to move the Arts faculty from Earlsfort Terrace to windswept suburban Belfield. There was serious concern, even among staff, that the *grand projet* was falling way behind schedule. Annoyingly, the Catholic church on the Belfield campus was completed long before the library. But we didn't take this lying down. John Feeney, the leading light of an avowedly Christian socialist group, and his cohorts had the effrontery to turn up with placards protesting against the consecration of the church. In the presence of Archbishop John Charles McQuaid, who was officiating on that auspicious occasion, Feeney's group pointed out that UCD was a constituent college of the National University of Ireland, which had been established in 1908 as non-denominational. But the college authorities had got round this restriction in its charter by dedicating the piece of land on which the church stood to the Archdiocese of Dublin in perpetuity, and as if by magic it was no longer legally part of the campus.

In February 1969, I was among the one hundred and fifty students who occupied the college's administration wing, to protest against the move to Belfield. We had gathered at lunchtime in the Physics Theatre, at the opposite end of the Earlsfort Terrace building, under an SDA banner, to debate a motion that there should be no move to Belfield until full library services were available; that UCD's governing body should be replaced by an elected staff/student committee; and that students should occupy the administration wing as soon as the meeting ended. This was proposed with great conviction by none other than Kevin Myers, long before his politics veered notably to the right. I'm not even sure that the motion was actually put to a vote, but led by Myers and lanky Dave Grafton we left the Physics Theatre, rushed along the corridor, through the Main Hall (now the National Concert Hall's foyer) and burst through the double doors of UCD's nerve centre, bolting them behind us.

Over the course of the next hour, we withstood an assault by grubby commerce students and persuaded startled staff to leave. Poor Paddy Keogh, UCD's impeccable head porter, didn't know what to do. Gardaí arrived, but then withdrew after the college authorities apparently indicated that they would prefer to sort things out internally. We then commandeered the college's Gestetner machines to churn out statements from the 'liberated zone', calling on our colleagues to resist the tyrannical regime at UCD, just as the students did in Paris during *les événements* some eight months earlier. Basil Miller, who also went on to become a journalist, stayed up all night with the rest of us, conducting seminars and printing Marxist tracts, as we sustained ourselves on fish and chips bought in a large batch from Dirty Dan's at Kelly's Corner.

It made the lead story in all the morning papers. 'The black flag of anarchy flew over UCD last night,' said the immortal first line of a report by Jim Farrelly in the *Irish Independent*. Outrageous! How dare they?! we thought. And then someone went out to check, only to find that there was indeed a black flag flying over the college. So two of our lads went up to take it down and replace it with a more appropriate red flag with 'SDA' inscribed on it in white letters, and we issued a press statement saying this had been done. The thing is that there were actual anarchists in Dublin then, who believed in overthrowing the State and giving real power to the people. I recall joining about thirty of them – all dressed in black jeans, black shirts and black jackets (often leather) – on a march to the Spanish Embassy in protest against the planned execution of Basque separatists. We were always marching against what we saw as abuses at home and abroad: to the US Embassy in protest against the Vietnam War, and through the city centre raising our voices in solidarity with the homeless.

On one such march in January 1969, organized by the Dublin Housing Action Committee to highlight the dire housing situation in the city, I witnessed gardaí lining up at the apex of D'Olier Street and Westmoreland Street, ostentatiously removing their identification tags and then baton-charging a crowd of us staging a sit-in on O'Connell Bridge. We all ran for cover wherever we could find it, and I saw three plainclothes Special Branch men beating up John Feeney outside the public toilets on Burgh Quay. The ugly scenes that day reminded me of what Brendan Behan once said about the guards in Dublin, that they 'were all lured down from the Kerry mountains with lumps of raw meat'. More seriously, the fracas on O'Connell Bridge confirmed our suspicions that the police force had been politicized and was now acting as the partisan agent of a wearyingly long-serving Fianna Fáil government.

Eddie O'Connor and the SRC took no part in the occupation, leaving that to us Bolsheviks – at least until it came to an end, which it did late on the second night, when we all came out of the 'liberated zone' to cheers from a crowd of students in the Main Hall and a mass meeting in the Great Hall. There were up to five thousand at these 'teach-ins' that continued all week. All sorts of people got involved, including Garret FitzGerald and Maurice Manning – both of whom became chancellors of the NUI – as well as Ruairi Quinn, then chair of the Labour Party branch in UCD, and Eddie O'Connor, who went on to make a fortune from wind energy.

The Academic Council set up a 'Committee of Inquiry into the Recent Disturbances in the College', with Robin Dudley Edwards as its sole member. He turned up every day to take his place in the council chamber, wearing baggy chinos, a light summer jacket and thin, psychedelic tie – probably because he was trying to pretend that he was on our side. After conducting his 'inquiry', the nutty professor wrote an infamous report blaming us for everything and suggesting we should be 'disciplined' for our roles in the 'disturbances'. None of us were, as far as I recall. But a steamroller was in motion and there seemed to be nothing more we could do to stop the move to Belfield. So we went out there, very reluctantly, in the autumn of 1969, as soon as the Arts Block was finished. It had been designed by Polish architect Andrzej Wejchert, who had won an international competition for the Belfield masterplan, drawing up his concept on the kitchen table of his mother's flat in Warsaw. The Restaurant Building, a modernist masterpiece by Robin Walker, was also up and running, but the huge, top-heavy Library by Sir Basil Spence was still under construction, so the basement of the Arts Block was pressed into service for library use. As for the

Students Union building, well, it might happen at some stage in the future. In short, Belfield was very much a work in progress and, in parts, a mucky building site.

It took us ages to persuade CIÉ to extend the No. 10 bus route to this college-in-the-making; in the meantime we had to get out at Donnybrook Church and walk the rest of the way. Worst of all, there was nowhere to get a pint. The Montrose Hotel, nearest licensed premises to the college, detested students and would only serve us half-pints, which we knew was inherently uneconomical. So we devised a cunning plan to build a student bar on campus. Ciarán Fahy, then president of the SRC, and myself as deputy president concocted the scheme for a modest prefab building and sought a meeting with the college's fearsome Secretary and Bursar, J. P. McHale, to seek funding for it. He refused to entertain the idea that UCD should provide money for the construction of any facility where students might get drunk.

When the meeting was finished, McHale – who ran the entire college out of his head in those pre-digital days – turned to me. 'Mr McDonald,' he said. 'Are you a communist?' I suppose he was thinking about my role in the SDA occupation. A champion bridge player, McHale was actually quite a shy man, and he posed the question in his characteristically diffident manner. I replied that I wasn't a communist exactly, but I believed in greater equality in society, or some such.

The irony was that, having been refused the college's support for a student pub, I became a rather effective capitalist. We raised substantial grants from Guinness and Cantrell & Cochrane, with the balance as a loan from Mercantile Credit. With this financial package in hand, we sought another meeting with McHale and, this time, rather surprised by our entrepreneurship, he consented to the plan and even offered to bridge the funding gap by giving us an interest-free college loan of £14,000 – the total cost, I recall – provided that it would be a 'beer-only' bar; he believed that spirits would have the same effect on students as 'firewater' did on Red Indians in the Wild West. We had lined up architect Aidan Powell, a former Machine member of the SRC, to design the Terrapin hut on a site facing the Restaurant Building and, while it was being built, we advertised the post of bar manager and proceeded to conduct interviews with the applicants. There was one outstanding candidate, Séamus Boylan, and we gave it to him. (As if to prove that we got it right, he remained on as a highly regarded bar manager until his retirement thirty years later.)

We then established the UCD Students Club and put on our best suits to appear before Dermot Gleeson's father, Circuit Court Judge John Gleeson, to make our application for a club licence. We got it no problem and the bar duly opened in August 1971, charging the same prices as ordinary pubs in town – 17 pence for a pint of Guinness, 18 pence for Smithwick's ale and 21 pence for Harp lager. At the official opening, I blushed with embarrassment at an unexpectedly generous tribute from McHale, who named me in his speech as 'the prime mover on the students' side in formulating and executing the idea', saying that UCD students were 'fortunate in having among their number one who has been willing and is still willing to devote himself wholeheartedly and unreservedly to an enterprise he believes will benefit his fellow students' – which was a bit unfair to Ciarán Fahy. I congratulated McHale for letting us go ahead with the project, commending the college's concession to 'the principle that students should run their own affairs'.

The bar we threw up in a few weeks had hard bench seats and very basic facilities, far removed from the soft sofas that would appear much later when the Students Union building was finally built, but at least it was open for business. Our Terrapin hut lasted for twenty years, ending its life as a computer lab before being demolished without trace. So much for my only venture into property development! Today, Belfield has at least four bars; and the Montrose Hotel, which treated students so badly, has now been converted into student housing, which represents some sort of justice. I still have my honorary life membership card – No. 000001 – as first chairman of the UCD Students Club.

Another bonus of being involved in student politics was the

opportunity it gave us to meet fellow students from other colleges, north and south of the Border, on their home turf. I recall travelling to Cork by car on one occasion and hiccupping all the way back to Dublin later that night after drinking far too many pints with UCC student leaders in some pub at the rear of their college. Ciarán Fahy and I represented UCD at the May Ball at Queen's University Belfast in 1969, which was attended by the Governor General of Northern Ireland, Lord Grey of Naunton. A novel aspect of the formal dinner in the Great Hall that year was the introduction by then Queen's SRC President Fred Taggart of a 'Toast to Ireland' after the traditional 'Toast to Her Majesty, the Queen'. Such were the deep divisions of those days that many of us – shamefully, in retrospect – didn't stand for the first toast, while many of those who did stand declined to do so when the second toast was called. Taggart, a liberal Protestant, was among the Queen's students who took part in the People's Democracy march from Belfast to Derry in January 1969, and were attacked by loyalists at Burntollet. Later that year, we were all delighted when Queen's psychology student and People's Democracy activist Bernadette Devlin took the Mid-Ulster seat in a by-election and became the youngest ever MP in the British House of Commons at the age of twenty-one.

We had formed an enduring alliance with Queen's at a marathon USI congress held at the Yeats Country Ryan Hotel in Rosses Point, Co. Sligo, in 1969, where London-born Nick Ross, one of the most handsome guys around, won the 'Perfect Student Body' title; he went on to become a well-known BBC broadcaster on radio and television. We became great friends with two other members of the Queen's delegation – blonde-haired Annie McCartney and her sidekick, René Cheong. Annie was from the Falls Road area of Belfast, living in a 'two-up, two-down' terraced house on Oranmore Street, with the gates of Clonard Monastery at the end of it. (Sadly, its *Coronation Street*-style housing has since been obliterated by the Northern Ireland Housing Executive, in favour of suburban-style houses with front gardens and driveways. I still can't face going back there to see it now.) Around the corner was Bombay Street, where Catholics had been burned out of their homes by a loyalist mob in August 1969. Yet the McCartneys' front door was always 'on the latch', as were most of the others, so that neighbours or children could drop in at will.

Clonard also had its share of shebeens, and I had the privilege of being brought in to one or two of them by Annie's dad, Joe McCartney, a man who enjoyed huge respect in the area; when you were with Joe, you felt safe even though Belfast was falling apart. (Of course, the city wasn't safe at all. In August 1972, one of our best friends, Kevin Finnegan, was repeatedly shot by a masked gunman while locking up his father's off-licence on Tate's Avenue, and was lucky to survive.)

The city-centre retail zone had to be railed off to guard against terrorist bombs, and everybody going through the gates was frisked by 'civilian feelies', as Annie called them. But at least you felt relatively secure once you got inside the protected area. Outside it, you could never really tell whether a parked car on any street was a potential bomb, as there were so many going off. Sometimes, we'd miss the last train back to Dublin on a Sunday night because the security forces would have thrown a cordon across Ormeau Road, checking every car. Disruption to rail services between Belfast and Dublin also intensified during the Troubles because the Provos regularly blew up Kilnasaggart Bridge near the border in south Armagh, forcing passengers onto buses between Portadown and Dundalk.

Marked differences in the roads were acutely embarrassing for us as Southerners. You'd leave Belfast on a motorway, with a decent road running south towards Newry, and you'd know immediately when you had crossed the Border – even at night – because the road surface suddenly became so rough. The British Army also began cratering minor roads, to make the Border less porous and require those crossing it to go through massive security installations on the main routes, such as those just south of Newry and Aughnacloy. In Belfast, we tended to stay in the area around Queen's, with side trips to Clonard in one of the IRA-approved black taxis that ferried people up and down the Falls Road after the city bus service was withdrawn; too many of its double-decker buses were being burned by republican rioters.

Back in Dublin, it was inevitable that there would be fallout from the Troubles up north, and it came in the form of the Arms Crisis. In the early hours of 6 May 1970, then Taoiseach Jack Lynch dismissed Charlie Haughey and Neil Blaney from the government over suspicions that they had been involved in a conspiracy to import arms illegally for the Provos; another republican-minded minister, Kevin Boland, resigned from the government in protest. News of the sackings took everyone by surprise, not least because Haughey – then Minister for Finance – had not been marked down as a hardliner on the North. Lynch was to make a statement in the Dáil at 10 o'clock that night, and both Ciarán Fahy and myself wanted to be there for it. So we asked Bill Leen, a retired Garda superintendent from Kerry who held the post of Warden at UCD (keeping an eye on the students, mainly), if he could get tickets for us and, sure enough, he did. Neither of us had ever been in the Dáil public gallery before, yet there we were hanging on the Taoiseach's every word and watching the stony-faced reactions of his former ministers, now consigned to the back benches. In the end, both Blaney and Haughey were acquitted of all charges in the Arms Trial. I learned much later that the architect Sam Stephenson, who had designed a traditional Irish bar for Haughey's palatial home in Kinsealy, used to drive him to the Four Courts for his trial.

Some of the most formidable student politicians came from UCG. They included Frank Flannery, who defeated me by 60 votes to 46 for the post of president of USI and went on to become Fine Gael's most professional 'handler' and founder of Rehab, as well as Pat Rabbitte and Eamon Gilmore, both of whom became leaders of the Labour Party, and the extraordinary Richard O'Toole, whose stint as president of the Soviet-backed International Union of Students in Prague rather surprisingly prepared him for a glittering career that embraced the Department of Foreign Affairs, the European Commission, the World Trade Organization and Goldman

Sachs International, as an acolyte of Peter Sutherland. Having failed to take the USI post, even with solid support from the Queen's delegation, I was persuaded to stand for presidency of the SRC in what turned out to be a three-way contest. I ended up heading the poll, but the other two candidates – Gerry Flynn and Tom Blenerhassett – had done a deal on second preferences and this resulted in me being defeated on the second count by 19 votes out of a total poll of nearly 4,500 by Flynn, who went on to become career guidance officer at my grandfather's old school, Rockwell College. I must admit that the result rather undermined my faith in proportional representation. My campaign manager, Dick Lincoln, was in tears, and so were many other supporters. I was the only left-wing candidate.

In retrospect, I'm actually quite glad that I lost the contest, because it pointed me towards journalism rather than politics. A group of us got together to set up a new student newspaper, as UCD was now without one following the demise of both *Awake* and *Campus*. Rather prosaically, we called ours *Student* and it was a huge success. Not only was it cheap to print – all we needed was an IBM 'golf ball' typewriter, sheets of Letraset for headlines and off-set litho for printing – but we even got permission to stay in the Arts Block overnight to produce the paper, rather than having to do it in someone's grotty basement bedsit with a coin meter for the electricity. We splashed stories about what was going on in college and outside it. One of the causes célèbres of the time was the occupation of Georgian houses at the corner of St Stephen's Green and Hume Street, to prevent their demolition by the Green Property Company, and I remember going to interview Duncan Stewart, Deirdre Kelly and others about the stand they were taking to protect Dublin's heritage.

Incredibly, *Student* was selling up to three thousand copies per issue, and we were rolling in money. So the editorial board – Peter Mair, Francis Mulhern, Ronan Brady, Tom Hayes and myself – used to treat ourselves to dinners at the Trocadero on Andrew Street, with its pictures of the stars; or the Robert Emmet Grill of the Russell Hotel on the corner of St Stephen's Green and Harcourt Street, which was great for steaks. My only regret was that Dublin's premier restaurant, Jammet's on Nassau Street, had already closed before we could eat there. But then, what we were used to was rather basic, such as the Coffee Inn on South Anne Street, the first place in Dublin to do pizza; Robert Roberts café on Grafton Street; and the Golden Spoon, in the basement of O'Connell Bridge House. Mair went on to become one of Europe's premier political scientists and professor of comparative politics at the European University, dying suddenly while on holiday in Ireland in August 2011. Mulhern went to Oxford and became a left-wing cultural critic and member of the editorial board of *New Left Review* while Brady became a journalist and NUJ activist. And Tom Hayes joined the Workers' Union of Ireland (since subsumed into SIPTU) as a branch officer before going over to the other side – first as a personnel officer for Linson Pharmaceuticals in Swords and later as a 'human resources' consultant based in Brussels.

We had very cordial relations with leading lights of the SRC in Trinity College, despite the traditional enmity between our two institutions. Trinity was a peculiar place then. Because of the Catholic Church's ban on its adherents attending the college without a 'special dispensation' from a bishop, it had remained, in effect, the Protestant university founded by Queen Elizabeth I. A third of its two thousand five hundred students then came from England, a third were Irish (including a large contingent of Protestants from up north), and a third came from overseas, usually from British Commonwealth countries. Certainly, it seemed quite 'foreign' to me at the time, like the reincarnation of an Oxford or Cambridge college in the middle of Dublin. Trinity had Fellows and Scholars, and august societies like the Hist and the Phil that were much older than our L&H; undergraduates had to wear academic gowns to attend Commons, where Grace before Meals would be recited in Oxbridge Latin, as it still is today; and student decorum was overseen by the voluble royalist Junior Dean, Professor R. B. McDowell.

Adrian Bourke (brother of Mary Bourke, later President Mary Robinson) was president of the SRC and had convinced the college authorities to make space on their board for him and his successors. But the ultra-respectable Bourke was unexpectedly defeated in his bid for a second term by Kerry Protestant Joe Revington, who cultivated the grass roots with his marvellous slogan, 'Vote for Joe, the man you know. Policies not personalities!' He had another advantage, in that his mother owned the racecourse in Tralee and he was never short of money. So he would take over the basement of the Suffolk Lounge from time to time for an almighty piss-up, with all drinks 'on the house'. (Revington later became special adviser to Dick Spring when he ran the Labour Party, and one of his duties was to organize busloads of grass-roots members from Kerry to flood party conferences in Dublin to vote in favour of going into coalition with Fine Gael, Fianna Fáil or whoever. It is also suspected that he was behind the big banner erected beyond the bridge at Abbeyfeale in 1982, proclaiming the preposterous message, 'Socialist Kerry Welcomes its New Leader.')

Other Trinity luminaries in our day included Shane Ross, with his unshakeable anglicized accent acquired at Rugby School; Jim Hamilton, a brilliant lawyer who went on to join the Attorney General's Office and later became Director of Public Prosecutions; and David Vipond, a firebrand Maoist agitator who conducted surreal exercises in 'mass democracy' on the steps of Trinity's Dining Hall. When Paul Tansey took over as president of Trinity's Students Union, it could always be trusted to produce at least four hundred students for a protest march, complete with appropriately worded placards, within an hour – whatever the *casus belli* happened to be at the time.

Out in UCD, however, the so-called 'Gentle Revolution' was over. Its end was marked by the intake of freshers in October 1969, notably Adrian Hardiman and his friend Michael McDowell, both of whom were very much on the political right and could articulate their positions rather well. McDowell took to wearing his FCA greatcoat to college as a provocation, we thought. Hardiman not only became Auditor of the L&H but also President of the SRC before going on to become a successful barrister, senior counsel and libertarian Supreme Court judge, while McDowell also prospered at the Bar, later becoming Attorney General, Minister for Justice and leader of the Progressive Democrats. With the Belfield Bar doing well and an arts degree in history and politics under my belt, I couldn't wait to get out of college. Having enjoyed summers working in Boston and New York, I decided to go back to New York to look for work. Indeed, I was in such a rush to go, in September 1971, that I left before the annual degree conferring, denying my parents the opportunity of seeing me dressed up in an academic gown and mortar board. That was a mean, uncaring thing to do after all the sacrifices they had made to put me through school and then through college. I still regret it to this day.

4

Hard to believe, but it's true: I started my journalistic career at the age of twenty-two as freelance New York correspondent for the *Irish Press*. But before that happened, life in the city was a struggle. I got a job with an Irish-owned security company doing night shifts guarding telephone installations at the nether end of Staten Island. It was not too bad in the autumn, but New York winters are bitterly cold and the only thing that stood between me and hypothermia, as I sat in the driver's cab of a telephone company truck, was a thin blanket. It also stuck in my craw that the real reason why the telephone installations needed to be guarded was that telephone company workers were on strike and the employers feared that they'd sabotage the equipment. One night, when it got really arctic, I just thought, What am I doing here? and decided to quit there and then, catching a night bus to the ferry terminal, then the boat to Manhattan and finally the No. 1 Broadway Local line home to the Upper West Side. I dropped my uniform back to the security firm in Midtown, but kept as a souvenir the solid nightstick they had given me.

After that, I was so desperate for income that I signed up with Avon, selling cosmetics from door to door in our apartment building – a nice way to meet the neighbours, but there wasn't much money in it. I was literally down to my last fifty cents when I called Jimmy Hanley, a friend from UCD, to see if he knew of anything going. He had been working in the Blarney Rock, an Irish bar on 33rd Street between Sixth and Seventh Avenues, near Madison Square Garden. As luck would have it, he was leaving to go home to Ireland, so he left his job on the Blarney Rock's sandwich counter to me. The pub was owned by Tommy Dwyer, a single-minded Irish-American with a short fuse, and it was populated by regular customers attracted by relatively cheap drink and the atmosphere of a modest neighbourhood bar. Pat Judge, who later set up as a solicitor in Castleknock, was the head barman, assisted by Larry and Tom – all three of them from Ireland. My job was to cook hunks of ham, pastrami and roast beef in the grungy back kitchen and then make sandwiches to order on rye, brown or white bread at a long counter facing the bar. It used to get mad busy if there was some big event on in Madison Square Garden, or when an Aer Lingus crew staying in the Pennsylvania Hotel opposite would descend on us, sometimes leaving the worse for wear. But the pay and tips were good: I was taking home $175 per week, which was a lot of money in those days.

Meanwhile, I had hopes of breaking into journalism. I had good contacts in the Irish papers through my involvement in student politics, and Michael Kirke, then education correspondent of the *Irish Press* (and, incidentally, a member of Opus Dei), passed me on to foreign editor Joe Carroll, who gave me the break in the spring of 1972. I bought a Remington portable typewriter, which I still have in case everything else breaks down, and set about becoming a proper journalist; I even managed to get an 'I' visa (for foreign press) to legitimize my stay in the United States. I had a wonderful time writing about Watergate, Irish Noraid, Broadway and off-Broadway shows, and off-beat stuff about New York City. I met Pete Hamill and Shirley MacLaine, interviewed the great Siobhán McKenna in the Gramercy Park Hotel and watched Senator Sam Ervin and the Watergate hearings on daytime TV.

I'll never forget interviewing Noraid's chief, Michael Flannery, in the bleak Irish ghetto of Astoria, in Queens. He had left Ireland in 1926, deeply disillusioned by Éamon de Valera's decision to establish Fianna Fáil and participate in Free State politics, and his mind was frozen in that era of 'betrayal'; he knew almost nothing about contemporary Ireland. This was when members of the New York City Police Department marching in the annual St Patrick's Day parade carried green banners fringed with gold tassels, bearing the message, 'ENGLAND GET OUT OF IRELAND'. Flannery believed that the 'armed struggle' would bring about a united Ireland, and he worked tirelessly to raise funds ostensibly for Sinn Féin but in reality for the Provisional IRA.

Good sources told me how they would pack coffins with Armalites and other weapons for dispatch on Aer Lingus flights to Ireland, banking on these not being discovered due to the traditional Irish respect for the dead. The Irish Deputy Consul General in New York at the time was Paddy McKernan, a brilliant and engaging diplomat whose job included keeping an eye on Noraid. He was nothing if not unconventional, with poster-size portraits of Marx and Lenin in the master bedroom of his Upper East Side apartment, which he happily showed me on a tour of the flat. But his early left-wing dalliance didn't stand in the way of McKernan's stellar career, which included posts as Irish Ambassador to both the EU and the US, as well as Secretary-General of the Department of Foreign Affairs.

I was sharing a rent-controlled apartment on Riverside Drive and 100th Street with an American friend, David Longmire, who was a dedicated remedial teacher for blind kids and, later, a professional therapist. Our twelve-storey brownstone had liveried doormen at the entrance and a communal basement laundry that doubled as a nuclear fallout shelter; there were tins of baked beans and packets of biscuits there from the 1950s, just in case NYC was nuked by the Soviets. New York City had an edge then, which it has lost since. It was dangerous. You could easily get mugged; someone advised me to carry at least $10 in my pocket at all times in case I had to give money to a heroin addict with a knife. Central Park was particularly risky, but I still went there quite regularly to check out its cruising area near the Museum of Natural History; you never knew who you might meet. And even though I was out at all hours of the day and night, I was never once mugged during the two years I was living in Manhattan.

Back in Ireland, things were going from bad to worse. Bloody Sunday in January 1972 was the lowest point, not only because of the indiscriminate killing of civilians by British paratroopers, but also the biased way in which it was reported by the *New York Times*, with far too much credence given to 'briefings' by British sources suggesting that it was really a battle rather than a massacre. If this was how the *Times* reported Ireland, a country I knew well, how could anyone have any confidence in its reporting of difficult situations in other parts of the world? But as the conflict in Northern Ireland intensified, I was moving away from the nationalist version of history we had all imbibed at school. I bought the first US edition of Conor Cruise O'Brien's magisterial work, *States of Ireland*, and began to grasp the essential truth that one million loyalists could not be coerced into a united Ireland. It purged me of any residue of republicanism (in the Irish sense), and I am indebted to the Cruiser for that.

I had spent my first Christmas away from home with my red-headed friend Maggie Hammond and her family on Long Island, but returned to Dublin for the festive season in 1972. Seeing I was on board the Aer Lingus jumbo jet, crew members I knew from the Blarney Rock invited me into the cockpit as we were flying into the dawn; I was astonished to discover that they were all sitting around drinking coffee and chatting, while the plane was on autopilot.

Tony Reddy, an SRC colleague from UCD with shoulder-length hair who became one of my best friends, came over for two summers to work for New York-based architect Paul Rudolph and stayed in our apartment. In September 1972, we got Greyhound bus tickets that offered foreign students unlimited travel in the continental US for three weeks at an all-in cost of $99 per person. We decided to head for the West Coast, as anyone would. Flying there is one thing, but going by road is a marathon journey. When we got to Chicago, exhausted, we realized we'd done only a third of it. In San Francisco, we booked into a budget hotel beside the Powell & Mason cable car turntable. Two young Indian guys were checking in at the same time. It turned out that they were both studying science at Bombay University, and one of them added that he also read people's palms to tell their future.

'But that's just rubbish,' I said. He looked offended, and then offered to read mine, as he obviously hoped to demolish my prejudice and demonstrate that palmistry was sound. We dropped our bags to our respective rooms and met again in the lobby, for a palm-reading session. The Indian student took hold of my left hand, examining my palm closely and telling me that I had a long 'life-line' and would live until I was quite old. I thought, That's a good start anyway. Then, he took my right hand and looked at the lines on my palm, telling me that I would do well in journalism, write books and even become famous one day. Not only that, but I would never be short of money – not rich, mind you, but comfortable. He did the same for Tony, telling him that he would become a very successful architect and multimillionaire. Tony thought it was all a load of nonsense, but I was intrigued, to put it mildly. The palmist went on to unnerve me even more by telling me that I was gay and that I would meet my 'life partner' in my own city within a few years. All of it was true, or turned out to be true. And Tony did indeed become a very successful architect and multimillionaire. (We will have to wait and see what age I make it to, but my dad would live to a hundred and one – and my Indian palmist friend could not have known that there was such longevity in the family genes.) I still don't know what to make of it all, although I was always fascinated by my Aquarius Zodiac sign and how closely its alleged attributes applied to me.

Given that I was so far away from friends and family, it was a vintage period for letter writing, and I still have all the letters I received and carbon copies of the ones I sent. I used to address my letters home, 'Dear Mam, Dad, Liam, Edel & Denis,' but it was invariably Mam who would reply, always starting hers with, 'My dear Frank,' in very clear handwriting and peppering them with 'P.G.' (Please God) and 'T.G.' (Thank God). Just before St Patrick's Day, she sent me a 'little bit of shamrock from our own garden', commenting that 'it is scarce this year, even though the weather has not been too severe'. It was a touching gesture, and I remember wearing that sprig of shamrock on my lapel for the big parade in New York.

When I told her in April 1973 that I had contracted dysentery, a disease I had always associated with the tropics, and then graphically listed the symptoms – 'vomiting, headaches, shivering, high temperatures, fever, diarrhoea, etc.', she replied, 'God help you, that was an awful dose you had. I hope you got a tonic from the doctor. There is nothing as weakening as dysentery . . . How much did your illness cost? We hear so much about the high cost of being sick in the US, is there insurance to guard against it?' In truth, it didn't cost much more than a visit to the doctor and some prescription drugs, but one of the real benefits was that I couldn't smoke because I was so ill. So when I told Mam that I was off cigarettes for a week or more and vowed to 'give them up for all time', she wrote, 'What a blessing it would be if you could remain off the cigs. Today's papers are full of the dangers of smoking. It appears that the tar content is worse than the nicotine. Continue to think of all the bad effects of smoking and also that soon smokers will be outlawed by society.' Sadly, my resolution didn't last.

Most of Mam's letters to me carried news about my siblings. Edel, who had started doing horticulture at the National Botanic Gardens in Glasnevin, 'gave us a wonderful surprise the other night when she came home for tea – she got first place in her Christmas exam'. She was worried about Liam, however. He had dropped out of UCD, where he had been doing science, and was now on the dole – something our parents found appalling. Then he got a job on a building site in Foxrock for presumably luxurious '£12,000 bungalows', but jacked it in after a day. 'I wish you saw the cut of him – he was muck & cement from head to toe – far from the gentleman I had reared him to be'.

There was another problem: Liam was living in a bedsit in Ranelagh with his macrobiotic girlfriend Maura Carey, from Youghal, Co. Cork, and she was expecting his baby. 'I can't understand why they have not got married,' Mam wrote. 'There is no need to tell you that Dad & I have spent many sleepless nights over this, and during one of those nights it occurred to me that it would be a good idea if we told our friends that they were married in a registry office in England last year and that only now they have considered being married in a church. The fact of them having the bedsitter has made this "cover-up" story all the more concrete, so to date it has gone down very well.'

Finally, a date was fixed for the wedding in the church on Beechwood Avenue in May 1973. 'It is only going to be a family affair and we have promised to take them to lunch at the Downshire [Arms Hotel] in Blessington afterwards,' my mother told me. Maura was seven months pregnant at that stage and there was no way of concealing it, but 'the whole thing changed from a "nightmare" to a fairytale' on the day. Liam had just managed to get work on a small farm in Ballinamona, near Oldcastle, Co. Meath, with a free house to live in with his new wife and £14 per week from the farmer, Jack Colgan, for looking after his cattle. His main business was a butcher's shop on Pearse Street in Dublin. 'The fact that Liam had a house to go to after the wedding put a different complexion on things and, when our relations and friends heard the good news, wedding presents started to arrive in quick succession.' Baby Nessa was born two months later in the Coombe Hospital. 'She is really gorgeous and would you believe she has my mouth, God help her. Otherwise she looks like Maura . . . Write soon as we worry a lot about you, but that's parents for you (foolish). God bless you. Love, Mam.'

(Liam and his new family lasted eighteen months in the damp old cottage in Ballinamona, eventually escaping from rural isolation and what he called 'the malaise of Ireland' in the mid-1970s by moving to London, Maura already pregnant with their second child, Murraigh. Liam got a job with the Post Office and they lived quite happily in a squat in Archway, before relocating to a terraced house of their own in ever-so-pretty Georgian Bath a few years later.)

Despite being separated from my family, I was ambivalent about returning to Dublin, as I told Tom Hayes in a letter, fearing that 'things will have changed utterly (as the poet said), but yet I realize that even if this is the case, my remaining abroad is a desertion of my country especially now that things are beginning to move [following Fianna Fáil's defeat in the 1973 general election]). On the other hand, I don't think I can stay in Dublin forever and simply settle down, etc. No matter where I am, I must always feel that I can just get up and go, drop what I'm doing and go and do something else, somewhere else.'

In May 1973 I got a phone call from Tim Pat Coogan, editor of the *Irish Press*, complimenting me on my dispatches from New York and offering me an unspecified job with the newspaper in Dublin. In a letter to him afterwards, I wrote that 'my primary commitment is to Ireland and things Irish. As a result, I feel a certain commitment to return home and involve myself in the goings-on there. Not, mind you, that I have any intention of becoming entangled in matters political. Rather, I would seek to observe events and, in so far as that is possible, to interpret them . . .'

By then, I had made my television début, taking part in a daytime talk show on cable TV in New York, on the subject of Northern Ireland. As I confessed to Annie McCartney in a letter, I took a 'moderate, almost Cruise O'Brien-ite line on the situation'. I was also a guest at the New York State Trial Lawyers Association's annual awards dinner at the Plaza Hotel in honour of Mayo-born Paul O'Dwyer, the great civil rights advocate. One of my contacts at the time was his legal partner Frank Durkan, and he helped me out when I ran into difficulties with a shipping agent over the consignment of a steamer trunk containing all the books, records, letters, clothes and other stuff I had accumulated from two years of living in Manhattan. I was also able to rely on the Irish Consulate to weigh in on my behalf, and the trunk eventually arrived at Dublin Port three months after I'd packed it.

I didn't even know what a subeditor was until I started working as one in the autumn of 1973. Although I had been freelance New York correspondent for eighteen months, I hadn't a clue about how the stuff I wrote was processed for publication. All I knew was that my copy was turned into a ticker tape at the Reuters office on Broadway not far from the Flatiron Building and then sent on to Dublin by Telex. Now suddenly, with no training whatever, I found myself on the subs desk in Burgh Quay one Sunday evening, having been escorted there by deputy editor Fintan Faulkner, an absolute gentleman. His younger brother Pádraig had been a Fianna Fáil minister and went on to become Ceann Comhairle of Dáil Éireann – but then, even the dogs in the street knew that the *Irish Press* was a Fianna Fáil paper. Fintan introduced me to chief sub John Garvey, who promptly gave me a 'two-of-eighteen' to do. Maurice Sweeney, whom I knew from *Campus*, helpfully explained that what this meant was a two-paragraph 'short', topped by a two-line heading in 18-point type – using a brief news story some reporter had done as my raw material. I soon got the hang of it. My starting salary was £28 per week, topped up by £11 in lieu of a productivity deal then being finalized between management and the NUJ chapel, headed by Niall Connolly. I'll never forget him pledging at a mandatory meeting in Liberty Hall that they weren't going to settle for anything less than a basic of £80 per week! It was almost unimaginable. (Connolly subsequently went over to the management side in the *Press*.)

As a sub, I had to get to know the *Irish Press* house style, which had its peculiarities. In obituaries of Old IRA veterans (*always* Fianna Fáil ones), it was the practice to say that they had fought somewhere-or-other in 1916, took part in the War of Independence and then 'remained on the Republican side' during the Civil War – clearly implying that those who joined the National Army were traitors. No wonder the paper was nicknamed *Pravda* by Conor Cruise O'Brien, then Minister for Posts and Telegraphs, who announced – menacingly – that he was keeping a file on its editorials and readers' letters about the situation in Northern Ireland. But the *Irish Press* was not propagandist in the way that *Pravda* was. Its political correspondent, Michael Mills, was a man of the utmost integrity and he reported the news from Leinster House in a strictly non-partisan way. Only when it came to elections was the paper pro-Fianna Fáil; its managing director, Vivion de Valera, son of the party's founder, was also Fianna Fáil TD for Dublin North West.

There was only one occasion that I can recall when news values were cast aside for political reasons. That was on the night of 21 November 1974, when twenty-one people were killed by IRA bombs in Birmingham. The front page should have been cleared for this atrocity. But much of it was given over to the State funeral of President Erskine Childers, who had died suddenly four days earlier. Colm Tóibín later told me a story about Childers addressing a large crowd of men in cloth caps on a damp night in the main square of Enniscorthy during the presidential election campaign, not much more than a year earlier. In his best English public-school accent, he said, 'I've been to Paris and I've been to Rome and I've seen the Taj Mahal. But believe me when I tell you that you're much better off where you are.' Nobody in that square believed him, I'm sure.

The *Irish Press* subs desk in the 1970s was populated by so many interesting characters – fellows who knew Latin or Greek, historians, literary types, alcoholics, poets and novelists. One of the assistant chief subs, John Banville, gave us all signed copies of *Long Lankin* – his first book, a collection of short stories – after it was remaindered by Secker & Warburg. Joyce scholar Terence Killeen was also on the subs desk then, along with the mild-mannered poet Hugh McFadden; Dermot Keogh, who went on to become professor of history at UCC; and the diminutive Derry man Séamus McGonagle, a great raconteur (when he was sober), artful cartoonist and author of a slim volume called *The Bicycle in Life, Love, War, and Literature*. It was a very enjoyable place to work. John Garvey, from Co. Down, was probably the most decent man I ever met as well as being a great journalist with an instinct for a good story. He was ably assisted by deputy chief sub Liam Moher, an edgy Cork man and former army officer who brought a sense of order to the place.

Other fine colleagues included John Spain, who became literary editor of the *Irish Independent*; the genial Galwegian Seán Conway; and future chief sub Seán Purcell, who also ended up in the *Irish Times*. We amused ourselves by thinking up joke headlines, using the *Irish Press* typefaces and font sizes; the winner by a country mile – coined by John Brophy – was 'Rabbit carnage as train hits magician'. Our half-hour break ('cutline' at 10 p.m.) was spent in local hostelries, with the hard chaws going to Mulligan's whereas we moderate drinkers went to Kennedy's on George's Quay. The only food available there was a bowl of soup or a toasted ham-and-cheese sandwich, served up in a piping-hot cellophane bag; that was pretty much the range of 'bar food' in Dublin in the 1970s. Another option was the Scotch House, a great old pub on the corner of Burgh Quay and Hawkins Street; it was later pulled down for a nondescript office block. There was also the old White Horse, at the corner of George's Quay, which was later transformed beyond recognition, ending up as yet another Starbucks; it was a favourite haunt of our colleagues, the printers who claimed direct descent from Gutenberg.

As a subeditor, you had to be conscious of the strong demarcation line between printers and journalists. This was most visible on 'the Stone', where we stood facing each other over the frame of a page as columns were filled with cooling hot metal and headlines formed from a matrix of steel letters. Before a page proof was produced, you got used to reading the headlines upside down *and* back to front. If you touched any of the metal, you were dead; that was exclusively the preserve of the compositors, those princes of the printing trade. They took precedence over the Linotype machinists who, by some alchemy, turned molten lead into columns of material to fill the pages, reading from the often heavily subbed stories sent down for printing by John Garvey after he had gone through them all. Behind Garvey sat the night editor, Jack Jones, whose main job was to lay out pages. A gentleman and good Protestant, he'd say things like, 'Would you mind awfully, old chap?' before asking you to do something or other – perhaps even taking a badly written report and rewriting it from top to bottom on one of the typewriters in the newsroom. I once did that right in front of the offending reporter.

Not long after I joined the *Irish Press* subs desk, the Burgh Quay building was redeveloped around us, with the exception of a Georgian house adjoining the Corn Exchange. This was where Tim Pat

Coogan had his office. At 8.30 one night, I popped in with an urgent query to find him sitting back in a wooden swivel chair, legs crossed on the desk, dictating his latest book to his secretary, Eileen Davis; she later married Donal Flanagan, a former Jesuit priest who was also a good colleague on the subs desk. Incredibly, the extensive construction work was not financed by a bank loan or anything like that, but rather by day-to-day receipts from the sale of newspapers – the *Irish Press*, *Evening Press* and *Sunday Press*. The latter was the biggest seller, allowing its editor Vincent Jennings – nicknamed 'Jenocide' long before he presided over the Irish Press Group's demise as managing director – to preen himself like a peacock. Foreign editor Julien de Kassel spoke impeccable English even though he came from Belgium; there was a rumour that he had been a Flemish collaborator with the Nazis during the Second World War, but few of us believed this calumny.

Equally exotic were the likes of Terry O'Sullivan, who penned 'Dubliner's Diary' for the *Evening Press*; he used to arrive in the office at around 8 p.m., always in a dinner jacket and dickie bow, to type up his account of an almost endless string of receptions every evening. The best line about this bizarre circuit of social engagements was not his, however, but rather that of his opposite number Séamus Kelly, who wrote 'An Irishman's Diary' in the *Irish Times* under the pseudonym of Quidnunc. After being at a lavish caviar-and-champagne reception in the Gresham to launch something or other, he was asked by his photographer if he'd be writing about it, and said, 'Certainly not. Let us stun them with our ingratitude!'

And then there was the larger-than-life figure of Con Houlihan, a great wordsmith from the wilds of Kerry, who wrote all his articles in longhand, leaving them to be typed up by the sports editor's secretary while he held court in Mulligan's or the Palace Bar, telling hilarious stories with his hand across his mouth, in an accent that strangers would not know. He used to say that he 'grew up speaking Hiberno-English: English woven on a Gaelic loom' and uttered such aphorisms as, 'A man who will misuse an apostrophe is capable of anything.'

On my way to work one evening in May 1974, I heard a loud bang. This, I soon learned, was one of the three car-bomb explosions that evening, in Parnell Street, Talbot Street and South Leinster Street. The city's emergency plan was activated and ambulances with sirens blaring were soon rushing the victims to hospital. Twenty-seven people were killed and a further seven perished when a car bomb went off in Monaghan later that evening. The atmosphere in Burgh Quay that night was sombre; after all, nobody knew whether relatives or friends were among the casualties, and it took a while before the names of those killed were released. Although a car bomb had exploded outside Liberty Hall in 1972, the widespread carnage in Dublin and Monaghan that day – caused by the UVF, it was suspected – brought 'the Troubles' to our doorsteps.

It was also while working as a sub that I realized Dublin was dying. Cycling home after finishing work at either 1 a.m. or 4 a.m., when the city centre is taken over by squawking seagulls, I began to notice derelict sites all over the place and reckoned that there was a story behind every hoarding. So I started writing about what was happening. I was greatly influenced by *A Future for Dublin*, a richly illustrated special issue of the London-based *Architectural Review* in 1974. Among many other things, its editor Kenneth Browne called attention to the Liffey quays as:

> the frontispiece to the city and the nation . . . grand, yet human in scale, varied yet orderly, they present a picture of a satisfactory city community; it is as though two ranks of people were lined up, mildly varying in their gifts, appearance and fortune, but happily agreed on basic values . . . If they are allowed to disintegrate, to be replaced by unsympathetic new buildings, the most memorable aspect of the city will be lost.

I've carried those words in my mind ever since. But first, I had to become a proper journalist and, in late 1976 after three years as a subeditor, I finally made a switch to the newsroom, working under Mick O'Kane and Dermot MacIntyre. O'Kane, who was from the

North, was the quiet man, while MacIntyre, his deputy, was always barking orders at us like a chef in a busy restaurant. I can still see him standing at the news desk at lunchtime, wolfing an apple; no doubt he thought lunch was for wimps. MacIntyre was news editor of the *Evening Press*, then in cut-throat competition with the *Evening Herald* for what was still a lucrative market. Everything became local. Famously, a banner headline 'IRISH NUNS SAFE' topped a story about forty-eight people dying in a 'bus plunge horror' somewhere in the north of Pakistan, I think.

I was rostered for everything in the news area – the Children's Court, the Dáil, day-to-day news stories and even the Yeats Summer School in Sligo, where I had to produce daily reports for the *Irish Press* and the *Evening Press*, based on lectures given by academics on often obscure aspects of W. B. Yeats's life and work. It had its compensations though, as there was a beautiful blond-haired English student at the summer school with whom I climbed Knocknarea to the cairn on top, with its breathtaking views over Sligo Bay.

I also found myself in the Special Criminal Court, covering the Sallins mail train robbery case. The suspects had appeared black-and-blue at habeas corpus hearings. One after the other, members of the gardaí got into the witness box to deny beating them up or having any knowledge of how the injuries were inflicted; their theory was that they had beaten each other up while sharing cells, or, in the case of one of them who had not shared a cell, that he had beaten himself up. (Arising from this case the *Irish Times* had the previous year broken the story of a 'heavy gang' operating within the Garda.) I noticed that one of the judges was falling asleep and mentioned this to defence counsel Séamus Sorahan SC. He told me he had seen it too, and himself and Paddy MacEntee SC would be making an application for a mistrial. Unsurprisingly, this was rejected by the three-judge court, so Sorahan and MacEntee appealed to the Supreme Court. To the utter incredulity of those of us who had seen Judge John O'Connor asleep, the highest court in the land held *as a matter of fact* that he had been alert all the time. Not long afterwards, the sleeping judge died from heart failure, and Nicky Kelly, Osgur Breatnach et al. had to be put on trial all over again. It was enough to convince me that justice and the law are not necessarily intertwined.

One of my biggest assignments as a fledgling reporter was to cover the St Patrick's Day parade in New York City and interview Judge James J. Comerford, long-serving chairman of the parade committee. It was regarded as so important that Tim Pat even took me to see Major de Valera in advance, in his grand office on O'Connell Street, where the Major gave me a little lecture about the political independence of the *Irish Press*. Naturally, I didn't believe a word of it. I only discovered afterwards that Comerford, who had emigrated from Co. Kilkenny in the mid-1920s, had been the *Irish Press* bagman in the US for many years. And it was through the Delaware-registered Irish Press Corporation, which held in trust the shares of thousands of Irish-American investors in his newspaper venture, that Éamon de Valera and his family were able to control the company for decades. (In this, the de Valeras were no different from Major T. B. McDowell, chairman and long-serving chief executive of the *Irish Times*. When its ownership was transferred to a trust in 1974, to protect the newspaper's independence, the Articles of Association specified that he would be the sole 'A' shareholder and, in the event of any attempt to remove him, the 'A' shareholder's vote would be equivalent to all of the others, plus one vote.)

I covered the launch of Fianna Fáil's general election manifesto in 1977, which promised the abolition of car tax and domestic rates as well as lots of other expensive giveaways; after reading the main points, I remember turning to Paul Tansey, who was reporting it for the *Irish Times*, and we both shook our heads in disbelief. At Fine Gael's ardfheis in the Mansion House on the eve of the election, I heard then Taoiseach Liam Cosgrave ranting about 'blow-ins', who could either 'blow out or blow up' – a reference to critics such as South African-born Kader Asmal, founder of the Irish Anti Apartheid Movement, and English-born Bruce Arnold, political columnist with the *Irish Independent*. After Fianna Fáil's landslide victory, I was in the Dáil press gallery when they descended on the place to take over. There weren't even enough seats on the government benches, so at least a dozen of them sat on the stairs, or wherever they could find, to avoid being bracketed with the outgoing Fine Gael and Labour lot.

In March 1978 I reported on the funeral of Micheál MacLiammóir, co-founder of the Gate Theatre with his partner Hilton Edwards. The pair of them were English, both born in London, but they had embraced Ireland with such enthusiasm that MacLiammóir (originally Alfred Willmore) not only changed his name to a fictitious Irish one, but also became fluent in the Irish language. I knew they were homosexuals, of course, and had seen MacLiammóir's marvellous one-man show *The Importance of Being Oscar* at the Gate more than once.

I had also heard the amusing story about how, shortly after the actor (who wore stage make-up all the time) was conferred with an honorary doctorate by the NUI, a PhD student doing a thesis on the Gate had telephoned their home on Harcourt Terrace, asking to speak to 'Dr MacLiammóir'. Hilton Edwards, who hadn't yet got his own honorary doctorate from Trinity, answered the phone. 'He's not here,' the great producer told him. 'Will Nurse Edwards do?' MacLiammóir's funeral, at University Church on St Stephen's Green, was attended by the then President, Patrick Hillery, and I witnessed a very touching scene when he went over to commiserate with Edwards as the surviving member of Ireland's best-known gay couple. Here was the first citizen of our State, where homosexual acts were still illegal, doing the decent thing by paying his respects to them on behalf of us all.

Probably due to years of denial about my own sexuality, I had none of that 'Look at me!' confidence you're meant to have going into a gay bar. It made my palms sweat with worry that someone I knew might see me in this compromising situation. I felt so awkward about it that I never entered one of those bars alone; it was *always* with a friend or two. And even then, I was not much good at it. The whole experience of leading a double life had left me emotionally, even psychically, scarred and it took me years to accept who and what I am. I'm still working on that, to be frank. Yes, that's it. To be Frank, a more authentic version of myself.

Some of my gay friends had started out as lovers, such as Alain Ficat, then deputy director of the Alliance Française here; or Gerard Cleary, a cute and caring dental student from Co. Mayo, who went on to become a dentist in London. Others were simply good friends, like the ever-entertaining Gary Quinlan, then First Secretary of the Australian Embassy in Dublin and later his country's High Commissioner in Singapore and Permanent Representative at the United Nations; Paul Murphy, a young surgeon from Galway, with a sense of humour that goes with the territory; and Ted Broderick, a bitchy civil servant in the Office of Public Works, who regularly hosted amusing dinner parties at his Oakley Court flat in Ranelagh.

We would go to Dublin's premier 'gay-friendly' bar, Bartley Dunne's on St Stephen's Street (where the Grafton Plaza Hotel was built), or Rice's on the corner of St Stephen's Green and South King Street (later swallowed up by that ghastly shopping centre). Another haunt was Duke Street, home to Tobin's, with its 1950s cocktail-bar interior (now the Duke, with fake 'snugs'), and the Bailey, which was a popular gathering place for more affluent gay guys on Saturday lunchtimes. One of the Bailey's regulars was the impish Glasgow-born RTÉ set designer Charles Self, whose effervescent life was overshadowed by the savage brutality of his murder in the mews house in Monkstown where he had hosted so many wild parties. Everyone who knew him, including me, was interviewed by gardaí after he was found dead in January 1982 from multiple stab wounds. Although a young male prostitute was his suspected killer, nobody was ever charged with the crime. Equally horrifying was the murder later that year of Declan Flynn, who was beaten to death in Fairview Park by 'queer-bashing' teenagers; they all got suspended sentences after being convicted of manslaughter, with Judge Seán Gannon declaring that 'this could never be regarded as murder' – a verdict branded at the time as 'a licence to kill'.

In the summer of 1975, I ran into a lovely French guy, Jean-Marc Gandit, who was in Dublin to brush up his English. At the time, he was working as a steward for Air Inter, the French internal airline, but he really wanted to be an opera tenor; I can still remember him singing an aria in the courtyard of an apartment building in Paris. Always seeking more meaning in his life, Jean-Marc turned to Tibetan Buddhism, spent years in a prayer stall at the Dalai Lama's retreat in Dharamshala, in the north of India, and is now lama (chief Buddhist monk) of Strasbourg with the adopted name of Tsultrim Guelek. It was through him that I met Helen Spillane, a friend of his from Trinity, who ended up marrying the criminal defence solicitor and humanitarian Garrett Sheehan, later a High Court judge and member of the Court of Appeal; he became my lawyer for a time, and we're still good friends.

There were some home-grown boyfriends, although none of the relationships lasted very long, for one reason or another; I suppose that's what happens when you're in your twenties. Iain was a moderate unionist medical student at Queen's who I liked a lot, even though he once wrote me a letter saying, 'I watched the Last Night of the Proms concert yesterday and tonight the Battle of Britain film – Great to be British, I thought.' I didn't tell Annie McCartney that I was consorting with someone like that, especially as her letters at the time were bristling with fear and loathing after the Ulster Workers Council strike brought down the power-sharing executive. 'The last lot of days here have been nightmarish with a real sickening realisation of just how polarised the two communities are,' she wrote in May 1974. (Annie had just got married to Iain – a popular name up North – a stunning long-haired medical student, who she met through Dramsoc at Queen's. They eventually settled in a listed Victorian terraced house on Rugby Road, overlooking the Botanic Gardens – at my instigation.) I think I compensated for (my) Iain with Tony, a nationalistically minded young teacher from Enniskillen, who was great fun and didn't see Dublin as a 'foreign' city at all.

Then there was Alain Boschetti, a lovely French-Moroccan guy, who I met in London and continued corresponding with even after he had returned to Agadir to work as *lycée* teacher. But my favourite was John, a tall trainee accountant, who I imagined as 'the One' even though we had only just met. He was bright, good-looking and fun to be with. We had gone to see *Cabaret* on our first date and were delighted by that scene in which Michael York, looking more beautiful than ever, loses it over Liza Minnelli's infatuation with the rich amoral aristocrat played by Helmut Griem. 'Oh, screw Maximilian!' he says. 'I do,' she replies, and then he darts back, with a knowing smile on his face, 'So do I.' Three weeks later, John stood me up. I had got tickets for *Godspell* at the Olympia Theatre and was waiting for him to turn up. As the minutes ticked away, with no sign of him, I went to a phone box to call his flat and the line went dead. I rang again and the same thing happened. He had hung up on me, twice. I was devastated. Nobody had ever done anything like that to me. As I recounted in a long letter to him later that night:

> I felt cold, so I went to a movie. I couldn't really concentrate on the drift of the film because I was too depressed . . . When it was over, I still felt cold. And sad. And alone. So I went into Trinity College and sat on a park bench beside the playing fields and tried as best I could to rationalize the night's events, to attempt to find a reason, an explanation for what had happened. It was impossible. I drew a blank . . . After all, even though we've known each other a short time, we seemed to get on well, even very well.

Maybe John just didn't like me any more. My angst-ridden letter went on to talk about how, in the 'gay world', it was hard to find people who might become really close.

> Most relationships tend to be quite fragile and one is left with the alternative of seeking 'casual' associations, usually in squalid and revolting loos. But this is the sort of dilemma that goes with being 'gay'. In Ireland, where one is forced to don a mask and pretend a lot, it is especially difficult. It is not an easy prospect and hardly makes for the most fulfilling kind of life. That is why last night was such a shattering experience. It would be a shame if our friendship was to end like this – without a glance, without a word.

I didn't hear from John for months. Eventually, he wrote me a letter apologizing for 'the rotten way in which I treated you during the summer'. He explained it by saying that 'it was really a question of confused identity, which I hope I have sorted out since then,' and asked if I would like to go out for a drink some night, saying, 'You can drop me a note. If not, I will understand.' I can't remember whether or not I accepted his belated invitation. Either way, it was the end of our all-too-brief affair.

By then, I had almost given up visiting relatives, mainly because some of them would keep asking whether I had found a 'nice girlfriend' yet, which was irritating, when what I really wanted was a nice *boyfriend*, although I couldn't bring myself to admit that to them. Gay discos were getting under way in Dublin, starting in a warehouse on Great Strand Street and moving on to a basement on the west side of Parnell Square, where a weekly event was run by the newly formed Irish Gay Rights Movement, led by Trinity lecturer David Norris; he was the first self-described homosexual to appear on Irish television in 1975, when he was interviewed by Áine O'Connor.

The following year, I was bemused by a huge controversy over the Gay Sweatshop repertory theatre company staging four overtly homosexual plays at the Project Arts Centre, then run by Jim Sheridan and John Stephenson. 'There were bomb threats, wooden rosaries and illustrations of flagellation scenes posted through the letter box, and people who had not even seen the plays were condemning them as filth,' as Gay Sweatshop's Philip Osment recalled. And because the Project had received grant aid from Dublin Corporation, city councillors came under pressure from groups like the League of Decency, Parent Concern and the Society to Outlaw Pornography to rescind this 'subsidy for perversion'. An elderly, deeply conservative Fianna Fáil councillor, Ned Brennan, suggested that the Project had been taken over by 'funny bunnies' while more liberal colleagues on the council were denounced in letters to the newspapers for promoting 'sodomy and lesbianism as art forms'. The members-only Irish Film Theatre in the basement

My parents, William and Maura, after their wedding at Corpus Christi Church on Griffith Avenue in September 1948.

My maternal grandad, F. X. Coghlan, a veteran of the 1916 Rising, with three of his seven sons – (*left to right*) Frank, Eamon and Dónal – at my parents' wedding.

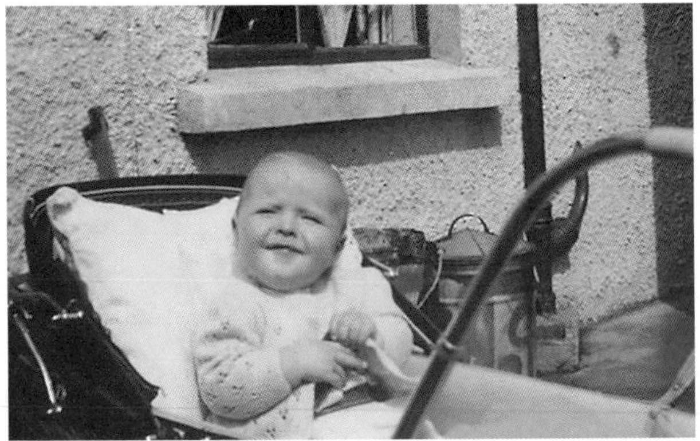

Above: Here I am in 1950 – I was born that January – parked outside the back door at home in Glenmore Road.

Left: By 1953 my brother Liam had arrived – he's on the tricycle and I'm on the rocking horse. Edel followed in 1954 and Denis in 1959.

At Granny McDonald's home on Malahide Road in 1951. She's at the door and my mother is in the deckchair.

Liam (*back*) and me (*front centre*) with our Hendrick cousins, Tom (*left*) and Paddy (*right*) in 1954. We had an annual two-week summer holiday at their home in Wexford and the four of us were the best of friends throughout our school days.

In my First Communion suit in front of the trellis ('the rustic') at Glenmore Road in 1957.

Me (*left*) and Liam, again at 'the rustic', on the day of my Confirmation in 1961.

The 1961 Confirmation class from St Vincent's CBS Primary School, Glasnevin. I am in the second row, second from the right.

Pretending to play a balalaika in a friend's house, wearing a pullover knitted by my mother – Christmas 1967.

With fellow UCD delegates Tom Hayes (*left*) and Seán Finlay (*right*) at the USI annual congress, Rosses Point, Co. Sligo, 1969.

The opening of UCD's first students' bar in August 1971 includes (*left to right*) me, Gerry Flynn (who defeated me for presidency of the Students' Representative Council), UCD Secretary and Bursar J. P. McHale, architect Aidan Powell and a drinks company rep.

Looking pensive in the summer of 1970, on a beach in Cape Cod.

My first and only time on horseback – western Massachusetts, 1970.

LOL in New York City, 1979.

With UCD friend Tony Reddy at the Grand Canyon in 1972.

Eamon on a bus in New York City, 1979.

Eamon and me on a canal barge in Ireland in the early 1980s.

For decades Bartley Dunne's on St Stephen's Street was one of Dublin's few 'gay-friendly' bars. It stood near St Stephen's Green, on the site of the Grafton Plaza Hotel.

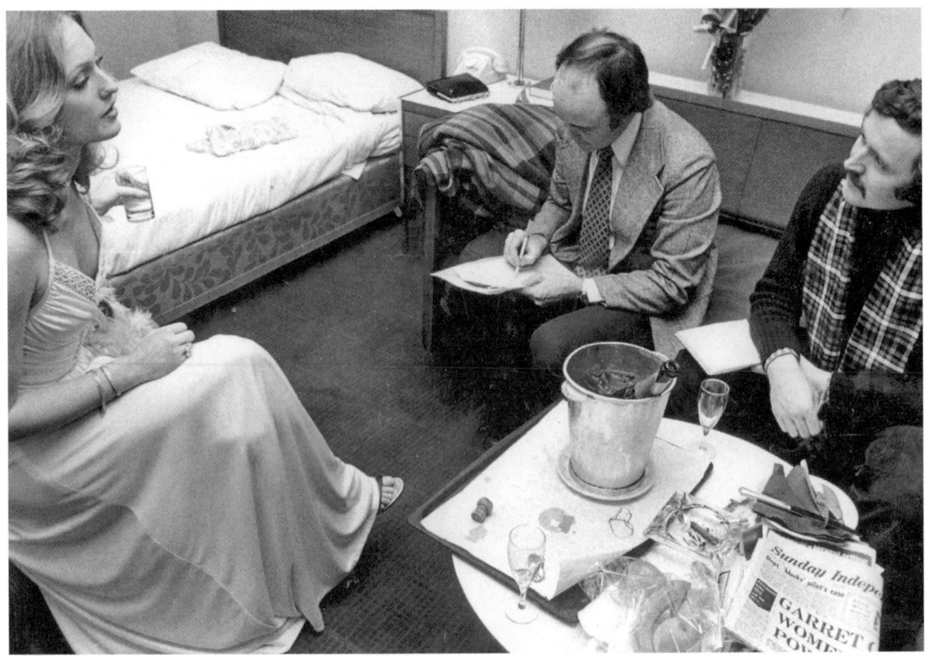

Life on the news round – here I am (*right*) in Jury's Hotel interviewing Miss World, Sweden's Mary Stävin, for the *Irish Press* when she visited Dublin in December 1977. I can't recall who the other journalist was.

Above: Looking tweedy in the *Irish Press* newsroom, 1978.

Right: With Irish peacekeeping troops in south Lebanon, 1980, reporting for the *Irish Times*.

of Irish Sugar's headquarters was also a target of the religious right because it was showing sexually explicit films such as Peter Brook's *Marat/Sade*, Derek Jarman's homoerotic *Sebastiane* and Pier Paolo Pasolini's *Salò, or the 120 Days of Sodom*. We took perverse pleasure in enjoying it all.

One Saturday night in September 1976, I was chatting to a friend, the diplomat Michael Hoey, outside the Royal College of Surgeons when a fresh-faced young fellow he already knew came along and joined in the conversation. His name was Eamon Slater, a telecoms technician then aged twenty-two (I was twenty-six at the time), and he was going to the IGRM disco on Parnell Square, so I said I might see him there later. Which I did, and we have been together ever since. We danced to glam-rock stuff like 'Don't Go Breaking My Heart' by Elton John and Kiki Dee, and then got a lift back to the place I had recently bought – a four-bedroom Edwardian end-of-terrace house on Casimir Road in Harold's Cross. There was practically nothing in it then apart from a bed, a table and some chairs, a chemical toilet, and an electric cooker plugged into an ordinary socket so you could only use two rings at a time. But I had got it for £12,500 – a whole £1,500 less than the asking price – on account of dry rot and rising damp.

Eamon still remembers the first meal I cooked for him, a notably poor attempt at spaghetti Bolognese, but we were in love so it didn't matter. He was much more 'out' than I was, and had even taken part in brave little protests outside the GPO with tall curly-haired Hugo McManus, who used to wear a long coloured woollen scarf and feather boa, holding 'Gays Are Angry' placards, to the bemusement and sometimes contempt of passers-by. A memorable weekend in Paris followed and then some great summer holidays island-hopping in Greece in 1977, travelling by train in the north of Italy in 1978 and hiring a station-wagon with Alain Ficat and Gary Quinlan for a marvellous road trip down California Route 1 from San Francisco to Los Angeles, via Monterey, Carmel, Big Sur, San Simeon and Santa Barbara, in September 1979.

Jimmy Maguire, one of the most wonderful guys around, was

living in LA then and brought us to all sorts of clubs. Sadly, he contracted HIV and died from Aids some years later. So did several other gay guys we knew, including the interior designer Eugene Fogarty, who had a magnificent Georgian house on Hume Street, and the Clonmel-born RTÉ DJ and TV presenter Vincent Hanley. They had all contracted the HIV virus before the British government commissioned its *Don't Die of Ignorance* TV commercial that scared the wits out of everyone. Narrated gravely by John Hurt, the forty-five-second advertisement about the deadly disease for which there was no known cure showed its dreaded acronym being chiselled on a large black slab, which fell backwards dramatically to become a tombstone. Aids really was a death sentence then, of course, and for a long time afterwards until anti-retroviral drugs became available.

Too late for Thom McGinty. The Glasgow-born mime artist – known as the Diceman – was one of the most memorable fixtures on Grafton Street for many years, dressed as Dracula or the Mona Lisa (complete with gilded picture frame) and even as a light bulb on occasion, giving a saucy grin and big wink at patrons who put money in his bag. Everyone loved him. Diagnosed with HIV in 1990, he died five years later at the age of forty-two. In a singularly appropriate gesture towards the place he had made his own, friends carried his coffin the length of Grafton Street as a throng of his many admirers – including me – gave the Diceman a final and richly deserved round of applause.

5

On a grey autumn evening in 1978, Caroline Walsh and I were sitting in her car outside the *Irish Press* offices on Burgh Quay when she suddenly said, 'What are you doing working here? You should be in the *Irish Times*!' (Later on, after she discovered I was gay, she exclaimed, 'What a waste!') Myself and Caroline, youngest of writer Mary Lavin's three daughters, had become good friends through meeting at press conferences and other events over the previous two years, but I could barely imagine myself with a job on the 'paper of record'. The only other *Irish Times* person I knew was Andrew Hamilton, the paper's ebullient motoring correspondent, who was an assistant news editor and also gay; he'd be as likely to be testing a new car in Marrakech, or some other exotic location, as helping to oversee the newsroom on Fleet Street. When a senior reporter's job came up, he encouraged me to apply even though the advertisement specified that good shorthand and typing were 'essential', whereas I could only type with two fingers (as I still do) and had no shorthand at all.

During the interview, with four of the *Times*'s editorial executives, I thought I was sunk when its legendary news editor, Donal Foley (author of the weekly 'Man Bites Dog' column and a native Irish speaker from Ring, Co. Waterford), asked me how good was my Gaeilge. I had to confess that it was a bit rusty after spending two years in New York, although I did point out that I had got honours in Irish in my Leaving Cert and actually did it in my first year at UCD. About two minutes later, Foley said, 'I've heard enough,' got up and walked out. But I ended up landing the job, mainly because he and the others liked my argumentative disposition in discussing contemporary issues such as what could, or should, be done about transport in Dublin. My *Evening Press* feature on the clapped-out suburban rail service between Howth and Bray had even prompted RTÉ producer John Kelleher to get me to do a test television report on this shambles, with a view to joining the *Seven Days* current affairs team, but they gave the job to Scotsman Forbes McFall instead. I'm glad they did because I thought television was very cumbersome compared to radio or print journalism.

So I joined the *Irish Times* in January 1979, and couldn't have been more pleased. Within a month, I was covering big stories, including the Whiddy Island disaster when the French oil tanker *Betelgeuse* blew up in Bantry Bay, with the loss of fifty lives. I can still vividly remember dictating my story to a copytaker in Dublin from a 'wind-up telephone' in a kiosk on the main street in Bantry. In August 1979, when Lord Mountbatten was assassinated by the Provisional IRA at Mullaghmore, Co. Sligo, I was sent off to cover that story too. For years, the last British Viceroy of India had spent his summer holidays at nearby Classiebawn Castle, but this time the IRA had booby-trapped his boat, *Shadow V*, and blew it up with a remote-control detonator. It pained me to think that not only had he met his end in such a terrible way, but also that the lives of others in his sea-fishing party, including two teenage boys, were wiped out.

Later on the same day, the IRA ambushed and killed eighteen British soldiers near Warrenpoint, Co. Down, in what seemed to mark a serious escalation in its campaign. Folk singer Liam Clancy was at the Beach Hotel in Mullaghmore that evening as we were having dinner and felt impelled to make a short speech. But instead of condemning outright the atrocity earlier in the day, within sight of the hotel, he waffled on about how Ireland's history was marked by a litany of 'tragedies'. I felt like giving him a piece of my mind, but managed to restrain myself. The following day, I was at Casement Aerodrome, Baldonnel, for a poignant ceremony with full military honours being rendered as Mountbatten's coffin, draped in the Union flag, was transferred to an RAF Hercules plane to be flown back to England. When will all this bloody business be over? I thought.

A month later, nearly everyone in the *Irish Times* was rostered to cover Pope John Paul II's visit to Ireland – the first by a reigning pontiff. Eamon and I had been on holidays in the US, and our return flight on a Pan Am 707 had to do a figure-of-eight over the country, as Aer Rianta had decreed that no plane could land at Dublin Airport within an hour of the Pope's arrival. As our plane finally made its descent, we flew in over the Phoenix Park and had a clear view of the million people gathered there, all arranged in neat corrals of one thousand each facing towards an elongated altar topped by a huge papal cross. The city itself was eerily empty. I had to pack my bag and head for Knock, Co. Mayo, where John Paul II was due to appear the following day. Needless to say, it poured rain there although this didn't dampen the spirits of some four hundred thousand fervent Catholics, including many in wheelchairs. The Pope later held an audience for the press corps at Cabra Convent, where the Papal Nunciature had been relocated from the former Under Secretary's Lodge in the Phoenix Park (since demolished), addressing and blessing us all from an internal first-floor balcony. (If anyone asked me about my own beliefs, I would describe myself as a 'recovering Catholic', in the sense that I was – and still am – recovering from having been a Catholic in the Ireland that I grew up in.)

At the time, I was working on a major series of articles that appeared under the heading 'Dublin – What Went Wrong?' Conor Brady, then features editor, had commissioned me to do it even though I was not much more than six months in the *Irish Times* and the paper already had a local government correspondent, Frank Kilfeather. It was in that golden era when journalists had the luxury of time to do original research – in my case, in the planning department of Dublin Corporation, its roads department and the Companies Office, as well as doing long interviews with some of the main players in the city.

I'll never forget one of the interviews – with Mr Ó Siochrú, an engineer nearing retirement, who was in charge of the road planning section's public office, then located in the Baxendale's building on Capel Street, above where PantiBar is now. It was in the 'bell and hatch' days of the public service – you had to ring a bell, then somebody inside would open the hatch to find out what you wanted. I asked to see all the long-term road plans, so Mr Ó Siochrú produced a folder of A1 drawings. What they showed was astonishing: the engineers had drawn 'setback lines' throughout the inner city, involving the presumed wholesale demolition of existing buildings, including nearly everything on both sides of the Liffey quays. What they wanted to do was to turn the quays into an six-lane dual carriageway with the River Liffey as its central median. My legs almost turned to jelly as I stood there in awe at their arrogance in treating the historic city merely as an obstacle to the movement of traffic, and asked Mr Ó Siochrú what could be done about all these plans.

'Do you see that window over there?' he said, gesturing to a window overlooking Great Strand Street. 'They should all be fecked out that window.' I told him that I couldn't agree with him more. My series, which ran for a full week in autumn 1979, documented how Dublin had fallen victim to the depredations of property speculators and roads engineers, and provoked quite a reaction; I won the Outstanding Work in Irish Journalism Award, then sponsored by Benson & Hedges, and there were three already-opened packets of 'Pure Gold' on every table at the awards lunch in the Berkeley Court Hotel, with the cigarettes invitingly arranged like a cathedral organ.

I was not yet thirty when Charles J. Haughey finally achieved his lifelong ambition of being elected as leader of Fianna Fáil and Taoiseach in December 1979. A few days later, I wrote a lengthy news feature on his wealth and lifestyle, under the cheeky heading, 'Life has been good to Charlie', describing him as 'the richest man to hold the office of Head of Government since the foundation of the State', with an estimated net worth approaching £3 million. At his victory press conference in Leinster House, Vincent Browne had asked Haughey if he would now disclose the sources of his wealth, to which he replied, 'Ask my bank manager,' so I was following the money, as it were.

There was his grand house, Abbeville in Co. Dublin, modified and enlarged by James Gandon, with four splendid reception rooms and stables to the side for his valuable horses, including one called Aristocracy. Then there was Inishvickillane, second largest of the otherwise uninhabited Blasket Islands, which he had bought for a relative song; he had built a holiday home there, powered by solar panels and a wind turbine. And his yacht, a converted trawler called *Celtic Mist*, which was usually moored at the marina in Howth and taken out for voyages around the coast to Co. Kerry.

'Mr Haughey is said to be an expert judge of champagne and vintage port, and he is also reputed to be a connoisseur of good claret,' I wrote. Not long afterwards, I heard that some Kerry construction workers had been marooned on Inishvickillane by bad weather while building an extension to the Haughey holiday home – or perhaps it was a swimming pool. Either way, they got thirsty and helped themselves to the expensive contents of his cellar. Overcome with remorse, they thought they'd get away with it by replenishing the stock of claret with a few cases of cheap Valpolicella from a supermarket in Dingle. Charlie must have been bemused by their naivety in believing that he wouldn't notice the difference.

There were rumours even then that Haughey's much-vaunted wealth might be hollow – specifically, that he had run up an overdraft of £1 million at Allied Irish Banks. For years, he had his account with AIB in the former headquarters of the Munster and Leinster Bank in Dame Street, next door to Dublin Castle. After a series of heaves against his leadership of Fianna Fáil, the bank calculated – wrongly, as it turned out – that Charlie's goose was cooked and decided to call in the debt, even threatening to take away his chequebook. I made contact with a very good source in AIB, who quietly confirmed these facts, and wrote a story for the *Irish Times*. To my amazement, it appeared below the fold on a left-hand inside page, apparently because our esteemed editor, Douglas Gageby, didn't want Haughey to be too prominently maligned. Gageby believed that the Taoiseach could yet play a crucial role in engineering peace in Northern Ireland and had developed this rather benign view of CJH under the influence of his close friend John Healy, author of the long-running 'Backbencher' column, for whom Haughey was the 'Golden Boy'. Years would pass before the full story emerged, including the fact that Michael Phelan, manager of the AIB branch in Dame Street, had written a letter to Haughey in December 1979 congratulating him on becoming Taoiseach and saying that 'the task you've taken on is daunting, but I've every faith in your ability to succeed in restoring confidence in this great little nation'.

On 14 February 1981, more than eight hundred young people were enjoying themselves at a Valentine's Day disco in the Stardust nightclub in Artane when it went on fire, killing forty-eight and injuring more than two hundred and forty. It happened in the early hours of a Saturday morning, and the *Irish Times* went into overdrive to remake the front page of the paper's city edition to bring the news of this immense tragedy to its readers. The effort was pulled together by Pat Smyllie, who manned the news desk in the wee hours. Conor O'Clery, then news editor, spent the entire weekend in the office coordinating coverage of the story, and the edition of the paper that appeared on Monday morning was one of the finest the *Irish Times* ever produced.

My own contribution was a front-page story highlighting our lackadaisical approach to fire safety. Among other things, it showed that the law under which fire brigades operated hadn't been updated since 1940, that most of the recommendations of a major report on the fire service in 1975 – including regular fire safety inspections – had yet to be implemented, that draft Building Regulations banning the use of highly combustible materials were still 'under discussion' after more than four years, that senior officials of the Department of the Environment had attempted to thwart a 1979 ministerial directive giving more independence to chief fire officers, and that at least two fire chiefs who had highlighted the multitude of problems confronting the service were forced out of office merely for speaking out to protect the public.

I then spent a full day in the Companies Office going through files relating to the Butterly family, who owned the Stardust. As usual, there was a maze of companies involved, including one called Mensaform Ltd, which had been set up in 1967 by accountants Haughey Boland & Company, with paterfamilias Patrick Butterly as one of its directors and shareholders. What I found particularly interesting was that one of Haughey Boland's partners, Des Traynor, was also a director of Mensaform Ltd and had taken a controlling interest in the company, holding 3,180 of the 5,000 £1 shares. I was aware that Traynor was closely associated with Charlie Haughey, but didn't mention this in the piece I wrote. They had both gone to St Joseph's CBS in Marino, and were later partners in Haughey Boland; it was known, too, that Traynor had long acted as Haughey's financial adviser. (Later, as managing director of merchant bank Guinness & Mahon (Ireland) Ltd, Traynor ran the notorious Ansbacher accounts, nominally housed in the Cayman Islands, on behalf of rich people in Ireland seeking to evade paying their fair share of tax at a time when the rest of us were being fleeced by the Revenue.) Nonetheless, the implication that Haughey himself – one of the local TDs – might have had a link to the Butterlys via Traynor so infuriated *Il Duce* that he got the ever-faithful Pádraig Ó hAnnracháin, Assistant Secretary in the Taoiseach's department, to complain to Douglas Gageby about my 'outrageous' story.

Worse still, the story had been lifted word for word by Vinnie Doyle, then editor of the *Irish Independent*, and printed in its city edition on the same day. I was shocked by the *Indo* pilfering my work and sued Doyle for plagiarism under the NUJ's Code of Conduct. My complaint went to an NUJ tribunal in London, which upheld it and fined Doyle £500 for his blatant act of plagiarism. Conor O'Clery was delighted by the outcome and told me to write it up for the *Irish Times* as a straightforward news report, which he passed on to his old friend Michael Keane, then news editor of the *Irish Press*, thus ensuring that the story appeared in both papers the following day. I was then sued by John Foley, secretary of the

NUJ's *Indo* chapel, for bringing the union into disrepute through the 'unauthorised disclosure' of its internal affairs – a charge I regarded as quite ridiculous, given the nature of our trade. In the end, I was fined £50, which O'Clery gamely agreed that I could put on my expenses.

After the Gallagher Group collapsed on 30 April 1982, I made a beeline for the Companies Office, going through returns from its interlocking miasma of fifty companies, all of which had their 'headquarters' at the Guinness & Mahon Cayman Trust, in the Cayman Islands, operated by the ubiquitous Des Traynor. The group was run by Patrick Gallagher, who had taken it over in 1974 at the tender age of twenty-two following the untimely death of his father, house-builder Matt Gallagher. Young Patrick had made millions over the years from property speculation, mainly around St Stephen's Green, but 'the man with the Midas touch' (as he was dubbed) had over-extended himself. Just before his empire fell apart, he was featured on the cover of *In Dublin* magazine as a King Kong-like cartoon character in a pinstriped suit and hard-hat clambering over the ruins, with the immortal headline, 'Patrick Gallagher – Property speculator & brat'.

The author of the story was Mary Raftery, who went on to make mould-breaking documentaries for RTÉ. Thanks to a planning permission granted on appeal by then Minister for Local Government Jimmy Tully, Gallagher had carried out one of the most despicable acts of destruction perpetrated in Dublin: the demolition of Deane and Woodward's Molesworth Hall and St Ann's Schools in 1978, to make way for an office block; it was shamelessly occupied for years as a Dublin outpost of the European Commission and Parliament. After the Gallagher Group collapsed, I felt particularly sorry for depositors who had lost their life savings in Merchant Banking Ltd, the Gallagher Group's 'piggybank' into which Patrick would dip regularly whenever he needed extra funds; none of those in the Republic got a penny back. Gallagher escaped scot-free in this jurisdiction, but he was later sentenced to two years' imprisonment for fraud and theft in Northern Ireland, where he got to know the inside of Magilligan before relocating to South Africa for a decade until his death in 2006, at the age of fifty-four.

In August 1982, it emerged that Ireland's most wanted man, Malcolm MacArthur – who was suspected of two murders – was staying at the home of the Attorney General, Patrick Connolly SC, at Pilot View in Dalkey. Not only that: the pair of them had attended a GAA match in Croke Park just a few days after MacArthur had strangled a nurse, Bridie Gargan, in the Phoenix Park. I ended up covering the political fallout from this astonishing story for the *Irish Times*. At a hastily convened press conference in Government Buildings, the Taoiseach was clearly grappling for the most appropriate set of words when he described it as a 'grotesque situation', an 'almost unbelievable mischance', a 'bizarre happening' and an 'unprecedented situation'. Conor Cruise O'Brien, then an acerbic opinion columnist for the newspaper, spotted the four adjectives – grotesque, unbelievable, bizarre and unprecedented – in my report and coined 'GUBU' as a generic term to describe what was going on under Haughey's watch.

Certainly, it applied to the bitter and unruly leadership heaves against Haughey, and the responses to them by *Il Duce* and his henchmen, which I was involved in covering. The intimidation going on, in public and in private, was shocking. I'll never forget an anguished Mary Colley, wife of Haughey's long-time foe George Colley, telling me about an abusive phone call she received late one night. 'I haven't the faintest idea who it was, but he went on for five minutes, using all the four-letter words in the book and some that I hadn't even heard before,' she said. The caller had also made specific threats against her husband's life. 'He said they would blow his head off, and other parts of his body as well . . . It was very frightening.' That story made the front page, under the heading, 'Senior party figures "ran hate campaign"'. This was all documented a year later by Joe Joyce and Peter Murtagh in their great book *The Boss*. Among many other things, it detailed serial abuses of power involving Haughey's Minister for Justice Seán Doherty, including tapping the phones of two political journalists – Bruce Arnold and Geraldine Kennedy – with the Taoiseach's full knowledge and consent, and the mysterious white HiAce van that used to turn up outside certain ministers' houses to spy on them.

During that period I got to know George Colley, although he remained quite cautious in talking to journalists about CJH, or anything else; the inimitable Bart Cronin was his press officer and front man. We were on a junket to Denmark together in 1980, to have a look at the first two experimental wind turbines erected on the west coast of Jutland, climbing internal steel ladders to get to their hubs. Then Minister for Energy, Colley was wearing a charcoal-grey coat with black velvet collar, of the type favoured by Fianna Fáil politicians, quite unlike long-haired Danish Environment Minister Erik Holst, who was in an anorak and looked like a radical student leader; they made an odd couple. Everyone on the Irish delegation was very impressed by the new turbines, then returned home and did nothing much while the Danes went on to develop the most profitable wind industry in Europe.

By comparison with the taciturn Colley, Albert Reynolds was disarmingly frank. I first met him when he was Minister for Transport in 1980–81. At one press conference, in response to a question from me, he promised that the first bus lanes in Dublin would be introduced 'by Easter' – and he was true to his word. We were out on Harold's Cross Road together at eight o'clock one morning to see it put into operation alongside the park, for a distance of a hundred metres or so. There seemed to be a Garda motorcyclist every twenty metres along the white line, and I congratulated the Garda Traffic Superintendent on this turnout, which was clearly a show of force on the first day. As soon as he was gone, Reynolds confided that he had 'fierce problems with the guards' and had to threaten that, if they didn't go out and paint the bus lane on the road by a certain date, he was going to get a tin of white paint and do it himself. 'And do you know something else? It's all illegal!' the minister told me. Apparently, in order for the bus lane in Harold's Cross and another one of equivalent length on Swords Road to be legal, every local authority in the Dublin area – including Balbriggan Town Commissioners – would have had to adopt a set of by-laws. Rather than wait for all these ducks to be put in a row, Reynolds just went ahead with it. In that case, it seemed to me that he was acting in the public interest, and his bold initiative laid the groundwork for the network of bus lanes we have today. But it later became clear that Albert was equally capable of facilitating private-sector interests, as he did for Goodman International by granting unlimited export guarantee insurance for its beef trade with countries outside the EU, notably Saddam Hussein's Iraq.

I was involved in doing something that seriously annoyed Fianna Fáil, although they didn't know it at the time. During that chaotic period of short-lived governments in 1981 and 1982, Ray Burke abused his position as Minister for the Environment to pack An Bord Pleanála with political appointees, including his own 'constituency adviser' Tony Lambert. Given that the appeals board had been established in 1977 to take politics out of planning, I was concerned that its independence had been compromised, so I contacted my old friend Joe Revington, who was now special adviser to Dick Spring, the new Minister for the Environment and leader of the Labour Party, to see what could be done about it.

We met for a pub lunch in Daly's Lounge on Eden Quay just after Christmas in 1982. Joe was as disturbed as I was by what had happened and said that Spring was minded to dismiss the members of An Bord Pleanála. I suggested that I would write an opinion piece in the *Irish Times* calling on him to do so, thereby ventilating the issue in public and preparing the ground for his intervention. The article appeared under the bald heading, 'Spring should dismiss planning appeals board'. When Spring announced new legislation to 'reconstitute' the board, introducing an arm's-length process for appointing its chair and members, Fianna Fáil went berserk. Haughey characterized it as a 'loathsome piece of politically motivated legislation to try to assert some mean vindictive party political policy', and led his deputies out of the Dáil in protest after 'the most unruly scenes seen in the chamber for many years', as

Denis Coghlan reported in the *Irish Times*. According to Pádraig Flynn, the only 'sin' committed by the Burke-appointed board members being replaced by Spring was that they had 'stroked for Fianna Fáil on ballot papers over a number of years'.

Around that time, there were dark suspicions about a sewerage scheme for Baldoyle that could open up the north fringe of the city – including Haughey's estate in Kinsealy – for development. It was redolent of the plot in *Chinatown*, in which a crooked wealthy businessman played by John Huston is involved in diverting the Los Angeles public water supply to the San Fernando Valley, where he has hundreds of acres of orange groves with development potential. In the Baldoyle case, the landowner was Endcamp Ltd, controlled by John Byrne, an old crony of Haughey, who had made his fortune building office blocks and letting them to State entities. As Byrne's property empire was nominally controlled by a parent company registered in the Cayman Islands, it was impossible to tell if rumours that Haughey was a 'sleeping partner' were true. One clear link between them was that Des Traynor was also a director of Byrne's vehicle, Carlisle Trust Ltd. Some two hundred acres of land were proposed for rezoning, to facilitate yet more of the suburban development that had helped turn Dublin into a doughnut city, with a nearly empty centre. Media reports, including my own in the *Irish Times*, put an end to that effort.

I had been dispatched to Lebanon for two weeks in 1980, when Irish troops serving with UNIFIL were in the line of fire; but I had no wish to become a war correspondent, so it was a relief to me when Kevin Myers was sent to Beirut two years later as Israeli tanks rolled in and jets relentlessly strafed and bombed the city. Such was the scope and ferocity of Israel's 'Operation Peace for Galilee' that the *Irish Times* was also carrying syndicated reports and analysis by Robert Fisk, as well as vividly colourful pieces from Myers. Except that there was a big problem: Fisk had just defected from the NUJ and joined the renegade Institute of Journalists. An order came through from NUJ headquarters in London that his copy was to be 'blacked' – in other words, nobody could lay their hands on it.

Douglas Gageby was absolutely furious and summoned us all to a meeting in the newsroom, where he got up onto one of the big oak desks and used it as a bully-pulpit to spell out his position in no uncertain terms. What the NUJ had ordered us to do, he said, was to refuse to handle the copy of a working journalist who was risking life and limb in a war situation. He felt so strongly about it that he even threatened to halt publication of the paper unless we stopped this nonsense and got back to our desks. You could have almost heard a pin drop when he finished up by saying, 'Now, if you'll excuse me, I have a paper to get out.' The *Irish Times* NUJ chapel, then headed by Chicago-born Mary Maher, was left with no option but to drop its blacklisting of Fisk, and we got back to work – with a subeditor processing Fisk's latest dispatch from the front in Beirut. It was a dramatic illustration of Gageby's authority; I always thought of him as a dead ringer for Ben Bradlee, managing editor of the *Washington Post*, as portrayed by Jason Robards in *All the President's Men*.

There was a great atmosphere of camaraderie in the *Irish Times* newsroom then, and we all felt very much part of a disparate team of self-starters, directed with quiet diplomacy and good humour by news editor Gerry Mulvey. One of his principal tasks was to compile the daily news schedule for the main editorial conference, then held at 3 o'clock in the afternoon; most days, it had a line saying, 'Martyn Turner's cartoon will be on the 5.30 p.m. bus from Newbridge,' and a messenger would be duly dispatched to collect it from Busáras. At our end of the newsroom, nearest the door, I sat opposite Kevin Myers by a window overlooking double-decker buses on Fleet Street, belching noxious diesel fumes, as he churned out another 'Irishman's Diary'. Behind me was Michael Foley, our media correspondent, for whom the Atex system's spellchecker was a real godsend. Mark Brennock, who went on to become political correspondent and one of my best friends, sat beside me, opposite Jim Cusack, the security correspondent from Belfast. The laconic Deaglán de Bréadún was also in our group, as were Kerry-born political pundit Michael O'Regan and, off and on, Mary Holland, veteran observer of the Troubles.

The banter, when it got going, was unbeatable. But we had to be careful of making a faux pas, such as splitting an infinitive, lest we get a dressing-down from Bruce Williamson, deputy editor and keeper of the English language on the *Irish Times*; he was the one who sat at the big oak desk in the Editor's Office, overlooked by a portrait of legendary editor R. M. 'Bertie' Smyllie, while Gageby sat at a bockety thing just inside the door; he didn't need any trappings, everyone knew that he ran the paper. He was, however, coming up to retirement, and there was a lot of jockeying for position to succeed him, mainly by Conor Brady and James Downey. The latter looked the likely winner, so there was consternation in some quarters when Brady got the nod in 1986. A master of office politics, he immediately got Downey off-site by giving him the job of London editor; but Eugene McEldowney managed to hold on to his job as news editor, despite having backed the wrong horse. Conor O'Clery might have been in the frame, but I'm sure he was glad he didn't go for the job, because he became one of the best foreign correspondents around, reporting from London, Moscow, Beijing, Washington and New York City – always in the right place at the right time.

Presiding over it all, largely unseen, was Major Thomas Blakeney McDowell, chairman of the Irish Times Trust and chief executive of its operating company, Irish Times Ltd. With his Savile Row three-piece suit, gold watch chain and monocle, he always struck me as a fully formed version of the White Rabbit in *Alice's Adventures in Wonderland*. He had a blue London taxi and a driver to convey him from his home – Grange Marches, above Rathfarnham – to his wood-panelled office in a converted shop on D'Olier Street, which resembled the interior of a London gentlemen's club, complete with a rack of folded (though perhaps not ironed) newspapers, including the *Daily Telegraph*, *Le Monde*, *Frankfurter Allgemeine* and *Corriere della Sera*.

I once wrote a Henry Root-style letter to the Major, complaining about the run-down state of the *Irish Times* buildings on D'Olier Street and telling him that I was being ribbed about it by city planners and even by some councillors. How could the paper criticize others for failing to maintain their buildings, if it wasn't looking after its own? I got a phone call from the Major's batman, company secretary Iain Pratt, saying, 'The Chairman would like to see you.' I asked when, and he said, 'Well, now, actually.' So I went down to his rather congested outer office, populated by attendants, and through a short, narrow corridor that led to the Major's inner sanctum. He rose from his Victorian throne-type chair (later donated by him to Geraldine Kennedy after she became editor; she used to sit in it for editorial conferences).

'Ah, Major McDowell – I haven't seen you in ages,' I said, shaking his hand.

With that, the monocle fell out of his eye socket, and he said, 'That doesn't mean I don't know what you're up to!'

Although he looked like a figure from a different age, he was not sentimental. When hot-metal printing had to go, it went, with the old Linotype machines donated to the Coptic Patriarch of Alexandria, for some obscure reason; Coptic priests even came to take them away. At least the printing press remained on the premises. Upgraded under Gageby's stewardship to a Uniman, the best of German machines, it occupied the basement, ground and first floors of a large part of the *Irish Times* complex, and you could feel the building vibrating when it was running at full tilt. That's what really brought it home to you that this was a real newspaper, and you'd see all the folded copies coming out on pegs to dispatch, with a fleet of vans and lorries to take bundles all over Ireland.

Dublin was driving me to distraction. The city had no sense of itself as a European capital. I calculated that derelict sites all over the inner city amounted to six times the size of St Stephen's Green. Its historic core was being wrecked, and nobody seemed to care. City councillors were being hoodwinked by Corporation officials, particularly in relation to the Corpo's devastating road plans. I had by now read Maurice Craig's masterpiece *Dublin 1660–1860*, first published in 1952, and couldn't believe that those who were responsible for looking after the city's built environment appeared to be so ignorant of its history, or worse. The population of the inner city had fallen in every census since 1926. Everyone who made decisions about the city now lived in the suburbs, so their perception was essentially suburban, usually framed by the windscreen of a car; for Corpo officials, it was a sort of colony that they drove in to administer every weekday. And they all had guaranteed parking spaces, in the basements of new office buildings or the cannibalized rear gardens of Georgian houses in and around Merrion Square. Dublin was nothing like Edinburgh, where the New Town laid out in the eighteenth century was still largely residential and populated by the professional classes.

Like Deirdre Kelly, who founded the Living City Group, I couldn't see any valid reason why the heart of Dublin couldn't be saved by repopulating it. So I set about documenting the extent of dereliction in the inner city and what lay behind it. Others were also chipping away at the bureaucratic monolith, notably *In Dublin* magazine, edited and published by John S. Doyle, who gave some of Ireland's finest journalists their first big breaks – the likes of Fintan O'Toole, Mary Raftery and Colm Tóibín. There was plenty to write about because the city was losing so many of its assets. The Russell Hotel, famous for haute cuisine, had closed down in 1974 and was demolished to make way for a dreary brick-clad office development called Stokes Place. The Royal Hibernian on Dawson Street became another casualty of 'progress' ten years later. The office complex that replaced this legendary hotel, characterized by developer Friends Provident as 'a terribly rambling place', was faced in light grey granite and the shopping mall at ground level was called Royal Hibernian Way – a name proposed, in a public competition, by the wife of then Chief Planning Officer Charles Aliaga-Kelly.

What grabbed people's imagination most of all was the discovery of Dublin's Viking origins at Wood Quay, where archaeologists led by Dr Pat Wallace (later director of the National Museum), were fighting a losing battle with the Corporation, which was determined to build its Civic Offices on the site. When Lord Mayor Paddy Belton was asked for his views on the controversy, he declared himself 'ignorant, and proud of it'. Through the Wood Quay campaign, I got to know such stalwarts as the volatile Alderman Kevin Byrne and the charming but steely Carmencita Hederman, who was also an alderman and enjoyed wearing her black tricorn hat and the green-and-blue robes of office that went with it. I didn't much care for any of this frumpery, sharing the view of John Kelly, a brilliant lawyer and often-acerbic Fine Gael politician, who once remarked that Éamon de Valera's City and County Management Act of 1955 had stripped local councillors of nearly all their powers and 'left them their tricorn hats, their chains, their gowns and their coaches'.

In September 1978 I had marched alongside the Reverend Professor F. X. Martin while covering the massive demonstration to save Wood Quay for the *Irish Press*. As usual, he was immaculately turned out in an Italian-tailored black tunic, with an academic gown and stripe over it; he may have been an Augustinian mendicant friar, but he had Visa and Diner's Club cards. I also met some of the campaign's leading protagonists, including his assistant Bride Rosney; barrister Mary Robinson, an outspoken member of Seanad Éireann on human rights issues; and her husband Nick, a good solicitor, cartoonist and architectural historian; they jointly represented F. X. in his successful effort to have the site designated as a national monument. Memorably, the High Court judge who made that decision, Liam Hamilton (later Chief Justice), insisted on walking the wattle pathways that had been excavated at Wood Quay – as I did myself – before delivering his judgment. But the Supreme Court overturned Hamilton's ruling, and the first phase of Dublin's most controversial building project went ahead.

One day in the spring of 1984, I received a letter from Fergal Tobin, commissioning editor at Gill & Macmillan, asking me if I would consider writing a book about the city. I had never thought of becoming an 'author', but I could see immediately that there was a need for a book that would tell the story of Dublin's demise. So I took nine months off work, six of them unpaid, to research and write *The Destruction of Dublin*, spending weeks during the summer of 1984 in the glorious reading room of the National Library on

Kildare Street, where I found there was some truth in what Douglas Gageby used to say: 'When you work for the *Irish Times*, you're not just writing news – you're writing history.' The grey boxes containing month-by-month microfilm of previous editions of the paper were often in tatters, while those containing records of the *Irish Press* or *Irish Independent* were in pristine condition.

I kept all the files I accumulated in two orange boxes in the dining room of 6 Casimir Road, and wrote in longhand before typing it all up on a rented IBM Selectric typewriter – the one with the famous 'golf ball'. About three-quarters of the way through, like a marathon runner, I hit a wall and felt that I couldn't go on. What helped me get over that hump was a realization that, if I didn't finish the book, this story of what happened to the city simply wouldn't be told. (Years later, at the request of a senior tax inspector, I turned over all my files to the Revenue so that they could chase a number of individuals and companies named in the book; a 'tidy sum' was netted in income tax arrears, I understand.)

Word got out around the *Irish Times* office that the book included three pages dealing with the paper's own property editor, Karl Jones, and his opposite number at the *Irish Independent*, Frank Cairns, both of whom were unapologetic cheerleaders for the development lobby. Gill & Macmillan provided a number of potential extracts from the book, but the *Irish Times* kept asking for more until it got its hands on the material about Jones and Cairns, in which they were named as members of a property syndicate – a conflict of interest that they had both denied. As a result, G&M got a solicitor's letter on behalf of Jones denying that he had been a member of the Grand Canal Syndicate, as it was called, and threatening to seek a High Court injunction to prevent publication. At a crisis meeting in the offices of Arthur Cox & Company on St Stephen's Green, the publishers' solicitors, I stormed out, saying that I was not going to have the contents of my book 'dictated by fucking lawyers'. By then, the book had already been printed and there were thousands of copies sitting in a warehouse at Inchicore. But even my own legal team, solicitor Garrett Sheehan and barrister

Michael McDowell, agreed that we needed more evidence to fight off Jones's legal challenge.

I was also under pressure in the office. Ken Gray, the deputy editor, told me that my credibility was on the line. Gageby summoned me to his inner sanctum and said, 'What you've done is outrageous. You have damned a colleague without telling his side of the story. He insists that he was never involved in any property syndicate.'

I replied, 'With all due respect, Mr Gageby, Karl Jones doesn't have a side of the story to tell that corresponds with the truth [in relation to his involvement in the Grand Canal Syndicate].' I also said it would have been invidious, in a book that named names from so many other professions, not to have dealt with the property editors. In fact, my motivation for presenting a more conservation-minded perspective in the news and features pages of the *Irish Times* derived from a desire to counterbalance the puff in the property pages. Jones had even sought to have me 'reined in' by taking news editor Eugene McEldowney to lunch in the Westbury Hotel, where my boss found him 'sitting at a table like a grand panjandrum'. Once, when I asked him to characterize his own role, Karl Jones said, 'I'm a journalist. At the same time, I am unashamedly pro-property. I represent the guys out there driving the bulldozers and investing their money in the future of this country. And contrary to any idle gossip around town, my page is not run like a bawdy house in New Orleans. It's more like Mount Melleray, I can assure you.' That's a direct quote from *The Destruction of Dublin*.

The book would not have come out if Jones's threatened injunction had been granted. With my back to the wall, I got on to the High Court Central Office, asking them to check if there was any documentation on file from a 1975 case in which the existence of an outfit called the Grand Canal Syndicate was disclosed. Set up by the architect Sam Stephenson, its members included his business partner Arthur Gibney, chartered surveyor Terry Sudway, and the two property editors I'd written about, Frank Cairns and Karl Jones. What we turned up was pure gold: not only did the musty file show that both Cairns and Jones were members of the syndicate, but they were in receipt of minutes of meetings, 'situation reports', profit-and-loss accounts – the lot. Michael McDowell then drafted a masterly letter detailing all the evidence we had, which Jones would have had to disclose to the High Court if he went ahead with his action against us. He knew then that we had him cold and, with no further legal proceedings, the book came out three days later. I remember seeing a whole stack of copies on a table in Fred Hanna's bookshop on Nassau Street and thinking, Oh my God. How are we going to get away with this?

The Destruction of Dublin was very well received. 'There is no use pretending that Frank McDonald is aiming at a dispassionate and judicial tone,' wrote the great Maurice Craig in the *Irish Times*. 'He is not. He is in a rage, and by the time the reader has finished he will be in a rage too.' Daithí Hanly, former Dublin City Architect, described it as 'the most important book about Dublin – about Ireland – that has been written this generation'. I was quite stunned by his accolade. And yes, I was indeed an angry young man, in a rage against those responsible for delivering such decay and destruction over the years.

A number of libel actions cost the publishers and myself money and these ongoing legal proceedings prevented Gill & Macmillan from reprinting the book. But I'll always remember the decency of the architect David Keane, later President of the RIAI. He could have sued – the book contained an erroneous claim that reflected poorly on him – but he merely required us to publish a retraction in the personal columns of the *Irish Times*.

Notwithstanding the stress and financial cost, at least the story was out now. Douglas Gageby brought a copy of *The Destruction of Dublin* on holiday to Lanzarote that Christmas and said to me, after he got back, that it 'throws a very interesting light on a subject that remained in the shade for too long'. I suppose that was his way of making it up with me. The truth is that he had a blind spot about the property pages of the *Irish Times* and appeared to believe that adulatory coverage of nearly every new development was necessary in order to sustain the advertising revenue being generated from the property sector. Frank Cairns was dismissed by the *Indo*, having previously given an assurance to his employers that he was not involved in the Grand Canal Syndicate; I was told that he went in one day shortly after the truth was revealed and found a note on his typewriter instructing him to report to the personnel department and collect his P45. Jones, on the other hand, was promoted to special reports editor and continued working for the *Irish Times* until his retirement.

When Dublin's legendary gay haunt, Bartley Dunne's pub, came up for sale in September 1985, deputy news editor Jack Fagan put me on the case. I interviewed Barry Dunne, who had run the pub for years with his late brother Gerry. Barry regaled me with a list of customers such as Liz Taylor and Richard Burton, Kim Novak, Laurence Harvey and Noël Coward. Late-1960s newspaper advertisements described Bartley Dunne's as 'unusual in character, continental in atmosphere. A breath of Paris, reminiscent of les Bistros. Cosmopolitan clientele. Left bank mood. Rendezvous of intelligentsia, Bohemian, literati, theatre personalities, socialites, beatniks, artists, aristocrats and fashionable young ladies, businessmen and professionals – from followers of Hippocrates to ambitious young advocates.'

There were prints on the walls of work by Cézanne, Monet and Picasso as well as Parisian theatre posters and photographs of film stars, and it was full of dimly lit nooks and crannies, adding just the right touch of interest and intrigue, I noted. As David Norris recalled, 'It was an Aladdin's cave to me, its wicker-clad Chianti bottles stiff with dribbled candlewax, tea chests covered in red-and-white chequered cloths, heavy scarlet velvet drapes and an immense collection of multicoloured liqueurs glinting away in their bottles.'

But when I put it to him, Barry Dunne flatly denied that it was a 'gay bar', even to me. 'We had a few who were that way inclined, but it was really nothing like the rumours,' he said. I thought this was a shocking betrayal of the pub's most faithful clientele, although I didn't say that in my report, which appeared under the heading,

'An oasis of exotica is put up for sale'. The proprietor was so pleased with it that he dispatched a case of vintage wine and spirits to my home a few days later. Some of this consignment lasted longer than Bartley Dunne's; within five years, all trace of the building was gone, rolled over by the Grafton Plaza Hotel and its kitsch Break for the Border nightclub.

The Late Late Show decided to feature *The Destruction of Dublin* in February 1986, with me in a black leather jacket, blue jeans, white shirt and thin canary-yellow tie, sitting beside Gay Byrne and facing a panel that included City Manager Frank Feely and architect Sam Stephenson. I had written terrible things about both of them but, whereas Feely took it personally, Sam remained as gregarious as ever, even though I had (wrongly) suggested that he had decamped to London after becoming a 'social pariah' in Dublin; a man who could begin a sentence, 'As Princess Margaret would say . . .' could never sink so low. A week or so later, Sam rang to invite me to supper in the flat he had at his offices in Bride Street. We got on really well and remained on the best of terms until his sudden death in November 2006.

You never knew who you'd end up sitting next to at the convivial dinner table jointly presided over by Sam and his second wife Caroline Sweetman in Ryevale House, Leixlip. One time it was Terry Keane, the *Sunday Independent* gossip columnist and mistress of Charlie Haughey, and on another occasion it was the incomparable Miranda Guinness, Countess of Iveagh, who brought us on a late-night tour of Farmleigh House on our way home. By then, Sam had abandoned the 'old-time religion' of modern architecture, declaring that he now went to bed with Palladio and got up with Lutyens. This became the title of a television documentary in 1988, directed by RTÉ drama producer John Lynch, who initially set out with a critical view of Stephenson, but after a lunch in London that ran through the afternoon and into dinner that evening the two were on much friendlier terms, and Lynch's unconventional documentary was delightful. As for Miranda, she did very well from the government's decision in 1999 to purchase Farmleigh for £23 million, with the intention of using it as a State guesthouse. She bought Wilbury Park, an early English Palladian mansion in Wiltshire, and threw herself enthusiastically into its restoration, inviting me over to see the results. Sadly, I didn't make it; she died there in 2010, from cancer, having bravely hosted her seventieth birthday party in the Guinness Storehouse's Gravity Bar five months earlier. I also believed that the government was wrong to buy Farmleigh, a quite undistinguished Victorian pile, when it should have bought Carton House, former seat of the Dukes of Leinster, in Maynooth.

I got to know another Guinness – Mariga – quite well. Princess Marie-Gabrielle von Urach-Württemberg had married the Hon. Desmond Guinness at Oxford in 1954 and moved into Carton, which they were renting from Lord Brocket. I knew them by reputation, of course. They had played leading roles in saving Castletown House in Celbridge, Ireland's largest and most magnificent Palladian mansion, as well as the Conolly Folly (an obelisk that can be seen from both Carton and Castletown), Tailors' Hall behind High Street in Dublin, and several other important eighteenth-century buildings. Desmond and Mariga were key players in establishing the Irish Georgian Society to campaign for the preservation of what is, after all, part of Ireland's heritage.

After the publication of *The Destruction of Dublin*, Mariga buttonholed me at some function and said she wanted to show me the state of Carton, which had fallen into the hands of Powerscreen Ltd, a Northern Ireland-based company that supplied specialized equipment for mining. She had a battered old Citroën DS – pronounced *Déesse* (French for goddess) – which she always referred to as her 'motor', and it was in this jalopy that we drove through the entrance gate without anything that resembled a permit, still less an invitation. Mariga pulled the car up right in front of the great house and we got out to peer through the windows, inspect the disused dairy done in the Dutch manner with decorative blue-and-white tiles from floor to ceiling, and visit the Shell Cottage, where Marianne Faithfull had lived for a time. But it wasn't only the fate of these buildings that concerned Mariga; she was positively lyrical about the demesne, which had been planted in the mid-eighteenth century by Lancelot 'Capability' Brown, under the direction of Emily FitzGerald, the first Duchess of Leinster. Any notion that this extraordinary landscape would be sacrificed for suburban housing or a golf resort (which is what it became) was anathema to her.

Some time later, I met Mariga at a 'Save Carton' public meeting in Maynooth. She was wearing a long tartan skirt, silk blouse, knitted cardigan and shawl, looking for all the world like Cathleen Ní Houlihan, with a wicker basket in her lap. Afterwards, she issued a generalized invitation to come back to Leixlip Castle for supper. Myself and former government minister and Labour Party strategist Justin Keating were the only ones who turned up, to find Mariga alone in the castle. By then, she was divorced from Desmond, who spent a lot of his time in London with his new wife Penny Cuthbertson, and was living in Leixlip without their consent. The staff were all Desmond's people and they even locked the fridge, so she had bottles of Soave cooling in a bath off the main bedroom, where in 1210 King John had reputedly slept one night.

Mariga had cooked spaghetti Bolognese and served it up to us in the library. There was a parrot in a cage with an open door and, every so often, the bird would pop out, fly around the room and land on the cornice of one of the bookshelves or even on Mariga's shoulder. She talked about her memories of being in Japan as a young girl, and childhood family holidays on a fjord in Norway, as well as about art, architecture and nearly everything else. We were so enchanted that it was after 2 a.m. before we realized it. There was a problem, however. Someone had locked the front door, so we had no obvious way of getting out. Absolutely unfazed, Mariga brought us back up to the library, pulled up one of the big sashes and invited us to jump out of the window. I went first, falling to the grassy ground about ten feet below, and then caught Justin Keating as he tumbled out. We picked ourselves up, waved to her and made our way back to Dublin by car.

Mariga didn't last much longer, sadly. In May 1989, she had a heart attack and died on what she would have called the 'mailboat' from Holyhead to Dún Laoghaire at the age of fifty-six. She was buried under the Conolly Folly, an inspired choice by her great friend Desmond FitzGerald, Knight of Glin. Maurice Craig drove me to her funeral Mass at the Catholic church in Maynooth, in his draughty Citroën Deux Chevaux.

I was fascinated by this other world of castles and stately homes, as we would have called the country mansions still occupied by titled folk. Accompanied by Eamon and our friend Betty Flanagan, I did a tour of Hidden Ireland houses for the *Irish Times*, discovering extraordinary places like Roundwood House, near Mountrath, Co. Laois; it had been saved by the Irish Georgian Society from the depredations of the Forestry Commission, whose budget to acquire the estate actually included an allocation for the demolition of this early Irish Palladian house. The State and its agencies couldn't give a hoot about protecting these remnants of the Ascendancy, as they were seen, and even demolished Coole Park in Co. Galway, the ancestral home of Lady Augusta Gregory, co-founder of the Abbey Theatre, after she had entrusted it to the nation; all that remains is the bare plinth on which it once stood.

Rockingham House, overlooking Lough Key in Co. Roscommon, was also demolished by the State after it was severely damaged by fire in 1957; a concrete tower, designed by UCD planning professor James Fehily, stands on the site like a large tombstone in the forest park. The wealthy King-Harman family, who had commissioned John Nash to design it, previously resided at the early eighteenth-century King House in Boyle, which later became a military barracks, and was derelict the first time I saw it in the 1980s; there was even a sycamore tree growing out of its sagging roof. When I called in to the new red-brick Garda station next door to enquire about the building, gesturing in its direction, the garda on duty there was flummoxed and asked, 'What building?'

I said, 'The big one, just there.'

To which he replied, 'Oh, *that*. It used to be the barracks, I think.'

So despite having an enormous presence in the town, King House had literally become invisible, although – mercifully – it was later restored by Roscommon County Council, which had been planning to pull it down as a 'dangerous building'.

Despite the success of Matt McNulty, then head of Dublin Tourism, in saving Malahide Castle and much of its Irish Jacobean furniture back in 1976, great houses were still falling prey to property speculators and developers with an eye on what was left of their estates. It was all documented by the Knight of Glin, David Griffin and Nick Robinson in *Vanishing Country Houses of Ireland*, published in 1988. 'The catalogue of destruction is almost endless, and it's not confined to the incendiary activities of so-called patriots during the early 1920s,' as I wrote in my review. 'What's so depressing is that we're still at it, wasting a precious part of our heritage for reasons of profit.' But Brian Molloy, a dedicated Georgian, managed to make Roundwood House habitable again. After his tragic death in 1978, the house was taken over by Frank and Rosemarie Kennan, and turned into a quirky, romantic B&B, with guests sharing a large dinner table after drinks in the library. Connie Aldridge had a similarly large table in the dining room of Mount Falcon Castle, near Ballina, and used to dish out soup to everyone from a big tureen, after they had already helped themselves to G&Ts at her 'honesty bar' below the staircase.

Palatial Hilton Park, near Clones, was another success story in the hospitality sector, with Johnny Madden as the genial host and his wife Lucy as chef in the kitchen. Their five children were also quite young at the time of our visit. The border with Northern Ireland is marked by a stream at the rear of their yard, and it's a mile to the front door whether you enter from the Clones gate or via the estate village of Scotshouse. Not far away, in Co. Armagh, former Speaker of the Stormont parliament Sir Norman Stronge and his son James had been killed when their ancestral home, Tynan Abbey, was fire-bombed by the Provisional IRA in 1981. Madden feared for his family's safety and sought a meeting with the Garda chief superintendent in Clones.

'You don't need to worry, Mr Madden. Sure your people bought their land,' he was told.

That was the bizarre thing. The chief superintendent knew, *as a matter of fact*, that Hilton Park had been purchased in 1734 by the Reverend Samuel Madden, a friend of Jonathan Swift. The clear implication was that, owing to this history, the IRA wouldn't set fire to Hilton Park; whereas Tynan Abbey, presumably, was believed to have been expropriated. Reverend Madden had bought the estate way back then for one of his sons, who was marrying a Protestant girl from Co. Tyrone. Her dowry consisted of a satchel full of acorns, which were planted to create a grove of oak trees that's still standing three centuries later. This unusual act, very much rooted in the soil, also rather charmingly confirmed my long-held view that there is a real difference between Protestants and Catholics on this island: Protestants saw it as their duty to pass on what they had inherited to the next generation in at least as good (if not better) condition, whereas Catholics sought to get what they could from the land, in the here-and-now. When I put it to Donald Caird, then Church of Ireland Archbishop of Dublin, that Protestants were disproportionately well-represented in Ireland's heritage organizations, he responded with the wry observation, 'Well, you have to remember that they once owned it all.'

Anyone living in a city or town couldn't fail to notice the proliferation of one-off houses in rural Ireland. Census data over the years showed a trend of population increases in rural townlands and a corresponding decline in the number of people living in towns and villages. The proverbial butchers, bakers and candlestick-makers who once lived above their shops had moved out, initially to new homes in what became known as 'ribbon development' on the approach roads and, later, to more dispersed locations all over the place. It happened to be cheaper to build your own house in the countryside than to buy one in a town or village, and this differential was compounded by hidden public subsidies for the bungalow builders in providing electricity, post, telecoms, school transport and other services.

And so it continues, such that there are about half a million 'one-off' houses in rural areas at the time of writing. The vast bulk of these homes were not designed by qualified architects, but rather plucked from pattern books such as *Bungalow Bliss*, by two-term Fianna Fáil Senator Jack Fitzsimons, that first appeared in 1971 and was so popular that it ran to twelve editions over the years. Nobody was writing about this phenomenon, so I coined the term 'Bungalow Blitz' for a series of articles in 1987 documenting what was, in effect, the suburbanization of rural Ireland. More and more people were now car-dependent, living as they did at a distance from shops, schools, churches and workplaces. This turned narrow rural roads into the most dangerous in Ireland – unsafe for both walking and cycling and particularly hazardous for anyone pushing a baby-buggy. It also had knock-on effects on towns and villages. As people moved out in greater numbers, the upper floors of once-inhabited shop buildings were left vacant with no sign of light after dusk. Ultimately, these buildings will become endangered through lack of use; many of them already are.

There were those, like my colleague Caroline Walsh, who believed that the 'Bungalow Blitz' series would change everything, simply by documenting what was going on. It certainly generated more letters to the editor than anything else in the *Irish Times* since Maeve Binchy wrote a rather disparaging colour piece about one of the royal weddings in London. But there was no prospect of changing the culture, particularly as some of the arguments were so atavistic. Thus, people had a 'right to build on their own land', they couldn't 'live off the scenery' and, in any case, dispersed housing was 'part of what we are'. Jim Connolly, founder of the Irish Rural Dwellers Association, once erupted like a volcano from the floor of a conference I was chairing in Glendalough, Co. Wicklow, accusing me of siding with the Royal (he pronounced it *Rile*) Town Planning Institute in London, which wanted to impose its 'foreign' standards on Ireland. By highlighting what was going on in nearly every rural townland, I had launched a 'metropolitan assault on rural Ireland', he (and others) claimed. Yet I'll never forget meeting an elderly woman whose life was transformed when she moved from an isolated bungalow in the countryside into a sheltered housing scheme in the middle of Gorey, Co. Wexford, within walking distance of the shops, post office, church and everything else. She couldn't have been more delighted by her new home.

The State was not entirely blind to the problem. An Foras Forbartha, the National Institute for Physical Planning and Construction Research, had been established in 1964 with support from the United Nations. In 1976, it produced a report showing that scattered rural housing cost the State up to five times more to service than housing in towns or cities. But the report was suppressed by then Minister for Local Government Jimmy Tully, a notorious facilitator of 'one-off' houses in Co. Meath. In 1982, Minister for the Environment Ray Burke decreed that 'the Foras' would move to Cork as a 'decentralization' initiative but staff successfully resisted it – much to his chagrin. Five years later, as part of a package of savage cuts by the Fianna Fáil minority government, the Foras was slated for abolition. Brendan O'Donoghue, then Assistant Secretary at the Department of the Environment, served as the undertaker, redeploying staff to a toothless Environmental Research Unit within the department itself or, later, to the EPA. The wily O'Donoghue went on to become Secretary-General of the department and later director of the National Library. But even he would agree that we could have done with the services of An Foras Forbartha in providing successive governments with good advice on the construction industry and building standards. The tragedy is that his political masters couldn't see that.

6

After *The Destruction of Dublin* was published, I became something of a public figure, identified at home and abroad with the city and its travails. I even got a letter from Spike Milligan, as manic as the man himself, expressing outrage that the Huguenot Cemetery in Merrion Row was about to be obliterated by another office development and asking me what I was going to do about it. I was glad to be able to write back to him at his home in Sussex, saying this was only a rumour and it had no basis in reality. (In fact, the Huguenot graveyard has since been enhanced by a set of railings, through which a beautiful carpet of bluebells can be seen every spring.)

Inevitably, I also became an activist and joined a group of like-minded people to organize the Dublin Crisis Conference in February 1986, in a determined effort to change public policy. The others included Victor Griffin, fearless Dean of St Patrick's Cathedral; David Norris, Joyce scholar and gay-rights campaigner; Larry Dillon, argumentative chairman of the Liberties Association; Deirdre Kelly, of the Living City Group; and Mick Rafferty, a community activist and right-hand man of Tony Gregory, future independent TD for the north inner city. We packed the Synod Hall in Christchurch Place for a whole weekend, with an impassioned keynote speech by me to kick it off, and even got the Taoiseach, Garret FitzGerald, to respond to the debate with a long and convoluted address that was broadly sympathetic to our cause. 'If you feel frustrated, so do I,' he said. 'Though I'm the Taoiseach of this country, I find it very hard often to see what course of action is open to me to achieve an objective in the areas you're concerned about through the systems and mechanisms that exist – whether it's in central or local government, the level of the officials or the community at large.' In the end, the conference unanimously adopted a composite resolution calling on the government and the Dublin local authorities to 'recognize and accept that the city *is* in crisis' and demanding a wide range of radical changes in policy, including the cancellation of all road plans in central Dublin, more emphasis on public transport, tax incentives to promote the rehabilitation of the city's architectural fabric and 'positive measures to encourage and facilitate public participation at all levels in the planning process'.

After all, the Corpo had ridden roughshod over public protests at Wood Quay, building bunker-like office blocks on what was widely acknowledged at the time as the most important Viking archaeological site in Europe. When I asked a taxi driver what he thought of the new Civic Offices, he took one look at the two bunkers, and said, 'It's a real *Guns of Navarone* job.' It was the best single line of architectural criticism I had ever heard, and summed up the extent to which Dublin Corporation was dug in against the people of Dublin. But then, the city's Latin motto *Obedientia Civium Urbis Felicitas* translates as 'the obedience of the citizenry [makes for] the happiness of the city'.

The Fine Gael–Labour coalition government responded to widely shared concerns about the decay of Dublin and other cities by giving us the Urban Renewal Act of 1986, with its scattergun scheme of tax incentives for development in 'designated areas', such as the gap-toothed Liffey quays. Dublin Corporation produced a brochure on the scheme with a flattering photograph of the semi-domed filling station at Usher's Quay on its cover, and put up billboards advertising derelict sites for sale saying 'Call Bill Lacey' – then assistant principal officer in the planning department – and giving a phone number to ring. UCD's School of Architecture contributed to the debate with its *Dublin City Quays* project, coordinated by Gerry Cahill, that put forward notional schemes for various sites by architects such as Yvonne Farrell, Shelley McNamara, Paul Keogh, Sheila O'Donnell, John Tuomey and Derek Tynan – all of whom would later be among the founders of Group 91, which came up with a plan to rebuild South Earl Street in the Liberties and devised an architectural framework plan for Temple Bar.

We ourselves followed up by producing a 'Manifesto for the City' and reconvening the Dublin Crisis Conference at the CIÉ Club on Marlborough Street in the run-up to the 1987 general election. Chaired by Olivia O'Leary, it drew nearly all the party leaders, including Garret FitzGerald, as bumbling as ever, and Charlie Haughey, whose arrival in the hall was not unlike that of a Mafia *capo*, surrounded by his henchmen. It was at this meeting that Haughey made his famous pledge to save Temple Bar, which was then threatened with having its heart ripped out by CIÉ to make way for a bus-and-rail transport hub. Describing the area as one of the oldest, most historic parts of Dublin, he said that he 'wouldn't let CIÉ near the place'.

Fianna Fáil went into coalition with the Progressive Democrats in 1989, and the party's deputy leader, Mary Harney, became Minister of State for Environmental Protection, piloting through legislation to establish the Environmental Protection Agency from her powder-blue office at the east end of the Custom House. Calling in to see her, I asked Harney why Pádraig Flynn had allocated her this suite far removed from the ministerial corridor at the west end. She said, 'Because he doesn't want me to see who he's meeting.' These people, as we later learned, included Sligo-born developer Tom Gilmartin, who had come over from Luton to advance plans for a huge motorway shopping centre at Quarryvale, on the M50, and another destructive scheme for Bachelors Walk. In time, it would be revealed that Gilmartin gave Flynn a cheque for £50,000 as a donation to Fianna Fáil, which the minister told him to make out to 'cash' and then lodged in his own bank account.

Even before that conversation with Harney, it was clear to me that we had still not won the argument about Dublin's future direction, either in broad terms or in detail, so I wrote another book, *Saving the City*, to drive home a sustainable development agenda, and even managed to get Bob Geldof to do a foreword, as he had become so outspoken about the wilful destruction of the city. (Geldof described me as 'a permanent thorn in the fat arse of municipal pretension'.) At a civic reception in his honour after the *Live Aid* spectacular in June 1985, he had talked about how Dublin had become 'increasingly brutalized' and reduced to a 'shambolic mess, at best'. Its mediocre new buildings 'can only be the product of backhanders, political corruption and moral degradation', he said. 'When a city is being destroyed by its custodians, then what are the people who live in it supposed to think?' Councillors and Corporation officials were appalled that Geldof had used a civic reception to criticize them in such a direct way, but that was always his style. They preferred the 'I ♥ Dublin' lectern, which would be wheeled out for public events such as the opening of a pocket park beside City Hall, on a long-term derelict site created by their own road engineers.

By then, I was writing about contemporary architecture, as well as historic buildings under threat of demolition and planning issues in general. My first tentative move in this new direction was a feature for the Arts page of the *Irish Times* on the Irish Civil Service Building Society's headquarters on D'Olier Street, a woeful piece of pastiche that replaced the Regent Hotel and broke the Wide Street Commissioners' continuous façade on that side of the street. Arts editor Fergus Linehan, who moonlighted writing witty scripts for shows starring his wife Rosaleen and Des Keogh, was quite happy to carry it.

Having spent countless hours over the years poring over plans at the public counter of Dublin Corporation's planning department in the Irish Life Centre on Lower Abbey Street, I had got to know how to read drawings. In time, I became conversant and comfortable with the language of architecture and was able to look at the work of architects knowledgeably as well as writing about it quite fluently. I tried to do that using a language that readers would understand, rather than sinking into the word soup of architectural jargon. What helped me most was that I had a 'good eye' for aesthetics and always took time to look up at buildings on city streets, whether old or new, whereas most people rarely take in anything above the shopfronts.

A rumour spread around that I was a 'failed architecture student from Bolton Street', but that was never true. As my friend Shane O'Toole later recalled, I would turn up regularly at evening events, organized by the Architectural Association of Ireland, which is run by younger members of the profession, to hear cutting-edge architects from home and abroad talking about their work. My punt, he said, was long-term research to deepen my understanding of the different forces that help to shape our environment.

'No Irish journalist had ploughed those furrows before, but it had to be done if he was to have any chance of playing a part in stitching his, and our, beloved but benighted city back together again,' as Shane put it. Although I detested the populist frolics of postmodernism, I accepted the thesis of Leon Krier and others that architects needed to consider context and get 'back to the street'. Indeed, that was the title of my friend Gerry Cahill's 1980 book on how to rescue the Liberties. More and more, I found myself hanging out with architects, some of whom are still among my best friends, but I never forgot the wider context of Ireland's corrupt political system and the damage it did to Dublin.

In *Saving the City* I documented the close links between Ray Burke and the developers Brennan and McGowan, for whom Burke had acted as both lobbyist and estate agent. One of the new members Burke had appointed to An Bord Pleanála in June 1981 was John P. Keenan, who had been principal architect for Brennan and McGowan, while another was Michael Cooke, a former building by-law inspector with Dublin County Council, who had also worked as a quantity surveyor for the then prolific house-builders. Keenan had designed Burke's detached house, Briargate in Swords, which was built for him by Brennan and McGowan. By the time the book was published in autumn 1989, Burke was Minister for Justice and another Garda investigation into planning corruption in Dublin was under way, following a series of articles in the *Irish Times* co-written by Security Correspondent Seán Flynn and myself.

One day, I decided it was my civic duty to talk to the gardaí involved, so I telephoned Garda Headquarters and asked to speak to Detective Superintendent Brendan Burns. I told him I had information that might be helpful to their inquiries and asked if we could meet to talk about it.

'How about this afternoon?' Burns replied. So I cycled up to the Phoenix Park and soon found myself ensconced in an upper room in the Garda's horrible office block, talking to Burns and two of his assistants about Liam Lawlor, George Redmond and Ray Burke. On whether Burke had got Briargate for free from Brennan and McGowan, the superintendent speculated that he 'could probably produce a fake mortgage' for the house, and said they would look into this transaction in detail.

As I was leaving, after being there for nearly two hours, I'll never forget what Burns said to me: 'What we're dealing with here is not just a few backhanders. What we're dealing with here is a nest of vipers.' I couldn't have agreed with him more. Yet the Garda investigation got nowhere, as usual. And when I wrote a background piece on Burke for the *Irish Times*, drawing on the research I had done for *Saving the City*, it was gutted and filleted in the Editor's Office, leaving little but the bare bones. The relevant section of the book was later read into the Dáil record by Labour's Pat Rabbitte as Fianna Fáil TDs bristled in their seats.

Throughout this period, Noel Carroll was the press spokesman for Dublin Corporation, often finding himself in the position of having to defend the indefensible, at the behest of City Manager Frank Feely. On occasion, he would unwittingly convey the authentic voice of an uncaring bureaucracy. When Hurricane Charley hit Dublin in August 1986, the Dodder burst its banks in Ballsbridge, causing terrible flooding. In nearby cottages, residents showed me watermarks up to a metre high on the walls of their living rooms and bedrooms, with wet muck all over the floors, yet there was no sign of the Fire Brigade or Civil Defence to help out. When I got on to Carroll about it, he came out with a classic Marie Antoinette-like line about how 'people who choose to live near rivers should expect to get their feet wet every so often'.

Not long afterwards, I ran into him in the Burlington Hotel, sitting with a couple of friends outside the ballroom where an Irish cabaret was in full swing.

'How can you listen to all that diddly-eye stuff?' I asked.

'That's my wife singing,' he replied, referring to the lovely Deirdre O'Callaghan. I wished the ground would open up so that I could simply vanish into it.

One August Bank Holiday weekend, I phoned Carroll, who had just returned from a trip to Barcelona with Deirdre, visiting one of their grown-up children. Frank Feely, meanwhile, was in Ballybunion playing golf. 'You should have gone to Ballybunion and he should have gone to Barcelona because then he might have found out something useful about how a great European city works,' I said. His surprisingly disparaging response made clear that he wasn't merely a mouthpiece for Feely. Our relationship improved after that, and I was even invited to dinner at Noel and Deirdre's home in Bride's Glen. (Carroll left Dublin Corporation in 1996 to become chief executive of Dublin Chamber of Commerce, but died from a heart attack on the running track in UCD Belfield in 1998, at the age of fifty-six.)

It was Frank Feely who gave us the bogus 'Dublin Millennium' in 1988, having spotted a mural in the City Hall's rotunda depicting Sitric, Viking King of Dublin, making peace with the Irish High King Máel Sechnaill in 988; the irony was that Sitric had only done so to save the city from destruction, as it had previously been sacked by the Irish on several occasions. And now we were being invited to celebrate the thousandth anniversary of his submission by the very people who were destroying the city from within. But at least the 'Aluminium', as Dublin wags quickly dubbed it, served the useful purpose of focusing attention on the historic city for the first time since the Civic Survey of the mid-1920s. Nonetheless, it was depressing to hear Feely declaring, in a panel discussion on Marian Finucane's RTÉ radio programme, that the first place he would take visitors to the city was the Dublin Mountains. When another participant, David Norris, started reeling off a list of the places he would take visitors – North Great George's Street, Trinity College, etc. – you could hear Feely saying, *sotto voce*, 'Oh, yeah, Trinity College,' as if he had just remembered it.

I was drawn into it all as an adjudicator for the Millennium Sculpture Symposium, which involved selecting a number of site-specific projects for key locations in the city centre. Jackie McKenna's *Two Women* – bronze figures seated on a stone bench with their shopping bags in Lower Liffey Street, where fast-talking Hector Grey used to conduct his auctions outside the Woollen Mills – were instantly dubbed 'the Hags with the Bags'. 'The Tart with the Cart' was Jeanne Rynhart's buxom bronze of Molly Malone, 'the Prick with the Stick' was Marjorie Fitzgibbon's statue of James Joyce in North Earl Street and, most notoriously of all, 'the Floozie in the Jacuzzi' was Eamonn O'Doherty's Anna Livia fountain in O'Connell Street, an allegorical representation of the River Liffey's course from the Wicklow Mountains to Dublin Bay.

(Later, while he was re-carving the weather-beaten statue of Christ the King from the apex of Cobh Cathedral in one of the back rooms of Ian Lumley's house on Henrietta Street, O'Doherty showed me a cartoon he had drawn on the theme. It featured the cross-section of a medieval castle with the queen having sex with a knave in the royal bedchamber and the king knocking on the door. The bubble coming from the queen's mouth said, 'Christ! The King.' Naturally, he hadn't shown it to his client, Bishop John Magee, who might not have recognized it as a witty example of lateral thinking.)

Meanwhile, I had been honoured with a Millennium Medal for my work in highlighting the city's architecture, but when it came to the presentation ceremony, then Lord Mayor Ben Briscoe – a self-seeking Fianna Fáil councillor who consistently supported the road engineers – was refusing to sign the certificate that came with the medal. Richard Burrows, chairman of Irish Distillers, which was sponsoring the awards, had to intervene at the last minute to persuade Briscoe to put his personal feelings aside and do his duty as Dublin's first citizen.

'Pro-development' councillors such as Briscoe – who double-jobbed as a TD – were unnerved by the emergence of a vocal lobby to defend the city, with Students Against the Destruction of Dublin as shock-troops reinforcing long-time campaigners like Deirdre Kelly and Dean Victor Griffin. Not only was the opposition well informed, but council meetings were now taking place against the backdrop of noisy protests outside City Hall, including one occasion when councillors could barely make themselves heard above the incessant din. SADD also took on the Sisters of Mercy when their hospital, the Mater, set its eyes on demolishing three Georgian houses on the south side of Eccles Street – having already laid waste to its north side. 'Mercenary Nuns Prey Not' read the huge banner they put up on the threatened buildings after taking up residence there, led by Ciarán Cuffe (later a Green Party city councillor, TD and Minister of State for Planning), Colm Murray (who became architecture officer with the Heritage Council) and Brian O'Brien (who went on to set up ecological architects Solearth). Their determined action ultimately resulted in the Mater renovating the three houses rather than pulling them down.

SADD also got involved in a campaign to save the former Debtors' Prison in Green Street. They set up a trust under the chairmanship of Niall McCarthy, one of Ireland's finest judges, who revelled in sending out begging letters to potential donors giving his address as 'Debtors' Prison, Green Street, Dublin 7', until he and his wife were both killed in a 1992 car accident in Spain. Although planning permission was secured for the prison's conversion to a mix of living and work spaces, the building has remained stubbornly derelict.

By far the biggest battle was fought over plans to turn Patrick Street, New Street and Lower Clanbrassil Street into a dual carriageway catering for suburban commuters. For years, Dublin Corporation had been preying on these historic streets by buying, blocking up and finally demolishing buildings that stood in the way of their plans – deliberately creating dereliction along the proposed route. Its road engineers were not true successors of the Wide Streets Commissioners, as they couldn't care less what, if anything, might be built along their bleak four-lane artery; that was someone else's department. Patrick Street was to become part of the 'Inner Tangent', branded by *In Dublin* magazine as 'the Road to God Knows Where', with the loss of everything on its west side for a dual carriageway that would have swept past the sunken door of St Patrick's Cathedral.

Dean Victor Griffin turned up at the pro-forma 'public inquiry' into the scheme in May 1985, demanding to be heard, as did many other objectors. The inquiry was a farce, however. Not once during the eight days it dragged on did the Department of the Environment engineering inspector, Michael Ward, ask a question of any of the Corporation's witnesses. He didn't consider the planning context, or how this particular scheme fitted into anything else, or any alternatives that would have a less devastating impact on the urban fabric. The purpose of such 'inquiries' was to give property owners along the proposed route an opportunity to object to compulsory purchase orders, as they have a constitutional right to do; they were not forums to debate transport or planning policies. I was reporting daily on this bizarre exercise for the *Irish Times* and was so appalled by what was going on that I took to the witness stand to denounce the scheme and read into the record all the Corporation's other road plans. Not that my intervention made a blind bit of difference: the inspector's report endorsed the scheme as proposed, without making any amendment to it, and the order was duly signed by Pádraig Flynn. Dean Griffin was incensed by the outcome and arranged to meet his 'old friend' Charlie Haughey out in Kinsealy, where they did a deal that resulted in a wide granite pavement being provided in front of St Patrick's, with the new road narrowed to a more respectful single carriageway as it passed the cathedral.

We all knew that what was being planned for Dublin by the road engineers was wrong, and there was a lot of evidence to show that we were right in seeking to restrain them. Martin Mogridge, a transport researcher in University College London, had produced a paper entitled *Travel in Towns: Jam Yesterday, Jam Today and Jam Tomorrow*, in which he argued that widening urban roads would only generate more traffic and that the only way to relieve congestion was to improve public transport. Mogridge's paper was dismissed at the time by Dublin Corporation's leading road engineer, Michael O'Sullivan, as an 'academic thesis'. In a televised debate on RTÉ's *Today Tonight*, in which I was also involved, he described himself as being 'in the do-function situation' – *sic* – which I took to mean that he had to deal with the real-world requirements of traffic in town.

Ultimately, the establishment in 1988 of the Dublin Transport Initiative – a genuine effort to achieve consensus, chaired by senior civil servant (and cyclist) Pat Mangan – put an end to the road plans that had caused such convulsions on the city council, placing the emphasis instead on improving public transport. Mangan was also fortunate in having Steer Davies Gleave as the DTI's consultants, with English-born transport planner Peter Ryan as project manager; I got on well with him and we had several lunches in Findlater's, a discreet Rathmines restaurant, to talk about it all.

'The road engineers knew they were on the back foot and brought us up to a hotel in Carrickmacross for three days in an effort to undermine the whole initiative,' he recalled. But they didn't succeed. Supported by key players such as Tom Coffey, chief executive of the Dublin City Centre Business Association, and Simon Perry, unconventional English-born professor of civil engineering at Trinity College, the DTI recommended a light-rail system similar to what many European cities were choosing at the time.

During the winter of 1988, the city was nearly suffocated by the worst smog in living memory, with pollution levels regularly breaching EU air-quality standards. As soon as the figures became available, the *Irish Times* published a weekly 'Dublin Smog Watch' slot to let everyone know how bad it really was. Pádraig Flynn invited me to his office in the Custom House for a pre-Christmas drink, and I raised the issue with him, saying the only solution was to ban bituminous coal.

'What about all the little old ladies?!' he said, parroting one of the propaganda points put out by the Coal Information Service, which ludicrously described burning smoky coal in open grates as 'part of Dublin's heritage'. The CIS had been set up by Coal Distributors

Ltd, whose chief executive John Reihill lived in Beechwell, a grand house at the entrance to Blackrock's main street. CDL virtually controlled the coal market in Ireland and showed no inclination to switch to smokeless fuels. And the government itself was at least partly responsible because it had given householders grants to install solid-fuel central heating in the wake of the oil crisis in 1973. The Davids taking on CDL's Goliath included Karin Dubsky, of the Clean Air Group (and later Coastwatch); and Dr Luke Clancy, an outspoken pulmonary physician in St James's Hospital, who insisted that bituminous coal had to be banned in the interest of public health. Dublin Corporation was going down the laborious route of designating 'smoke control areas', starting with Ballyfermot, and it could have taken decades to cover the entire city. So Mary Harney cut through the bureaucratic red tape by simply banning the sale and distribution of bituminous coal in the Dublin area. Harney was also responsible for establishing the EPA and could talk knowledgeably about the pending legislation without any resort to a script, making her most unusual among ministers.

It took four years for Haughey to make good on his promise to rejuvenate Temple Bar, but he certainly did so with the Temple Bar Renewal and Development Act of 1991, which established two State companies – Temple Bar Properties Ltd and Temple Bar Renewal Ltd – to oversee the area stretching from Fishamble Street to Westmoreland Street and from Dame Street to the quays. The first body was to act as a development company while the second, chaired *ex officio* by the Lord Mayor, was supposed to vet projects to ensure that they were compatible; without the approval of Temple Bar Renewal, developers couldn't avail themselves of an attractive package of tax incentives under the legislation. Launching the initiative in Government Buildings, Haughey was in *Uno Duce, una voce* mode as he took his place on one side of Eric Pearce's vast oval table in the Sycamore Room, with the press corps on the other. Around three walls, ranging behind the Taoiseach, a variety of public servants from central and local government sat in reverential silence as he droned on about how 'wonderful' and 'marvellous'

Temple Bar would be in the future, with the two State companies under his own department's wing and one of its assistant secretaries, the dynamic Paddy Teahon, acting as managing director of Temple Bar Properties.

Questions were invited by Haughey's press secretary, P. J. Mara, and somebody (it wasn't me) asked why the Taoiseach had appointed his brother Seán as a director of the company. Haughey looked furious at the impertinence of the question, saying he had only done so because his brother happened to be Assistant City Manager in charge of the Roads Department. I remarked that the choice was ironic; Seán Haughey had publicly opposed re-laying 'cobblestones' in Temple Bar because women in high-heeled shoes would fall on them and then sue the city for compensation. Whereupon the Assistant City Manager rose from his seat, pointing towards me and saying, 'That's not true!' At this stage, I thought that our great leader was about to storm out in protest over his big announcement veering off so unexpectedly in the wrong direction. And after a few more questions, it was all over.

'That was a rough session,' Mara said to me as he gathered up his papers. 'Are you going for a pint?'

We repaired to the Dáil bar, and Mara told one uproarious story after another about the high jinks he had with *'El Diablo'*, which is how he used to refer to his boss in casual conversation. By then, of course, Mara was a household name through actor Owen Roe's depiction of him on RTÉ Radio One's savagely satirical sketch show, *Scrap Saturday*. It was P. J., we later learned, who tipped off Donaghmede publican Martin Keane about tax incentives in Temple Bar one night in the Shelbourne Hotel's Horseshoe Bar, shortly before the legislation was published.

'He said if you've any money, go down there and spend it. Then Haughey came in for a pint. I asked him if the Temple Bar thing was correct. That's effing right, says he,' Keane told the *Irish Times*. Armed with this insider information, he bought an old building on the corner of Fleet Street and Anglesea Street (now the money-spinning Oliver St John Gogarty pub) as well as the building next door and Bloom's Hotel, and became one of the multimillionaire oligarchs of Dublin's 'cultural quarter'.

Other cities, including London, had woken up to the development potential of redundant dockland areas, and Dublin caught up with this trend in 1987, starting with the Custom House Docks. A development authority, under the chairmanship of former planning consultant Frank Benson, had been set up by the Fine Gael–Labour government, and it prepared a master plan for the 27-acre site. The next step was to seek tenders from developers, and I was told by a very reliable source that one of the bidders had flown in to Dublin with a briefcase full of cash, met his Irish contact in the Shelbourne Hotel and asked him, 'Who do I give this to?'

It is not known whether the money was indeed handed over or, if so, to whom. But such was Ireland's reputation for corruption that the bidder involved felt that it was worth a try. Benson was under tremendous pressure, but stuck to his guns, and the contract was awarded to a consortium led by Mark Kavanagh, of the long-established Irish development firm Hardwicke Ltd, in partnership with British Land, whose tender had been ranked first in the adjudicators' report. The master plan for the Custom House Docks, prepared under the direction of architect Seán Ó Laoire, had already been compromised by Charlie Haughey's capricious decision to locate the Irish Museum of Modern Art in the Royal Hospital, Kilmainham, rather than in the historic Stack A warehouse in the docks, as originally envisaged. This last-minute switch came about after the Taoiseach's artistic adviser, poet Anthony Cronin, had seen the Reina Sofía museum in Madrid, installed in a seventeenth-century palace, and thought this use would be a good fit for the Royal Hospital. It didn't seem to occur to him that Spain had lots of major seventeenth-century civil buildings, whereas we only had one – the refuge for old soldiers commissioned by King Charles II.

Padraig Ó hUiginn, Machiavellian Secretary-General of the Taoiseach's Department, went along with Cronin's view and they jointly persuaded Charlie Haughey that this was the way to go. As a result, the centre of Dublin was robbed of a contemporary art museum, and Stack A – where the Crimean War banquet was held in 1856 – languished for years until it was finally renovated at a cost of €45 million for CHQ, a ghost shopping mall eventually snapped up by an Irish-American billionaire, former Coca-Cola boss Neville Isdell, for less than a quarter of that public investment.

I made a point of attending the official opening in March 1990 of the West Link toll bridge, because I knew that Haughey would be there and I wanted to talk to him about what the government should be doing for Dublin's year as European City of Culture in 1991. Bizarrely, the Taoiseach and his hangers-on, as well as other politicians, officials and the press corps, were conveyed across the new bridge on a double-decker bus. I was sitting upstairs beside Morgan Sheehy, the brilliant Arup engineer who had designed the bridge, and introduced him to Haughey, who congratulated him on a job well done. Half-jokingly, I asked the Taoiseach when he had last been on a bus in Dublin, and he tried to pretend that he had been on the No. 42 to Malahide the previous weekend.

'Would you go on out of that,' I said. 'I bet the last time you were a fare-paying passenger on a bus was in the early 1950s.'

He laughed, and then turned serious. 'You're far too negative about Dublin. Everyone who comes back remarks on how much it has improved.'

I didn't disagree, but said that far too much of value was still being lost, arguing that the City of Culture gig should be used to reverse this trend and leave a legacy of lasting value. I told him that I had sent a submission on this to Pádraig Flynn on New Year's Day and still hadn't got a response.

'Send it to me, and we'll talk then,' Haughey said.

About a week later, I found a note in my pigeonhole at the office, saying, 'Please ring C. J. Haughey at 01 67 . . .' – his phone number in the Taoiseach's department. I did and was immediately put through to *El Diablo* himself. An appointment was made for the following afternoon at 3 p.m. in the old Taoiseach's office, then located in the north wing of Government Buildings; it was as dowdy as a parish priest's parlour. I thought I'd get fifteen minutes to make my pitch for projects such as the restoration of Francis Johnston's great triple-tiered steeple on St George's Church. Instead, over the next hour or so, Haughey and I had a wide-ranging discussion.

'You never give me any credit!' he said, glowering at me.

'For what?' I asked.

'St Doulagh's Church in Kinsealy, for example. I'm a great supporter of its restoration,' he said proudly. At one point, he brought me over to the window to view the ongoing work on Government Buildings, which was his own *grand projet*. A tracked digger was operating in the courtyard excavating a site for the ceremonial fountain that would become so familiar in the future; one could just imagine his friend François Mitterrand's limousine sweeping around it and the French President being greeted by our own Napoleon on the great flight of stone steps. When we were finished, I was surprised to discover former Deputy Garda Commissioner Joe Ainsworth waiting in the anteroom for his (presumably delayed) meeting with the Taoiseach. God only knows what Ainsworth, who had been central to the tapping of journalists' telephones, was doing there.

The public mood in Ireland was changing. Through Italia '90, we managed to reclaim our flag after years of seeing it draped over the coffins of IRA men: now it could be waved with enthusiasm for a heroic soccer team trained by an Englishman, Jack Charlton. And then there was the election of Mary Robinson as President in November 1990. For the first time that anyone could remember, the Angelus bells didn't ring on radio or television at 6 p.m. because RTÉ had to go live to the RDS for the declaration of the result after a particularly dramatic election campaign. With Charlie Haughey, runner-up Brian Lenihan and Labour Party leader Dick Spring standing behind her, this amazing woman brought us all to our feet when she congratulated Mná na hÉireann, saying that 'instead of rocking the cradle, they rocked the system'.

I was delighted, because right after Spring pulled a political master stroke in persuading Robinson to stand, I had sent her a cheque for £50 and a letter saying I looked forward to seeing her installed in Áras an Uachtaráin – more in hope than expectation, I must admit. But she made it, and that event marked the beginning of a shift in Ireland towards a more pluralist society, no longer dominated by the Catholic Church. I was also thrilled to get a personal invitation to Robinson's inauguration in Dublin Castle – a gesture, I later discovered from her brilliant adviser Bride Rosney, that Haughey had queried at the time, only to be told that I was a friend of the new President. So I entered St Patrick's Hall on that chilly day in December and walked up to the front, waving to Conor Brady along the way. What he made of my one-upmanship is anybody's guess.

The most touching thing Robinson did was to place a bright light in one of the upstairs front windows of the Áras, to show the many recent emigrants from Ireland that they had not been forgotten. With queues for Morrison visas outside the US Embassy in Ballsbridge, Gay Byrne rowed in with a *Late Late Show* panel discussion about the dire state of Ireland's economy. One Dublin Jackeen in the audience threw in his three ha'pence-worth, saying, 'Well, I think what we should do is to hand this country back to the Queen of England tomorrow morning . . . and apologize for the damage.' He was half-joking, but I could see his point.

Conor Brady, who had been editor of the *Irish Times* since 1986, was a bundle of contradictions. Innately conservative, he was the son of a senior police officer and had been editor of the *Garda Review*. Yet he wasn't afraid of change, responding to readers' concerns and making inspired appointments, particularly to foreign posts, as the paper's circulation grew and grew. Compelling columnists such as Nuala O'Faolain were hired to hold up a mirror to Irish society, and later the paper was among the first in the world to establish an online presence. One of Brady's standard questions was, 'Where do you see yourself in five years' time?' to which I was never able to give a satisfactory answer, other than saying something along the lines of, 'Still doing what I'm doing now, I suppose.' Perhaps he himself always had a chart mapping his career on the wall of his study in De Vesci Terrace, Monkstown, but I never did.

Séamus Martin, who went on to become Moscow correspondent, used to say, 'You'd go in to see Brady to talk to him about something that was bothering you, looking for reassurance, and he would apply the usual emollients. It was like having a Chinese meal: you were instantly satisfied, but half an hour later you couldn't remember what you ate.'

Brady also had his Rottweilers in managing editors Seán Olson and Don Buckley, whose function was to tell people that they needed to pull up their socks. An invitation to coffee in Bewley's of Westmoreland Street from Buckley almost always meant you were in trouble, which is why the café became known as 'the Killing Fields'. Michael Foley was taken there to be told that he was 'useless' as media correspondent, which came as a real shock to the son of Donal Foley. He rushed back to the office, easily outpacing Buckley, who had a bad leg, and went straight up to the Editor's Office to tell Brady what had transpired. 'Where could Don have got such an idea?' he said to Foley, as if the whole thing was a figment of someone's fervid imagination.

Not long after brick-sized car phones became available, Brady got one for his company-supplied Jaguar, and he kept a Part 1 telephone directory in the back window, presumably to let people know he was up to speed with new technology. Like Gageby, he had an aversion to anything that might be perceived as a gratuitous insult to members of the government. Thus, in a piece about the completion of the Government Buildings renovation, my line about how the helicopter pad on the roof 'had not been designed for a Ceauşescu-style getaway' was omitted. Perhaps it was too soon after our Christmas dinners were spoiled by the sight of Nicolae and Elena Ceauşescu's corpses after their summary trial and execution in December 1989. As it happens, I was impressed by what the OPW architects (Klaus Unger, Angela Rolfe and the late David Byers) had achieved with a quite limited budget of £17.4 million, and made my views clear to P. J. Mara.

'Do you see that fellow over there?' he asked, pointing to the Taoiseach. 'Go over and tell him that the Man from Del Monte says yes.' I never thought of myself in those terms, but did as instructed and got a broad smile and limp handshake from *Il Duce* in return.

Apart from issues involving 'taste', Brady was meticulous about the use of grammar and would frequently send out round-robin emails highlighting various horrors and cautioning against repeating them. He also instituted the 'Corrections and Clarifications' slot, which reached its apogee in August 1991 when one of the 'clarifications' read as follows: 'In yesterday's report of the Merriman Summer School, Prof. Denis Donoghue was quoted as seeking an openness to the "otherness of the self". This should have read the "otherness of the Other".'

When I reported to Brady that Dublin Fire Brigade ambulances had called to my home in Harold's Cross three times in as many months – always around 1 a.m. or so – saying they had a report that there was someone injured in the house, he offered to hire a private detective to investigate the matter. I didn't pursue it, feeling relieved that it wasn't a hearse.

In *Saving the City*, I had called for a new vision of Dublin as it prepared to assume the mantle of European Cultural Capital in 1991, but the year itself panned out as something of a damp squib. On spurious 'health and safety' grounds, the Department of Justice vetoed proposals for fireworks over the Custom House to mark its bicentenary, so we had to settle for a lacklustre laser show instead. The building, James Gandon's masterpiece, had been restored just in time for the celebrations by conservation architect David Slattery, with whom I regularly had boozy lunches in Éamonn Ó Catháin's Shay Beano restaurant on Lower Stephen Street. As Slattery explained, rusty iron cramps holding the blocks of Portland stone in place had expanded due to rainwater penetration and this, in turn, cracked the stone, causing pieces of it to fall off. The fire that engulfed the building in 1920, following an IRA attack, was so hot that it actually melted the lead strips Gandon had wrapped the cramps in to prevent corrosion, but this unseen damage only came to light seventy years later. We were up on the scaffolding, standing right underneath the huge cornice, which projects one metre from the building's façade.

'So what's been holding this up all these years?' I asked.

He replied, 'The only thing that's been holding it up is the memory of being there!'

Things in Dublin were so bleak then that you had to laugh, and barbed humour became part of the armoury of more radical conservationists, such as Ian Lumley, An Taisce's Heritage Officer. In 1990, he set up the ad hoc Dublin Urban Salvation Front and held its inaugural meeting in the seriously distressed Georgian house he had bought in Henrietta Street. Inspired by an editorial in *Apollo*, the London-based art magazine, which warned that the ruination of Ireland's heritage was heading in the Ceauşescu direction, Lumley came up with the wheeze of having triennial 'Nicolae Ceauşescu Memorial Awards for the Destruction of Dublin'. Naturally, I was among the select gathering for the awards ceremony, wryly reported by Séamus Martin in the *Irish Times*, at which twenty 'Ceauşescu Memorial Certificates' were presented *in absentia* to a variety of public officials, developers and institutions. As Lumley threw another spare chair leg or two on the open fire, this mock-serious event culminated in the presentation of 'Supreme Ceauşescu Memorial Order of Merit' awards – the Bronzed Aluminium Medal to the Fianna Fáil group in Dublin City Council, for 'whipping through the disastrous road schemes'; the Silver Tinfoil Medal to Charlie Haughey for 'treating the city as little better than a quarry for the construction industry'; and, finally, the Croagh Patrick Fool's Gold Medal to Pádraig Flynn for 'blatantly refusing to conform to Ireland's Council of Europe obligations . . . to bring Irish building preservation law in line with European practice'. All in all, it was a hilarious night in Henrietta Street.

There was also a whiff of corruption in the regions, especially after urban renewal tax incentives were extended to key towns in 1990 by Pádraig Flynn. So I decided to take a tour of some of these places, to see what was going on, which was not an easy thing for a

Dubliner to do because nothing was ever quite as it seemed in provincial towns. In Castlebar, Flynn's home town, I couldn't have had a better-informed guide than former Fine Gael councillor Frank Durkan, who had been branded 'the Maggot Durkan' years earlier by fellow Mayo man and Minister for Justice Mícheál Ó Móráin – in the Dáil, no less. He pointed out that the Welcome Inn, where Fianna Fáil always held its meetings, was at the core of Castlebar's urban renewal designated area even though Mayo County Council's planners had not included it in the area they recommended for designation. The same turned out to be true in Tralee, Co. Kerry, where the Brandon Hotel – owned by John Byrne, Charlie Haughey's long-time crony – was one of the main beneficiaries; Tralee Urban District Council had merely recommended the redundant 'Marts' area. Or take the curious case of Longford's main street, where a hotel owned by Jim Reynolds, Albert's brother, managed to get away with installing a full suite of male and female toilets beneath the adjoining 1793 courthouse. When Mae Sexton, who was leading a campaign against plans to demolish the courthouse, told me about this extraordinary arrangement, I could barely believe it and had to check it out myself.

My investigative stories meant that I was often in contact with the *Irish Times* lawyers, Hayes & Sons, then run by a careful Protestant called Adrian Glover; he once said about a piece I had written, 'I'm afraid that I must condemn it,' or words to that effect. I got on much better with his colleague, Andrew O'Rorke, who I knew from UCD, where he had been the secretary of Fianna Fáil's Kevin Barry Cumann. I was also well aware that he served on the party's National Executive for many years, even while he was advising the *Irish Times* on libel issues. But his involvement in Fianna Fáil never coloured his professional role as a lawyer, even in dealing with stories that reflected badly on the party or its leading figures, and he became an acknowledged expert on Ireland's arcane defamation laws.

O'Rorke would also turn up, on occasion, at Conor Brady's 'shout-ins' – intermittent gatherings of *Irish Times* journalists, at which everything could be discussed in an open forum. I used one of these occasions to criticize what I regarded as 'nervous nellyism' in the upper echelons of the paper, as exemplified by its disinclination to publish a story I had culled from the Merchant Banking Ltd liquidator's report showing that Charlie Haughey had received 'loans' of more than £18,000 from the 'bank'. The relevant extract from that lengthy report by liquidator Paddy Shortall had been passed on to me by Mary Raftery, whose brilliant hour-long documentary, *The Gallagher Story*, was featured on RTÉ1's *Today Tonight* current affairs programme. Even though the Haughey 'loans' were among those listed in the report, RTÉ management decided that no reference to them could be made in the documentary, citing legal advice. Given that Haughey was still Taoiseach, it seemed to me that this was merely a smokescreen for their own fear of *Il Duce* and what he might do to you. The fact is that nearly everyone was afraid of CJH.

In 1991, when Noelle Campbell-Sharp launched her project to create the Cill Rialaig international artists' retreat near Bolus Head in Co. Kerry, she lined up Charlie Haughey to lay the foundation stone. It was a wet and blustery day when the invited guests – including Terry Keane, CJH's mistress and Noelle's good friend – gathered for a champagne reception in the Ballinskelligs Hotel, but there was no sign of the Taoiseach.

'See if you can find him,' Noelle said to *Irish Times* photographer Frank Miller and myself.

So we set out along the boreens thereabouts and eventually spotted his Mercedes-Benz and a Special Branch car parked in one of the valleys in front of a cottage with turf smoke wafting from its single chimney. Inside, we found CJH chatting amiably to an old woman, probably a lifelong Fianna Fáiler.

'Are you not going up to Bolus Head, Taoiseach? They're all waiting for you,' I said.

'Yes, indeed I am,' Haughey replied. 'Do you know where it is?'

We had been up there already, and I said, 'Sure we do.'

So we got into our car, he into his and the two Special Branch men into theirs, forming a small convoy along the boreens until we reached the ruined pre-Famine cottages that Noelle planned to transform into her artists' retreat. Standing there, in this elemental landscape on the edge of Ireland, CJH paid tribute to her 'indefatigable' spirit and expressed the hope that Cill Rialaig would be developed 'in harmony with the local community'. Later, he was the guest of honour at a banquet in the former Waterville Lake Hotel where more than one hundred potential donors grazed on a lavish buffet of caviar, oysters, dressed salmon, fillet steak and a sumptuous selection of *patisserie*. I wrote a caustic piece in the *Irish Times*, under the heading, 'Making a feast of a famine', which quoted objectors as saying that the project represented 'the pillage of Cill Rialaig'. They were wrong about that, and so was I. It turned out to be an outstanding success, attracting some two thousand five hundred artists from all over the world to spend time living and working in the cottages renovated by architect Alfred Cochrane. I was happy to acknowledge that in a piece published in the *Irish Times* twenty years later, retracting my initial doubts.

7

Early in 1992, an American called Arthur Pennell contacted the *Irish Times*. He was making an explosive claim: his partner, Annie Murphy, had previously been in a relationship with the Bishop of Galway, Eamonn Casey, and had borne him a son. For a number of months, the story was known to very few members of the staff. Apart from Conor Brady himself, they included Conor O'Clery, then based in New York, who had interviewed Murphy and Pennell at length on several occasions; religious affairs correspondent Andy Pollak; and news editor John Armstrong, who was coordinating their work on it. Major McDowell was undoubtedly kept informed as well. At some point, I happened to meet Andy at Connolly Station, as I got off a train from Belfast that he was waiting to get on. Remarking that I hadn't seen him for a while, I asked if he was working on anything special.

'It's all hush-hush,' he said. I was intrigued and pressed him further. 'Well . . . it's about a bishop who had a baby,' he replied.

'Wow! It must be either Casey or [Brendan] Comiskey,' I said. But he wouldn't confirm that it was the Bishop of Galway rather than the Bishop of Ferns.

Once the *Irish Times*, working from interviews and also from documentary evidence, was finally ready to publish the story in May 1992, it felt the need to put in place a strategy to avoid any accusation that the historically Protestant newspaper was having a go at the Catholic Church. The reporting focused on how Casey had dipped into diocesan funds to pay for his son Peter's upkeep and education in the US. On RTÉ's *Morning Ireland*, Andy Pollak had to stick to the line that the *Irish Times* had no interest in Bishop Casey's private life, merely in his stewardship of diocesan funds. Yet the two things were inextricably intertwined. There is no more uncomfortable place than a radio studio in such a scenario; Brady, as author of this defensive strategy, should have been the one in the hot seat, rather than Pollak. Even before the story was published, Casey – who knew it was coming – had tendered his resignation and was already en route to Latin America, where he spent several years working with missionaries in rural Ecuador.

Douglas Gageby once told me that he eschewed hobnobbing with the great and good, in case their activities might need to be covered by the *Irish Times* at some point. Conor Brady took a different approach. He was a member of an informal 'First Tuesday Club', which used to convene for lunch in one or other of the city's top restaurants on the first Tuesday of every month. Others included the likes of Michael Colgan, then director of the Gate Theatre; Paul McGuinness, worldly-wise manager of U2; and Laura Magahy, who had worked her way up from chief executive of the Irish Film Centre to managing director of Temple Bar Properties at the age of thirty. No doubt these gatherings were a barrel of laughs, but I believed that they had the potential to colour editorial decisions in the *Irish Times*. In particular, I felt it could compromise our ability to examine what was really going on in the development of Temple Bar as Dublin's 'cultural quarter', where the proliferation of pubs was already getting out of hand. (In fact it didn't, as far as I could see.)

Brady liked a bit of grandeur; he originated the *Irish Times*/Harvard University Colloquium, held in alternate years in Dublin and Boston, at which world leaders – including Robert Mugabe, the tyrannical President of Zimbabwe, in 1997 – gave invitees the benefit of their wisdom. Organized down to the last detail by Seán Hogan, whose main job was letters editor, these events were reported extensively in the paper, as if it was aiming for a global reach. And to some extent, it was. Brady's empire-building involved establishing bureaus in such far-flung places as Washington DC, Moscow, Beijing, Berlin and Johannesburg, as well as maintaining long-established correspondents in London, Paris, Brussels and Rome. Nobody could doubt that the journalism they all produced was first class, but the 'reach' might be seen as a bit presumptuous for a newspaper published on a small island at the edge of Europe.

However, Brady deserved credit for commissioning Carol Coulter to spend a month in England on the Birmingham Six case, having read Chris Mullin's 1986 book, *Error of Judgment: The Truth About the Birmingham Bombings*, which convinced him that the six men who had been sentenced to life imprisonment for these outrages were wrongfully convicted. That was courageous, especially given that the *Irish Times* had lost circulation for exposing the Garda 'Heavy Gang' in the mid-1970s during Fergus Pyle's brief period in the editor's chair. I always thought that the Birmingham Six were fitted up by the West Midlands police and the British judiciary, none more so than Lord Denning, Master of the Rolls; in 1980, he rejected their appeal on the basis that it would be an 'appalling vista' if they won, as it would call into question the actions taken by the police in extracting their 'confessions'. After he issued that woefully wrong judgment, I regarded Denning as no different from Peter Cook's classic take-off of an outrageously biased judge in the Jeremy Thorpe case, instructing jurors to ignore the evidence of his one-time boyfriend Norman Scott on the grounds that he was a 'scrounger, parasite, pervert, a worm, a self-professed player of the pink oboe . . .'

Land rezoning in Co. Dublin was a cauldron of corruption that, by 1993, seemed to be bubbling over. So I went to my first-ever features conference to request a full page a day for a week for a series of articles on what was going on, in collaboration with Mark Brennock. (At the time, there were so many conferences and meetings in the office that one of the *Irish Times* techies, Michael Cunningham, put up spoof notices all over the place saying, 'Feeling lonely or depressed? Hold a meeting.' The text went on to enumerate the advantages, before concluding with a slogan: 'Meetings – the practical alternative to work!' Deputy editor Eoin McVey, then in charge of administration, was kept busy taking the notices down.)

Having got the nod from Conor Brady for a page a day, with maps and pictures, I left the meeting to get on with my work. And what a can of worms we unearthed about the skulduggery that was happening week after week in the Dublin County Council chamber on Upper O'Connell Street. In one of her opinion columns, Nuala O'Faolain had characterized the council as 'the real estate agency that represents us', with the power to turn green fields into gold – simply by voting to rezone this or that parcel of land for development, whatever the views of its own professional planners. The small 'public gallery' was heaving with estate agents, developers, landowners and lobbyists, watching every move like seasoned Las Vegas gamblers. You could nearly smell it in the air, that unmistakable whiff of corruption, and at times I felt impelled to make an inappropriate intervention, along the lines of, 'With some honourable exceptions, most of the councillors seated here should be taken from this place straight to Mountjoy.' Mark and I talked to many of those involved in this squalid circus, including a developer's agent and other sources who confirmed that key councillors were being bribed to vote the right way.

'There is a certain number of people in that council chamber who put a value on their votes,' the developer's agent told us. 'They are the power brokers who can bring five votes with you, or five against you, depending on how they're looked after.' Asked how it worked, he said it was on the basis of 'straight cash in brown paper bags'.

For legal reasons, we were unable to name any sitting councillors in the series. We got some flak for naming one former councillor, Seán Walsh TD, who had died four years earlier, leaving £250,000 in cash. Mark regretted identifying him, but I thought he was fair game even though it involved breaking the Irish taboo about 'speaking ill of the dead'. Former Tánaiste John Wilson, in a short, pompous letter for publication, wrote, 'No doubt the *Irish Times* lawyers told Brennock and McDonald that they could with impunity traduce the late Seán Walsh. The dead don't sue. They should ponder the words of Edmund Burke – "It is not what a lawyer tells me I *may* do, but what humanity, reason and justice tells me I *ought* to do." Sir, your editorship is a disgrace.' That broadside from Wilson must have made Conor Brady's lips curl.

We also mentioned Gráinne Mallon, a senior planner in north Co. Dublin and wife of Kevin Mallon, one of the three senior Provos who had been dramatically sprung from Mountjoy by helicopter in 1973. While she was on a 'career break' from her council post, she had set up as a freelance planning consultant and became one of the many involved in making land rezoning submissions on behalf of private landowners. I thought it was quite improper that somebody who was merely on leave of absence from a public authority would sell her services to landowners in this way. Clearly, it involved a potential conflict of interest as she herself might have to adjudicate on subsequent planning applications, made on foot of successful rezonings, after returning to her council post. When the *Irish Times* received a solicitor's letter on behalf of Mallon, threatening to seek damages, I spent a week at the Fingal planning department's public counter going through some three thousand files to dig out information on her. Afterwards, I compiled a thirty-five-page memorandum to the newspaper's lawyers, detailing a raft of questionable recommendations she had made – including one to grant outline planning permission to her nephew for a house in Howth, without declaring this close family connection. The libel action was dropped.

As the economy started heating up, a Dundalk man called Liam Carroll was building a lot of apartments that seemed remarkably substandard. After Carroll's company, Zoe Developments, had completed 'Arran Square', on Arran Quay, I went to see it, armed with a measuring tape. The scheme had just been finished and some of the internal plaster was still wet on the walls as I walked along one of the narrow (4 foot 11 inch) artificially lit corridors and into flats so small that all the furniture was three-quarter scaled to make it look bigger. Every one of these apartments was 'single-aspect' (windows only in one direction), all the bathrooms and kitchens were mechanically ventilated, and there was no storage – not even in the hot press, because the upper part of every one was occupied by a heavy-duty PVC cold water tank. There was nowhere to put a hoover, other than in the bottom of one of the flimsy built-in wardrobes where shoes are usually kept. And the 180 shoebox flats were all contained behind a mock-Georgian façade, worked up by Zoe's team of architectural technicians with help from Dublin Corporation planner Dermot Kelly, who performed the same role for Zoe when it came to redevelop Bachelors Walk in similar style.

I thought it was appalling that Carroll, an industrial engineer by training, had such low standards; and yet he became the main engine of urban renewal in Dublin, with the collaboration of city planners. So I spent a couple of hours in the planning department going through files, establishing as a matter of fact that Zoe Developments Ltd didn't employ any architects at the time, and then wrote a feature-length article on how it was building 'the tenements of the 21st century'. It took two months to get it into the Arts page of the *Irish Times*, then edited by Paddy Woodworth. He was nervous about it; the paper's lawyers were consulted and the Editor's Office got involved. Zoe's estate agents – Hooke & MacDonald – were big advertisers in the property supplement, and that must have been a consideration. Eventually, an edited version of the original hard-hitting piece appeared, with the reference to Carroll not employing architects unaccountably excised. Still, I like to think that it had some impact on then Minister of State for Housing and Planning Liz McManus, a trained architect herself, prompting her to promulgate improved minimum standards for apartment design. They weren't *that* great, but at least it was a step in the right direction.

Too late for Bachelors Walk, however. Arguably the most important of the Liffey quays because of its high visibility, its eighteenth-century houses had been hacked about mercilessly over the years and then earmarked by Tom Gilmartin and British developers Arlington Securities for a madcap shopping centre, with a city bus station on its roof. This improbable scheme got nowhere – even the planners thought it raised 'civic design issues' – and the entire site fell into the hands of Liam Carroll. Fearing that he would cover it with blocks of shoebox flats, I bearded him at one of his many building sites, suggesting that Bachelors Walk deserved better and he really should sponsor an architectural competition to find the best design. But he insisted that 'architects are only interested in designing penthouses for fellows with Mercs' – a preposterously prejudiced view that had no basis in reality.

Carroll went on to do his worst, squeezing in 330 apartments, with 'neo-Georgian' façades on the main frontage, topped by *faux* chimneys. He was even allowed to demolish a very rare example of Egyptian art deco, the former Dublin United Tramway Company's headquarters, replacing it with a woeful piece of pastiche. However, Hooke & MacDonald had no problem offloading all the flats, mainly to 'Section 23' investors, lured by full-page advertisements in the *Irish Times* property supplement and the usual adulatory report on Liam Carroll's latest 'sales coup'.

Around the country, bitter battles erupted over plans by the Office of Public Works for a series of 'interpretative centres' in highly sensitive landscapes, and I was among those who thought the very idea of locating such facilities in the middle of protected areas was crazy. In the case of Mullaghmore, right in the heart of the Burren in Co. Clare, campaigners included film-makers Lelia Doolan and Éamon de Buitléar, Dr Emer Colleran of An Taisce, and the remarkable Father John O'Donoghue, who spoke of its karst limestone landscape in mystical terms: there was no way the OPW could achieve its ambitions, because it was flying in the face of God's creation. On the other hand, there were those in Co. Clare who strongly backed the plan, no matter what. The impetus for the 'interpretative centres' had derived from the availability of EU funding for such things, under the tourism heading.

I got on very well with the OPW's press officer, Chris Flynn, and he drove me down there for a site visit. In February 1993, the Burren Action Group won a High Court ruling that the OPW had acted illegally in starting construction of the visitor centre within sight of the folded mountain of Mullaghmore and, in an immense slap in the face for central government, struck down the State's exemption from planning control. Eventually, the project was halted by Michael D. Higgins, after he became Minister for Arts and Culture.

There were more pleasant diversions. A gang of us got tickets for Neil Young's concert at Slane Castle in 1993, with access to the 'VIP enclosure'. I knew Henry Mountcharles, having first met him in the mid-1980s when he was running a restaurant in the castle's vaulted cellars, taking orders for food and drink, which I thought represented a curious role reversal for an aristocrat. Mark Brennock and Yetti Redmond had their wedding reception at Slane Castle in 1990, and Henry was on hand then too, overseeing the catering arrangements. A year later, fire nearly destroyed the castle, and I was on the scene the following day while it was still smouldering. Henry had just returned from Our Lady of Lourdes Hospital in Drogheda, after being treated for smoke inhalation, and brought me on a tour of the severely damaged interiors, which were still dripping wet from Meath Fire Brigade 'emptying the River Boyne into the place', as he put it. 'You know that U2 recorded one of their albums here – *The Unforgettable Fire*, of course!' he spluttered, laughing at the bitter irony.

The castle was undergoing restoration when Neil Young played in its vast natural amphitheatre in July 1993. We were all sitting around in a circle after having an al-fresco lunch, smoking some American weed that someone had brought along. Suddenly, this fellow in an anorak and jeans jumped into the circle, flashed his badge and said, 'Drugs Squad,' seizing a roach and putting it into a plastic evidence bag. It would be only a matter of time, I feared, before we were all put in a Black Maria and conveyed to a special sitting of the District Court in Navan. Then it would be all over the papers. The detective started asking everyone in our group for their names and professions – netting a BBC drama producer, a playwright and novelist, a hospital consultant from Belfast, a lecturer in sociology from the US, a history professor, an RTÉ radio producer, a psychiatrist and two senior journalists with the *Irish Times*. It was quite a haul. But he only had a roach as evidence, so he gave up, allowing us to enjoy the rest of the concert in peace.

My old friend Annie McCartney accompanied me to an event that turned out to be even more bizarre. The 17th Earl of Pembroke, a tall man and the unmistakably aristocratic successor in title to Strongbow, had come to Dublin to present the Pembroke Estate's Irish papers to the National Archives, including wonderful drawings in colour of its characteristic cottages. To mark this occasion, the Knight of Glin threw a celebratory drinks party at his Dublin home on Waterloo Road. Among the guests was the then chairman of the National Archives, Mr Justice Hugh O'Flaherty of the Supreme Court, who sat in a winged armchair looking very judicial.

'Gin or whisk?' the Knight would ask each of us as he went around the room, topping up glasses several times in many cases, before announcing, 'Let's all go to the Coq Hardi for dinner!' The restaurant's upper room, where Charlie Haughey had often dined discreetly with Terry Keane, had been booked in advance and we were greeted by *chef patron* John Howard. By that stage, most of the company (twelve of us) were quite merry if not drunk, and we sat down to a sumptuous meal, washed down with good wine, with the presumably staggering bill covered by the Plain People of Ireland. When it got to the port and brandy stage, Hugh O'Flaherty turned around to me and said, 'You know I'm a judge in the X case appeal. What do you think?' I was stunned, never having had my views canvassed previously by a judge of the superior courts, but managed to retain my composure.

The X case was one of the most explosive dramas in Irish legal history. In 1992, the Attorney General, Harry Whelehan, had made an application to the High Court to prohibit a fourteen-year-old girl, who had been raped and impregnated, from going to England for an abortion. The application was upheld by Mr Justice Declan Costello, who said it was the court's duty to protect the life of the unborn, having regard to the Eighth Amendment to the Constitution. His ruling was overturned by a four-to-one majority in the Supreme Court (including Hugh O'Flaherty) on the grounds that there was a 'real and substantial risk' to the life of the girl, who was suicidal.

The appeal to which O'Flaherty referred related not to the Supreme Court's ruling regarding X's right to travel for an abortion, but to the rapist's appeal against his fourteen-year sentence.

All I could think of saying, under the circumstances, was, 'Well, Hugh, it must be very difficult to disentangle the fate of an individual from the huge controversy that erupted over the X case' – which, after I reported the matter to him in an email the following day, Conor Brady described as 'a good answer for 1 a.m.' Even though a lot of drink was taken that night, the appalling vista conjured up by the encounter I had in Le Coq Hardi was that judges might be taking such soundings on a regular basis at dinner tables on Dublin's Southside or, indeed, anywhere.

(Or perhaps it was just O'Flaherty. In late 1998, he was approached on the street by a neighbour's son who was accompanied by a female friend. Twelve months earlier the young woman's brother, Philip Sheedy, had been jailed for four years for causing the death of a woman while driving drunk. On foot of the conversation with Sheedy's sister, O'Flaherty made representations on his behalf, which resulted in Sheedy's sentence being reviewed and him being released by Circuit Court Judge Cyril Kelly. He had served thirteen months. When this came to light, O'Flaherty, Kelly and Dublin County Registrar, Michael Quinlan, were forced to resign. Sheedy was well connected to Fianna Fáil. The Dublin West TD, Brian Lenihan, had provided a character reference at his trial. Psychologist Don Lydon, a Fianna Fáil senator, provided two psychological reports for the court. Builder Joe Burke, for whom Sheedy, an architect, had worked, visited him in prison; Burke was a former Fianna Fáil city councillor and long-time close associate of Taoiseach Bertie Ahern. And Ahern himself made a representation on Sheedy's behalf to the Department of Justice. All this came out and caused massive public controversy in what became known as the 'Sheedy Affair'. Sheedy himself returned to prison to continue his sentence.)

By the early nineties, Eamon and I had decided that Harold's Cross was too far from the city centre and we really should move into town. Duncan, our adorable little Cairn terrier, had died, much to our distress, and this meant that we were free to consider apartment living. Casimir Road was also changing. The little old ladies were dying off, houses that had been in flats were reverting to family homes and younger couples with kids and big cars were moving in. 'Hearse, skip and Volvo, in that order,' was how Eamon summed it up. The road was clogged with cars and there were rows over parking spaces. This didn't affect us, since we never had a car and pretty much cycled everywhere, at a time when few did; the only 'cycle lanes' in Dublin then were the narrow spaces between double yellow lines.

Neither were we particularly concerned about perceptions of us as a gay couple living in a traditional residential area. Thanks to Máire Geoghegan-Quinn as Minister for Justice, the law had been changed in 1993, making homosexual acts no longer illegal in Ireland. She was finally giving effect to a 1988 European Court of Human Rights ruling, in the celebrated Norris v Ireland case, that the 1861 Offences Against the Person Act was in breach of the European Convention on Human Rights and should be repealed. With a clear eye on the prize, Geoghegan-Quinn scheduled the Dáil debate on this sensitive matter when she knew that South Tipperary Fianna Fáil TD Noel Davern, an implacable opponent of reform, was out of the country on a parliamentary junket, and the measure was then passed with little opposition. Once it had become law, removing the aura of criminality that had tainted us for so long, it was really quite liberating and I gradually realized that I no longer cared whether anyone knew I was gay.

I had also been writing for years about the need to repopulate the heart of Dublin, so the time had come to put my money where my mouth was, as it were. Temple Bar seemed to be the best prospect, given that there was a real commitment to high-quality architecture and building conservation – though the State development agency wasn't even sure that there would be a market for apartments in the new 'cultural quarter'. I told Owen Hickey, property director of Temple Bar Properties, that I'd be prepared to buy an apartment from them in a mid-nineteenth-century building on Temple Lane that would end up overlooking the proposed Curved Street. A deal couldn't be done, however, because the company's policy was to sell apartments on a 'first come, first served' basis, having fixed the price for each, so we ended up queueing for a week to make sure of getting the 'duplex penthouse', as it was described. We rented a clunky mobile phone to keep in contact, organizing a small rota of friends to help out with the queueing, and the builders kindly allowed us to camp out in their site office on the ground floor, in between bags of cement. I thought I'd get a chance to read several long novels, but Owen jogged by the door on the first day and asked what I was doing for lunch.

'I'm queueing for the flat!' I said.

'Ah, feck it,' he replied. 'Let's go to Frères Jacques and I'll deem that you're queueing there.' Maeve Jennings, who had project-managed the innovative Green Building two doors away, joined us and we had a good lunch with a bottle of Gevrey-Chambertin, in big balloon glasses.

Our purchase made the news – much to my amazement. 'Apartment critic pays £195k for luxury loft in Temple Bar', said the headline across eight columns on an inside page in the *Irish Independent*. Ryan Tubridy, then a cub reporter for RTÉ, turned up to do a radio interview about it, and Duncan Stewart featured the apartment in his *About the House* television series. It was also written up by the *RTÉ Guide*, *Image* magazine, the RIAI *Journal* and other publications.

I popped in to the Telecom Éireann office on the corner of Anglesea Street and College Green to arrange to get a telephone installed.

'Temple Lane. Where's that?' the fellow behind the counter asked.

'Just two blocks from here,' I replied.

'Oh, I'll have to get an engineer's report so,' he said.

I was mystified by his response, and asked why such a thing would be necessary.

'Oh, there's a lot of people moving into this area, and they're all looking for telephones,' he explained.

'Well, that was in the plan to develop Temple Bar,' I pointed out.

It was clear that the whole thing was news to him. So I decided to write another Henry Root-style letter to Alfie Kane, then chief executive of Telecom Éireann, recounting the conversation I had with that fellow in the Anglesea Street office, saying I needed a telephone for my work as an *Irish Times* journalist, and ending with the flourish, 'As V. I. Lenin would have said, what is to be done? Yours sincerely . . .'

The following day I got a phone call from someone in Kane's office saying, 'About this phone you want installed in Temple Lane – would tomorrow afternoon be OK?'

We were absolutely delighted to get the flat, even though there wasn't a single grocery store in the area then – no Spar, no Centra, no SuperValu or anything else. That was bound to change over time as the once run-down and laid-back bohemian district was remade as a 'bustling cultural, residential and small business precinct that will attract visitors in significant numbers'. The hype was quite overwhelming, especially after Laura Magahy became TBP's managing director, working closely with Patricia Quinn as culture and finance director; the pair of them were always so well turned out that they became known as the 'Linen & Lipstick Sisters'. They were 'driven by a vision; we know what we want and we are going to get it', as Quinn said quite openly in 1993. They also played their cards close to the chest. 'That's the dark side of our good qualities. We give the necessary information to the right people at the right time,' she told the *Irish Times*.

Three years later, before moving on to become director of the Arts Council, Quinn edited a lavishly illustrated book to celebrate TBP's achievements – already garlanded by a slew of architectural, planning and urban design awards. The book was called *Temple Bar: The Power of an Idea*; some cynic suggested a more apt title would have been *Temple Bar: The Idea of the Power.* Behind the scenes, TBP was directly involved in creating four super-pubs – Fitzsimons

Hotel, the Porterhouse, the Front Lounge and the Czech Inn – as well as facilitating the expansion of others, including the 'iconic' Temple Bar pub, which used to consist of a single room but now extends to at least 1,000 square metres. Turning the area into the 'Temple of Bars', as former An Taisce chairman Michael Smith once dubbed it, was never part of the official agenda; indeed, the word 'pubs' was barely mentioned back in 1991.

And Temple Bar Renewal, TBP's 'sister company', didn't exercise its primary function to veto schemes that would have a 'detrimental impact' on the area, largely based on ultra-cautious advice given by Finian Matthews, principal officer in the Department of the Environment, who sat on its board. Neither did the city planners have any hesitation in granting permission for new pubs and extensions to existing licensed premises. As a result, nearly an acre of extra drinking space was added to the district, effectively sealing its fate. Yet the High Court ruled in 1998 that if Temple Bar Renewal believed that granting approval for any project 'would be detrimental to a suitable mix of uses in the area . . . [then] it was mandatory upon them to refuse the approval'. In other words, TBR always had the statutory power to control the spread of pubs in Temple Bar, rather than simply rubber-stamping them.

One day, as the Fitzsimons Hotel was being finished, Nuala O'Faolain and I were walking past on our way to lunch in the Clarence and peered through the front door. We were invited in by Kevin Fitzsimons, a builder who fully appreciated the value of tax incentives for developments in Temple Bar. He brought us on a tour of the new hotel, showing us a top-floor room at the corner with a projecting window. Nuala was very impressed, remarking, 'If you had friends coming and not enough space to put them up, they could stay here and they'd have a lovely view of the Ha'penny Bridge.' I asked Fitzsimons how many hotel bedrooms you needed to lever a licence, and he said twenty, which was the exact number in his new establishment.

'You must be the first builder I've met who isn't from Cavan,' Nuala said.

'Ah, but I am from Cavan,' he replied with a broad grin.

With the way tax incentives were structured, 100 per cent of the project's capital cost could be written off against tax while double-rent allowances and rates relief for ten years were available to the operating company, also controlled by Fitzsimons. Later on, not long before his untimely death from cancer, Kevin told me that he and his brother Aidan, who's now running the 'hotel', had managed to get work in the US during the 1980s when there was precious little construction happening in Ireland. How did they get green cards? Well, they simply set up a registered building company in Boston, which then 'invited' them to come over – a classic Cavan ruse. The Fitzsimons Hotel went on to brand itself as a 'party venue with roof terrace . . . live on 5 floors . . . 7 nights a week . . . live acts/bands and DJs . . . late-night bar and club'. And like the other super-pubs in Temple Bar, it's a goldmine.

In July 1995, a firm of Newry solicitors, Donnelly Neary & Donnelly, placed an arresting advertisement in the personal columns of the *Irish Times* offering a £10,000 reward for information leading to convictions for land-rezoning corruption in Co. Dublin. The backers of this extraordinary initiative were anonymous, but I knew from the start that they were two campaigning barristers – Michael Smith, of An Taisce, and Colm Mac Eochaidh, who went on to become a High Court judge and, later, a judge of the EU's General Court in Luxembourg. The reason why they had to engage a firm in Newry was that no solicitor in the Republic would act for them, given the extreme sensitivity of the matter.

'This is not blackmail,' they declared in a press statement two months later. 'It is the resort of persons forced to take action in an arena which outside of a banana republic should be the realm of government.'

But the Rainbow Coalition of Fine Gael, Labour and Democratic Left seemed to have little interest in inquiring into land-rezoning corruption. This became clear after I approached Tim Collins, then special adviser to Minister for the Environment Brendan Howlin and later chief executive of Newstalk radio, seeking a meeting to brief the minister on some of the explosive allegations being made by Smith and Mac Eochaidh's informants. When we met, it was a damp squib. Although Howlin said he was 'totally committed to rooting out corruption' in the planning process, he was 'not prepared to do so on the basis of threats from anonymous sources'. He even declined to meet the two barristers on a confidential basis after they had put out feelers to engage his interest in what they were uncovering. And that was that, at least for the moment.

Fierce battles over the fate of Dublin's architecture resumed as the Irish economy entered its 'Celtic Tiger' phase. One of the most prominent of these rows revolved around plans by Treasury Holdings to demolish several historic buildings and retain the façades of others on a triangular site bounded by College Street, Fleet Street and Westmoreland Street. Treasury, owned and operated by Richard Barrett and Johnny Ronan, already had planning permission for an office development on the site, with an equivalent level of demolition and façade retention, and they were taking an each-way bet by securing approval from An Bord Pleanála in December 1996 for a luxury hotel. I was convinced that a hotel would be preferable to an office block, but An Taisce was vehemently opposed to *any* redevelopment that would sacrifice even unlisted historic buildings.

Michael Smith set up a company called Lancefort Ltd to frustrate Treasury's plans by taking legal action in the High Court, and was joined in this enterprise by Colm Mac Eochaidh and An Taisce's Heritage Officer, Ian Lumley. Exaggerated claims were made that the College Street scheme was 'the most destructive in Dublin for years', based on the alleged fact that eleven buildings were to be gutted or demolished. But this figure derived from Smith's double-counting of corner buildings; the former Scottish Widows building on the corner of College Street and Westmoreland Street was counted twice because it had façades to both streets, as was the former Pearl Insurance building on the corner of Fleet

Street and Westmoreland Street. Lancefort's legal challenge failed, but Smith wouldn't let go. He concluded that I was a traitor to the cause of conservation and let rip in a piece for *Magill* magazine, implying that I was in the pocket of Treasury Holdings; it resulted in the entire January 1999 issue being pulped on legal advice. Emily O'Reilly, *Magill* editor at the time and now the EU's Ombudsman, later told me their lawyers had warned that, if Smith's piece was published, I could have won £100,000 in damages had I sued them for defamation. Certainly, it was odd to find myself at the receiving end of an abortive press attack and to have my reputation defended by lawyers acting for another publication.

Meanwhile, CIÉ set up a project team to plan a light-rail network, headed by Cork-born engineer Donal Mangan. At the time, a three-branch network was envisaged, linking Ballymun, Dundrum and Tallaght with the city centre. But the Ballymun line was later dropped, largely because very few people living there had cars so they would only be switching from buses to trams. There was a press trip to France to see light-rail systems in Grenoble and Strasbourg, stopping off in Lyon along the way. But there was nothing that Mangan or his press officer Eamonn Brady could do to convince one particular journo that it was the right thing for Dublin. Although dead set against the light-rail project and with no working knowledge of French, he took to scanning restaurant menus to find the dearest dish, which he would then order quite shamelessly without even knowing what it was. He got his comeuppance in Lyon's legendary Brasserie Georges, when he was presented with a sliced pig's head on a plate and yelped in horror at the sight of it. 'There really is a God,' someone commented on seeing his discomfiture.

Mangan, Brady, planning consultant Bernard McHugh and I used to gather for lunch regularly in Tosca, on Suffolk Street, to discuss progress on the light-rail project, especially after it ran into opposition from the usual dark forces – as well as former Taoiseach Garret FitzGerald. He became convinced that trams wouldn't be able to turn the tight corner at Dawson Street and Nassau Street and told me that he had measured the radius early one morning in an effort to prove his point.

After Fianna Fáil and the Progressive Democrats returned to government in 1997 with Bertie Ahern as our beaming Taoiseach, the whole project was subject to a 'review' by Mary O'Rourke, the Minister for Public Enterprise with responsibility for most of the semi-State companies, including CIÉ. In May 1998, the Cabinet decided to scrap the city-centre link and opt instead for two free-standing light-rail lines, one linking Tallaght with Connolly Station and the other running from Sandyford to St Stephen's Green. Ministers, including Tánaiste Mary Harney, simply couldn't get their heads around the idea of taking road space on Dawson Street from cars and giving it to trams. In a spectacular example of political cowardice, the government had capitulated to lobbying from reactionary vested interests – the AA, Dublin Chamber of Commerce and IBEC – leaving us with a plan that made little or no sense. O'Rourke held a press briefing on the new plan, which envisaged going underground in the city centre, between St Stephen's Green and Broadstone, and used a crude diagram, almost a back-of-the-envelope job, to illustrate it. As I wrote in the *Irish Times*, this was a 'gutless response to irrational fears that there would be a huge political backlash over the disruption caused by construction of CIÉ's on-street alternative' and by the long-term operation of Luas, as the light-rail project came to be called.

When it came to roads, there were no limits at all. With the 'Celtic Tiger' boom in full swing, and EU funding plentiful, the FF–PD government decided to go ahead with a major motorway programme. The National Roads Authority's *Road Needs Study*, published in 1998, had merely recommended that existing routes be upgraded to motorways, dual carriageways or high-quality single carriageways, with bypasses built to relieve congestion in towns along the way. But this definitive study was effectively binned by Noel Dempsey, then Minister for the Environment, in favour of building new motorways running parallel to the existing main roads. The principal reason was that, with so many 'one-off' houses along these roads that would need to be acquired compulsorily for demolition, the political cost would have been prohibitive. It apparently never occurred to Dempsey or the road planners that an entirely new network of motorways could have been more creatively configured, to avoid pointing them all in the direction of Dublin, like the spokes of a wheel. It also didn't seem to occur to anyone that the motorway programme would undermine the viability of what's left of Ireland's once extensive railway network, whittled down over the decades by successive governments, by making it faster to travel by car than inter-city train.

Even though I've never been a motorist, it's impossible not to be impressed by the ease of travel on motorways, even if the scenery tends towards boring sameness on every route. I well remember the first stretch of motorway to be completed in Ireland in 1984 – the Naas Bypass – and how John Mulcahy, then managing director of chartered surveyors Jones Lang Wootton, 'did the ton' on it – 100 miles per hour – in his red Porsche on the way back from a planning conference in Cork while I sat glued to the passenger seat, so low down and close to the smooth blacktop that I felt like Ayrton Senna's guardian angel. Mulcahy and I, ostensibly polar opposites, used to meet periodically for gossipy lunches in a lesser-known French restaurant on Upper Stephen Street, where neither of us was likely to be seen by our respective 'constituencies'; we had a common interest in rescuing Dublin from dereliction. But I could see the dangers of spending €8 billion or more on a full-scale motorway programme that would reinforce the already overwhelming dominance of Dublin – with the Greater Dublin Area accounting for 40 per cent of the State's population – and this would make nonsense of the spurious claims being made by Dempsey, among others, about 'balanced regional development'.

I was also concerned that we were putting all our eggs in the roads basket and locking ourselves into long-term car dependency, thus making it doubly difficult for the transport sector to make any meaningful contribution to reducing carbon emissions. Given that well over 90 per cent of all freight in Ireland is carried by road, there was obviously a trade imperative behind the motorways, which explained the EU's interest in funding them. For years, the Liffey quays were clogged by trucks heading to and from Dublin Port, so there was a clear argument for a tunnel to take them away from the riverfront. Ciarán Blair, then chief engineer with National Toll Roads plc – operators of both the East Link and West Link toll bridges – put forward a brilliant plan for just such a tunnel, which would have provided a direct route from the fulcrum of the M50 to the port, along the line of the Liffey; but it didn't get anywhere. Instead, a more awkward north–south alignment was chosen for the Dublin Port Tunnel, mainly to preserve the long-standing objective of providing the city with an eastern bypass motorway, of which the tunnel itself would be the first phase. Bertie Ahern, whose main agenda was to relieve traffic congestion in Drumcondra, also faced down opposition from Marino residents who were worried about its impact on their homes, although it was quite easy for him to do that as they weren't his constituents. But at least the tunnel all but eliminated the unedifying spectacle of most of our imports and exports being trundled up and down the Liffey quays.

Another long-running road saga that was resolved around this time dated back to the eighties. In Sligo, the road engineers were determined to run the N4 right through the town centre as a four-lane dual carriageway, claiming this would help to solve the town's traffic problems. I got involved in the controversy after receiving a plaintive letter from Gabrielle Finan, a long-time resident of the doomed area, and went to Sligo to meet her and survey the territory that would be rent asunder by the proposed 'inner relief road'. For years, this wonderful woman and her neighbours had been 'living under the threat of this hammer falling on our heads', with forty 'lovely old houses' as well as numerous commercial premises earmarked for demolition. I was so appalled by this prospect that I sought a meeting with the then Environment Minister Michael Smith – a decent and honourable Roscrea man – and helped to persuade him to reject the scheme, adding my voice to a petition signed by five thousand objectors. But the review he ordered, which was carried out by private sector civil engineering consultants, endorsed the original plan with virtually no modifications. There was the usual pro-forma 'public inquiry' into the so-called Inner Relief Route and, to his eternal shame, Noel Dempsey eventually approved it. And did it bring any 'relief' to traffic in the town? *Pas du tout*, as they'd say in France.

Neither did Dempsey have any doubts about running the M3 motorway through the ancient royal landscape of Tara, in the heart of his own Co. Meath constituency, despite pleas from archaeologists and many others, including Nobel laureate Seamus Heaney. The great poet said it would literally 'desacralise' an area invested with great spiritual significance for centuries, on a par with Delphi in Greece or Stonehenge in England: 'If ever there was a place that deserved to be preserved in the name of the dead generations from pre-historic times up to historic times up to completely recently – it was Tara.'

Apart from his motorway myopia, I thought Dempsey was actually quite a good Minister for the Environment, and not only because he hosted a Christmas lunch every year for environment correspondents in the Commons, an upmarket restaurant that thrived for a time in the basement of Newman House. He was virtually alone in advocating a root-and-branch reform of the Irish electoral system, by getting rid of multi-seat constituencies so that TDs could concentrate on national issues instead of competing with each other to do as many favours as possible for individual constituents. Among other things, he pioneered new planning legislation that gave statutory protection for the first time to listed historic buildings. It was unveiled by Dempsey and then Minister for Arts and Heritage Síle de Valera in a very appropriate setting – the meticulously restored house on North Great George's Street of china specialist Desiree Shortt.

One notable absentee was Senator David Norris, despite the fact that he lives right across the street. He had fallen out with Shortt over her opposition to his ill-advised plan to erect a set of Regency gates from Santry Court at the bottom of North Great George's Street – to 'keep out the riff-raff', as one critic of the scheme claimed at the time. After I wrote a jaundiced piece about it in the *Irish Times*, Norris was furious and we have rarely spoken since. (I had also been taken aback by what happened after the National Gay Federation's Hirschfeld Centre on Fownes Street was closed down when fire gutted the building in 1987. Having invested proceeds from the sale of his family home in Greystones to develop it as Dublin's premier gay venue, Norris claimed ownership of the property. Some of his NGF colleagues disagreed, claiming the money was merely a 'loan', and the case went to court, but was later settled on undisclosed terms.)

Still, nobody who heard it will ever forget Norris fulminating on RTÉ radio over the appointment of Thomist theologian Desmond Connell as Archbishop of Dublin in 1988. In an interview with Pat Kenny, the Senator said that the new Archbishop 'may know everything there is to know about angels, but you can take it from me that he knows sweet fuck all about fairies!' Six years later, Connell must have been quite uncomfortable presiding at the funeral in Baldoyle of a sixty-eight-year-old priest who had died from a heart attack in the Incognito sauna on a laneway off Aungier Street. I remember seeing an elderly woman in her Sunday best staring in utter disbelief at the banner headline in the *Sunday World* at a newsagent's in Harold's Cross: 'PRIEST FOUND DEAD IN GAY SAUNA'. The owner of the sauna, Liam Ledwidge, claimed that up to twenty Catholic priests were among Incognito's regular patrons.

8

In November 1996, the journalist Sam Smyth broke a sensational story about how Ben Dunne, scion of the family behind Dunnes Stores, had funded major construction work at former Minister for Transport and Communications Michael Lowry's Regency house in Co. Tipperary as 'payment in kind' for the supply of refrigeration equipment for the retail chain. These revelations, which led to Lowry's resignation two days later, were followed by even more extraordinary claims that Dunne had made a number of large payments to Charlie Haughey. It was only as a result of a bitter feud between Dunne and his elder sister Margaret Heffernan over the control of Dunnes Stores that all this had come into the public domain, and there was no way of avoiding a tribunal of inquiry. Judge Brian McCracken was appointed as its sole member in February 1997 and expeditiously produced his report just seven months later.

The tribunal's public hearings at Dublin Castle were a real draw, with much of the interest focused on Heffernan, who turned up dressed entirely in black, like a 'Mafia widow', as Miriam Lord wrote in a colour piece for the *Irish Independent*. On the day that Haughey was due to give his evidence, I had an appointment to meet Kevin O'Sullivan, manager of Dún Laoghaire–Rathdown County Council, but cancelled it so that I could go to Dublin Castle instead. There was just no way I would pass up this unique opportunity of seeing CJH 'in the dock'.

George's Hall was crowded, with every seat taken, but a tribunal official helpfully escorted me upstairs to a small gallery where those of us lucky enough to get seats had a great view of the entire proceedings. Haughey, who was in the front row below, was called to give evidence and took his place in the witness box, listening intently to a long recitation of his often glittering career by tribunal barrister Denis McCullough SC, who concluded that he had 'indeed done the State some service'. With that, a shaft of sunlight broke through the part-glazed roof and fell upon CJH, and on him alone, illuminating his face as he answered a series of questions about his dealings with Ben Dunne. (None of the media reports of the hearing referred to the shaft of light, which I found quite extraordinary.)

Naturally, Haughey denied that the £1 million or more he had received from Dunne had anything to do with an advantageous ruling by the Revenue on the Dunne family trust's tax status. In his report, Judge McCracken found that Haughey had given untruthful evidence under oath and that Lowry had been knowingly assisted by Ben Dunne in evading tax. A subsequent prosecution of CJH for obstructing the tribunal had to be abandoned after prejudicial comments by Tánaiste Mary Harney to the effect that he should be put in jail.

Much more was to come. Despite dogs in the street knowing about Ray Burke's corrupt political career, Bertie Ahern had given him the plum job of Minister for Foreign Affairs. But publication by the *Sunday Tribune* of claims by James Gogarty, retired managing director of Joseph Murphy Structural Engineering, that he had witnessed a bribe of £30,000 being paid to Burke at his Swords home made the minister's position in Iveagh House untenable and forced the government to establish another tribunal of inquiry, headed by Judge Feargus Flood, in November 1997.

I knew Pat Hanratty SC, one of the newly appointed tribunal barristers along with former Garda officer John Gallagher SC, and felt it was my duty to brief them on what I knew about the veritable Augean stables that was Dublin County Council. We arranged to meet for lunch in the Old Dublin restaurant on Francis Street as soon as it reopened after Christmas, and the two barristers booked a private room upstairs, in the interest of discretion. I asked them to bring along a list of councillors, which they did, and then we went through it in detail. In a classic piece of felon-setting, I pointed out which councillors I believed were taking bribes, and gave Gallagher and Hanratty every bit of information I had about the corrupt land-rezoning decisions those councillors had taken against all planning advice. The room was cold, and every so often Gallagher would get up to toast his bum in front of a fire in the grate before coming back to the table for more good food and wicked allegations.

A long time would pass before the Planning Tribunal got into high gear by holding its first public sessions, and a much longer time before it produced even an interim report. But I made it clear in a speech at the General Council of County Councils annual conference in Sligo in 1998 that I welcomed its establishment, saying I looked forward to seeing corrupt councillors sent to jail. This was greeted by shouts of 'Shame on you!' by some of them.

I had put together a horror slide show illustrating the damage we were doing to Ireland's landscapes with the proliferation of increasingly large and vulgar 'McMansions' in rural areas, and presented it at a conference in Belfast in 1999 organized by the Northern Ireland Environment and Heritage Service. I hailed the range of statutory protections of important landscapes north of the border, saying tourists in the future would at least be able to visit parts of Ireland still in relatively pristine condition even after the rest of it had been wilfully destroyed. Up there, the planners had designated extensive Areas of Outstanding Natural Beauty to protect the Mournes, the Glens of Antrim and several other sensitive landscapes. Down here, it was effectively 'open season' outside the relatively few State-owned National Parks.

Officials from the Department of the Environment in Dublin, who were at the conference, took it very badly. It was as if I had hung out all our dirty linen for the Northerners to see, in a spectacular act of treachery. Dave Fadden, with whom I had clashed over the crazy 'interpretative centres', at least stayed around to talk. But John Sadlier, who used to run the department's ENFO service in Andrew Street, couldn't even bring himself to do that. As

I approached them in the Stormont Hotel, he said, 'There's a bad smell here. I'm going outside to get some fresh air.'

A couple of years later, after Peter Robinson became the North's Minister for Regional Development, I got a call from his office inviting me to join a 'round table' at the Ramada Inn in south Belfast to discuss challenges facing the countryside and give him the benefit of our advice. As we had dinner, I was sitting opposite Robinson and found him very well informed and not at all bigoted, even though he had been Ian Paisley's deputy for many years. He seemed to be a different man from the young hothead who had taken part in a loyalist 'invasion' of the border village of Clontibret, Co. Monaghan, back in 1986.

By then, the 'Celtic Tiger' had the Republic gripped in its claws, and it was not a pretty sight; Ireland's environment, built and natural, was 'taking a frightful mauling from that same ravenous beast', as I wrote in an *Irish Times* opinion column in August 1999. 'DIGGER BUCKET TEETH IN STOCK', screamed a hand-scrawled sign on a shop outside Castlebar: the shop was, I wrote, selling 'steel dentures for the buckets of JCBs, to replace the teeth worn out excavating sites for ostentatious bungalows, unsustainable clusters of holiday homes, homogenized Euro-trash shopping malls or whatever else the Celtic Tiger requires in the way of development'.

The economic boom brought benefits to many, but I felt it was doing terrible damage to our psyche. In Dublin, people were noticeably walking faster on the footpaths, as if on the way to making their next million. In the column, I recalled coming back from Barcelona the previous month, via London Heathrow, on a late-night British Midland flight. Across the aisle from me was a young man who spent the entire time poring over what I could see was a draft agreement on the importation into Ireland of pizza bases from Canada. When he was asked what he would like to drink, he said, 'I know what I'd like, but I'll just have a cup of tea, thanks.' I thought, We're really losing it if young Irish businessmen can't put their work away at that hour of the night (it was after 11 p.m.); at least I was reading one of Colm Tóibín's novels and ordering Bloody Marys.

My column caught the attention of the *Sunday Independent*; it was always looking for an excuse to heap odium and ridicule on the *Irish Times*, not least because of the high moral tone adopted by the 'Old Lady of D'Olier Street'.

So Éilis O'Hanlon penned a scathing riposte to what I had written. 'Let the Celtic Tiger types eat cake', said the headline over her article, which had a strapline branding me as 'the Marie Antoinette of Irish journalism'. The piece itself quoted from a feature in *Beyond the Hall Door* magazine on my 'architect-designed Temple Bar apartment', with its 'abundance of space and light . . . in the dining area, an Arne Jacobsen-style table and chairs take centre stage sitting on a large Turkish rug from Empires . . . at the other end of the room, luxurious Italian sofas from Bob Bushell dominate the living room . . . a state-of-the-art Siematic kitchen is tucked away in one corner of the room [while] a mysterious door opens to reveal every apartment-dweller's dream – a roof garden.' Perhaps the young man I had seen working late on that plane, O'Hanlon wrote, 'has simply realised that, if he wants to enjoy the same cushy lifestyle as Frank McDonald – Temple Bar apartment, roof garden, fine furnishings, and all – then he is unlikely to get it drinking Bloody Marys and reading books by Colm Tóibín.' Above O'Hanlon's rant was another pro-Celtic Tiger piece by right-wing columnist Mary Ellen Synon, headed, 'Nothing wrong with BMWs and blondes'; the *Sindo* was a cheerleader for the lot.

The boom did bring some tangible benefits to Dublin, as more funding became available to the city council. Under the dynamic leadership of John Fitzgerald, who had taken over as City Manager in 1996, much of the extra money was invested in public projects such as the Liffey Boardwalk, the 'rejuvenation' of O'Connell Street, the remaking of Smithfield with its gas braziers on tall lighting masts, the Millennium Footbridge and the restoration of City Hall and the Ha'penny Bridge. Movers and shakers in the new regime included City Architect Jim Barrett, Chief Planning Officer Dick Gleeson and Director of Traffic Owen Keegan, who went on to become Dún Laoghaire–Rathdown's county manager before taking over as chief executive of Dublin City Council in 2013.

I got on with them all, because I could see that real progress was being made after decades of bureaucratic torpor. Keegan, to his credit, pressed on with plans for a bus corridor on the Stillorgan dual carriageway in the face of opposition from the usual suspects, who had predicted traffic chaos; the dire warnings proved to be so much hot air. Fitzgerald held public meetings in the expansive Civic Offices foyer to hear people's views, gave the go-ahead to all sorts of projects and supplemented the council's press office with his own PR consultant, Mary Murphy. An accomplished professional, schooled in Carr Communications, she helped to project an entirely new image of 'the Corpo' as a forward-looking public body, engaged with the city and its citizens. There was a renewed sense of Dublin as a European capital, competing with the rest of them, rather than a living relic of the '800 years of oppression'.

Not everything the council tried in these years worked out so well. Fitzgerald bypassed standard procurement procedures to award gilt-edged commissions to Spanish 'starchitect' Santiago Calatrava for two bridges over the Liffey, upriver at Blackhall Place and downriver in Docklands. One resentful local architect paraphrased Lady Bracknell: 'To have one Calatrava bridge may be regarded as a misfortune; to have two looks like carelessness.' Nobody could dispute that the pivoted harp-like Samuel Beckett Bridge in the Docklands quickly became a symbol of the new Dublin, but the James Joyce Bridge further upriver seemed overwrought and did nothing to lift the area, other than redistributing traffic.

Then there was the saga of the Dublin Spire. Obviously, *something* was needed to replace O'Connell Street's missing centrepiece more than three decades after Nelson's Pillar was blown up, so an open competition was held to find the best design. It produced a collection of weird and wonderful ideas – from an enormous tattered Tricolour shot through by machine-gun fire to a 'Love Elevator' featuring the romantic musings of Irish poets, plus lots of objects in the shape of obelisks, sails, rockets, spires and spirals. I had no doubt that the competition jury was right to choose London-based architect Ian Ritchie's stainless-steel spire, soaring to a height of 120 metres. Claims that it would 'ruin' the proportions of O'Connell Street were nonsensical, given that it was so slim in profile. And there was the rub: unlike Nelson's Pillar, there would be no public access to any viewing platform, because there was none. The jury claimed, with a nod to the Ryanair Generation, that 'the aerial view is available to all who travel by air'. But this was far too glib. 'There is a big difference between viewing a city from the air, when it appears almost like a large, lumpy carpet, and seeing it from close-up through the intimacy of viewing rooftops and streets from a height,' I wrote at the time.

Much more controversial was Fitzgerald's promotion of plans for a municipal incinerator to deal with Dublin's growing waste-disposal problems. The 'Kill Dump' at Arthurstown, Co. Kildare, was running out of space for baled refuse, and a new waste-management strategy proposed that we should have a 'waste-to-energy' incinerator to relieve the impending crisis. Inevitably, this involved Mary Murphy organizing a few 'information visits' for journalists to view similar municipal facilities in Copenhagen, Vienna and Amsterdam, where we would all peer through thick glass into the fires of Hell as their waste was reduced to ashes. Vienna's Spittelau incinerator was tricked out by Austrian eco-architect Friedensreich Hundertwasser as a colourful, wacky art installation with a golden ball on its chimney. It supplies district heating for 60,000 homes and lets everyone know about its real-time emissions via a huge digital display board.

After one of the trips, I had lunch with Murphy and Fitzgerald in the Mermaid Café on Dame Street to talk about the incinerator proposal for Dublin.

'Where do you think it should go?' the city manager asked me.

'Poolbeg,' I replied, without hesitation.

My reasoning was that the long peninsula jutting out into Dublin Bay already had a major power station and sewage treatment works, so it would make sense to locate the plant alongside them. Plus, Poolbeg was uninhabited and, therefore, would be less likely to generate objections, since there wasn't anyone living right next door. At the time, the plan devised by consultant engineer

P. J. Rudden, of RPS Cairns, envisaged an incinerator with a capacity of some 200,000 tonnes of waste per annum. Nobody foresaw then that it would become a gargantuan beast requiring three times as much waste to 'feed' it round the clock, with much of this being trucked to Poolbeg from all over the country; economies of scale simply made it so. If it had been left to city councillors, this wouldn't have happened because they voted against the plan several times, as Labour's Dermot Lacey repeatedly pointed out. But Noel Dempsey took away their reserved power to determine waste-management policy and vested it instead in city and county managers who could be counted on to take orders from the Custom House.

In 1998, Crampton Buildings in Temple Bar – an apartment complex built in the 1890s by Dublin Artisan Dwellings – was up for sale by its Isle of Man-based owners, and there was a danger that the place would end up in the hands of rapacious developers. At dinner in the Clarence's Tea Room with Laura Magahy, John Fitzgerald and Noel Dempsey, I suggested that Dublin Corporation should acquire the forty flats on the upper floors, with funding from the Department of the Environment, to protect long-time residents. Fitzgerald readily agreed and, to his credit, so did Dempsey. As a result, £3.5 million was made available to fund the purchase, thus sparing the tenants from falling into the clutches of Treasury Holdings, which would almost certainly have turfed them out and renovated the flats as upmarket apartments; it had already bought all the ground-floor retail units, including the Elephant & Castle restaurant. The tenants were delighted and, for a time, the courtyard became a lovely oasis of trees and shrubs, with its own wormery to compost organic waste. Crampton Buildings eventually got a makeover from Dublin City Council, although the sanitized treatment, replete with 'health and safety' paraphernalia, robbed it of nearly all the greenery that made it so attractive.

Around that time the news desk often rostered me for regular reporting shifts, even though I was supposed to be the paper's full-time environment correspondent. It got so out of hand that one day

I ended up in the middle of a blazing row in the newsroom. I went to Michael Austen, then human resources manager, to complain that I was stressed out. Austen was sympathetic after I explained the situation to him over a couple of glasses of wine in the Clarence Hotel's Octagon Bar. I was so unwell and unable to function that my doctor, Niall Joyce, had to give me a series of medical certs. I stayed away from the office for three or four weeks, until eventually Conor Brady got the message that I was not going to put up with it. He agreed I would no longer have to do ordinary shifts and could even work from home, emailing my stories to the *Irish Times* from down the street in Temple Bar. Thank goodness for the advent of email!

Brady had much more pressing concerns, not least his determination to prevent Major McDowell parachuting his daughter, solicitor Karen Erwin, into a leadership role in the company. He managed to enlist the support of those of us who served on the paper's largely advisory Editorial Committee to join with him in resisting any attempt by the Major to make his daughter managing director, in succession to the long-serving and widely respected Louis O'Neill. Instead, Brady engineered the unlikely appointment of Nicholas ('Call me Nick') Chapman, an English military historian who found himself on a steep learning curve in coming to grips with Ireland, its history and culture; he barely lasted two years and then initiated High Court proceedings to prevent his dismissal, which the *Irish Times* had to report before settling the case on undisclosed terms.

Because of its central location, the flat in Temple Bar was often more like a railway station, with so many friends dropping in for coffee or a glass of wine or two. I toyed with the notion of writing Armistead Maupin-style *Tales of Temple Bar* but gave it up because I was so busy and, in any case, it seemed that Dublin's 'cultural quarter' wasn't going to become a real neighbourhood in any sense. Sure, we knew our immediate neighbours and a few others elsewhere, but that was about it. The area was already going bad, largely due to the proliferation of bars. Beautiful bevelled and frosted-glass panels in our building's front doorway were kicked in or otherwise smashed so regularly by drunken vandals that we gave up replacing them, settling for sheeted steel panels instead. Eamon returned one night to find a couple shagging in the entrance hall; the girl was on her hands and knees facing the wall, with a young Geordie guy giving it to her from behind. 'OK, mate?' he said to Eamon, apparently without missing a stroke. They had even hung their clothes on the handlebars of our bicycles. Only in Temple Bar, I thought.

Night after night, especially at weekends, drunks would piss in our doorway, leaving trails of urine on the footpath. I caught one of them in the act, and emptied a bucket of cold water on top of him from four floors up; he nearly jumped out of his skin in shock. Sometimes, the more despicable drunks would pee through our letter box, leaving a small lake of urine beneath a perforated rubber mat on the hall floor. On one occasion, someone defecated in a corner of the doorway, and we didn't have the stomach to clean it up. I think we left it there as a testament to the low life that was infesting the area, until the rain washed it away. Teenagers also got kicks from ringing our bell; the very idea that there was a set of six buttons you could press seemed to be so novel and irresistible to them.

Such carry-on would be unimaginable in, say, Berlin or Copenhagen; it suggests that we as a people are just down out of the trees in terms of urban living, because we don't even know the basic rules of coexistence. When dozens of Goths with Southside accents congregated in Curved Street right in front of our building, Eamon devised a system using piezoelectric tweeters, aimed at the crowd below from our top floor, that generated ultrasound at about 20 kilohertz – above the range of adult hearing but perceptible to those with younger ears. This seemed to have the desired effect of making them feel quite uncomfortable and they relocated en masse to the Central Bank Plaza.

*

The Soil Vent Pipe

by hieronymous
email: nevingettsofee@hotmail.com

In the eighties, Eamon had started an electronics company called Introl that developed a very useful call-barring device to prevent au pairs or employees making long-distance calls for free; it was even featured by Gay Byrne on *The Late Late Show*. But his older business partner was an alcoholic and it all turned bad. Later on, after we had moved to Temple Bar, Eamon did the three-month certificate course at Ballymaloe Cookery School and then set up a catering operation called the Portable Food Company in partnership with Brian Yore, who was living with us at the time. So when it came to my parents' golden wedding anniversary in September 1998, we were more than capable of catering for it at home.

Everyone in the family came along. My brother Liam brought his brood – Nessa, Murraigh, Seán, Jamie and Arran – all of whom had grown up in England but still cheered for Ireland at rugby matches. My sister Edel, her husband Paul and their two daughters, Kate and Jane, were also there, as was my youngest brother Denis. For Eamon, it was like doing dinner for the in-laws. Even though we never talked about it, my parents knew that he and I were a couple. 'Frank is a gay bachelor,' my mother once told a relative, 'with the emphasis on *gay*.' She had enjoyed looking after our Cairn terrier while we were away, in Ireland or abroad, taking Duncan for 'walkies' in the Phoenix Park on a daily basis. Dad was no daw either; he knew that Eamon was my 'boyfriend', as he told Edel years later. There was an extraordinary set of parallels between Eamon's family and mine: both of our mothers were called Maura; we ourselves were the eldest of four children – three boys and a girl; and the youngest in each case was called Denis.

The dinner in Temple Bar was the last great family celebration before something terrible happened – my mother's sudden illness. In December 1999, as I was writing my third book, *The Construction of Dublin*, I got a phone call from Liam telling me that Mam had been taken to A&E at the Mater Hospital after suffering a major stroke. I could barely believe it. She had done everything for us over the years and now she was lying on a hospital trolley, paralysed on her left side, looking so helpless and vulnerable.

'Are you not sorry that you never had children?' she asked me, out of the blue, when I called in to see her that afternoon. I didn't know quite what to say, apart from uttering some platitude about how the books were my 'children', or something like that.

Mam spent the rest of her life in a wheelchair, with Dad looking after her and the rest of us helping out in whatever way we could. Physiotherapy, which she called 'pummelling', came too late to make any difference to her overwhelming disability. And as she remained compos mentis, depression about her dependence on others became her daily reality. Gone was the gregarious woman we knew so well, who loved telling stories to give us a laugh. Driven by despair, she herself used to say it would have been better if the stroke had killed her, instead of becoming a 'burden' for Dad and the rest of us. I found it very hard to come to terms with her plight, as there was almost nothing I could do.

I was also run off my feet, juggling far too many things. There were the AIB Better Ireland Awards, for which Professor Frank Convery from UCD and myself formed the environmental component of the jury; our lunch meetings at Bankcentre in Ballsbridge gave us an insight into the pampered world of bankers and high-class catering. I was also on the jury for the Gulbenkian Museum of the Year Awards, coordinated by the fastidious Aidan Walsh with the aim of raising the standards of museums throughout Ireland. Then there was the International Institute for the Urban Environment, founded in Delft by the visionary Dutch architect and planner Tjeerd Deelstra with a mission to make cities more environmentally sustainable; when Dresden gave some consideration to getting rid of its tramways, to make more room for cars in the wake of German reunification, he invited its transport planners to Delft and convinced them to hang on to the trams.

I edited a book, *The Ecological Footprint of Cities*, for the institute based on the proceedings of a 1997 conference at Theatre de Balie in Amsterdam. My takeaway from that stimulating event was something that the ecologist William Rees said about how the world's economy is merely a division of the ecosphere, rather than the other way around; this is particularly useful to remember when you hear economists talking *in vacuo* about GDP growth rates. I was also regularly invited to chair or speak at public meetings, help out students with environmental theses, do radio interviews, take part in TV debates and other events, and too often I said yes. Conor Brady requested to be kept informed about my 'out-of-office' engagements, and I had to send him a list of stuff on a monthly basis; I think he took a dim view of journalists-turned-activists like me. In any case, as I approached my fiftieth birthday, work was taking over my life and I was going grey. One day, after news editor Niall Kiely had shaved off all his facial hair, I thought he looked almost naked, and said so to my colleagues Alison O'Connor and Catherine Cleary, both then in their twenties.

'How long have you had your moustache?' Catherine asked.

'Since I was twenty-one or twenty-two,' I said, trying to remember.

'Ah, so your moustache is older than us!' Alison quipped, as the pair of them chuckled on the way out to lunch. I shaved it off the following day.

Leafing through my diary for 1999, I counted a total of nearly eighty gigs and thought, I don't have a life that's separate from what I do. So I resolved there and then to cut back. 'Just Say No' became my resolution for the Millennium. This allowed me to reclaim my life and opened the door to a whole new chapter filled with bright young things; some of them became my closest friends and remain so to this day.

9

Early in 2000, Treasury Holdings was pulling out all the stops to progress an enormous office and commercial development along North Wall Quay, associated with the proposed Convention Centre at Spencer Dock. Johnny Ronan had even managed to persuade award-winning expatriate architect Kevin Roche and his team in Connecticut to design this mega-project and was waving his chequebook around Sheriff Street East in a bid to persuade people to sell their homes to Treasury. He even – as he later told me himself – thought the gay angle could be played by getting Richard Barrett, who's gay, to take me to dinner in Shanahan's, the expensive American-style steakhouse on St Stephen's Green, to smooth-talk me into supporting the scheme. But I remained stubbornly sceptical, characterizing it as 'Grimsville'; that resulted in a very angry phone call from Johnny. And even though Richard resembled the actor Jude Law, I wasn't tempted. We did become good friends, however.

At An Bord Pleanála's lengthy oral hearing on Treasury's plans in the Gresham Hotel's ballroom, which I was covering for the *Irish Times*, I encountered the former government Press Secretary Frank Dunlop, who was doing PR for the developers. When it began dealing with geological evidence, we went for a coffee break. Dunlop was due to testify at the Planning Tribunal, as he had played such an active role in lobbying for parcels of land in Co. Dublin to be rezoned for development, more often than not against planning advice. When I asked him if he was looking forward to it, Dunlop was his usual chirpy self, brushing it off as if the tribunal was just another gig. But when I pressed him on whether he was going to tell the truth, he turned serious and said, 'Well, there's one question I'll have to answer, if they ask me.'

Naturally, I was curious to find out what that key question was, so I asked him.

'Did any politicians ask me for money,' he replied.

Aha, I thought, that's useful to know. So I rang tribunal barrister Pat Hanratty SC and left a message on his mobile phone about my conversation with Dunlop.

At the end of Dunlop's first day in the witness box, this was the question that broke the camel's back, along with another about his 'war chest' of secret bank accounts from which corrupt councillors were being paid for their support. At first, Dunlop did not give truthful answers. Judge Feargus Flood warned him that he could be jailed for contempt if he didn't tell all he knew. The following day, he began listing names and detailing payments he made to get Quarryvale rezoned for what became the Liffey Valley Shopping Centre, which was now being planned by Cork-born developer Owen O'Callaghan after he bought out Tom Gilmartin's interest. (The greediest of all was Liam Lawlor TD, who amassed tens of thousands of pounds in bribes while he was a councillor. Not for nothing was he nicknamed 'Mr Big'.) Dunlop became ill and had to be excused from the witness box. He was so shaken by the experience that he emerged from the Printworks Building in Dublin Castle more ashen-faced than anyone I had ever seen.

At last, the truth was out about planning corruption in Dublin. I had thought this day would never come, and felt like opening a bottle of champagne to celebrate. A few days later, Conor Brady called me into his office to talk about it all and offered to upgrade me to Environment Editor, with an extra £5,000 a year. Perhaps the timing was just a coincidence, but I saw the offer as a gesture to make up for having believed for so long – as even some of my own friends did – that I might be exaggerating the extent of corruption in the planning process. But when Dunlop was eventually jailed for bribery and corruption, it struck me that not one of the councillors who took his bribes faced any real penalty apart from public opprobrium; they should *all* have been prosecuted and, if convicted, sent to jail.

*

For years, I had resisted getting a mobile phone because I couldn't stand the idea of being at everyone's beck and call all the time. Mairín McGrath and her colleagues on the *Irish Times* switchboard were my protectors, never once giving out my home number. It was only at Hanover's Expo 2000 that I realized that my phobia was untenable. My good friend Shane O'Toole, then writing about architecture for the *Sunday Times* Irish edition, and I had travelled to Hanover to see what new ideas the world had to offer. We also wanted to visit Murray Ó Laoire's Irish pavilion, where someone had the bright idea of digitizing daily satellite pictures of Ireland's weather and then running them all in fast-moving sequence, showing an unfortunate island being so persistently battered by Atlantic fronts that it seemed virtually uninhabitable; perhaps it was not lost on the Germans that we were protecting them from the worst. At some point on our tour, we were on top of the Deutsche Telekom tower in the middle of the fairground when I had to borrow Shane's mobile to make three phone calls, one after the other. I remember saying to him, 'Jeez, I'm just going to have to get one of these things after all,' and I did so as soon as we returned to Dublin. It was a pretty basic Nokia 6310, issued by the *Irish Times*, perfectly adequate for telephone calls and short text messages. Little did I know at that stage that the new phone in my breast pocket would become so central to my life.

Those of us who knew Deirdre Kelly well were devastated to discover that she had developed a particularly virulent form of cancer and didn't have long to live. Myself and *Irish Times* photographer Pat Langan, who had taken all the black-and-white pictures for her 1976 book, *Hands Off Dublin*, called to Our Lady's Hospice in Harold's Cross to pay our last respects. Deirdre was already in a coma, lying on the flat of her back in a bed in a private room, gasping for breath, with her devoted husband Aidan and their grown-up children by her side. It was difficult for us to see Deirdre like this, struggling with the inevitable, and we felt we were intruding into the realm of private grief, but Aidan reassured us that she would have wanted us to be there. I leaned down to get close, speaking clearly into her left ear, telling her that she had been an inspiration to me over the years and that she herself had put Dublin's inner city on the map of people's consciousness once again. I believe she may have heard what I said.

Deirdre died not long afterwards and the family asked me to deliver a eulogy at her packed funeral in the great domed church of Rathmines. (Nine years later, I was invited to speak at the unveiling of a memorial to her on the triangle in Ranelagh, noting that she would have been the first to object to the placement of its aluminium pyramid so close to a tree. Another element of the memorial, a bicycle on its side beneath a triangular glazed cut-out in the pavement, was rendered meaningless due to lack of maintenance by Dublin City Council; it has since been replaced.)

By then, I was finishing *The Construction of Dublin*, detailing how fast the city was changing in the boom years: its expansion into the Leinster countryside; its notions about a high-rise future; its disastrous transport planning. It was one of a number of books attempting to grapple with the first half of the Celtic Tiger period; the one I liked best was not *The Pope's Children* by David McWilliams, for all of its clever generics (remember 'Breakfast Roll Man'?), but Ann Marie Hourihane's *She Moves Through the Boom*, an extraordinarily well-observed snapshot of Ireland and its people in the grip of Mammon. As for my own book, I thought it wise to call Richard Barrett in advance to let him know that there was stuff in it about Treasury Holdings that he wouldn't like, but that none of this was motivated by an ounce of malice.

'Sure I know that,' he said, to my relief. Nobody sued me this time, and City Manager John Fitzgerald even agreed to launch the book at a big reception in the Civic Offices at Wood Quay, remarking that its title was much more positive than that of my first book – the obverse, indeed. But I intended the word 'construction' to signify more than bricks and mortar; it was also about what we meant by 'Dublin' now, given that so many towns within a 100-kilometre radius were becoming dormitories for people commuting to work in the capital. And all this was happening in direct contravention of the 1999 Strategic Planning Guidelines for the Greater Dublin Area, which emphasized the primary importance of consolidating the metropolitan area.

I had first observed the phenomenon in the mid-1990s, passing through Rochfortbridge in Co. Westmeath, where several housing estates had been tacked onto its edges like bits of Ballinteer and there was barely a single car outside any house because the occupants were all at work in Dublin, 80 kilometres away. When I put this to Seán Carey, Assistant City Manager in charge of planning and development at the time, he took a laissez-faire view. The sprawl would only stop, he believed, when all the houses then being built far from Dublin lost their resale value over time. My own contention was that such unsustainable development should be nipped in the bud, but this was simply not on the agenda.

Neither was there any constraint on rip-roaring house-building in other parts of the country, way beyond the capital's obese commuter belt. Letterkenny, the largest town in Co. Donegal, became a classic example of 'Celtic Tiger' development. Suburban housing estates were popping up in random fields on hillsides around the town, which has only one coherent street. In a sponsored *Irish Times* supplement on Derry, I contrasted its remarkable urban form with the chaos of Letterkenny, and ended up debating the issue on Highland Radio with the town's then Fianna Fáil mayor. His line was that I had only written what I wrote because Derry was paying for the supplement. This was a very serious charge to level against a journalist, because it suggested that the view I had expressed was not a genuinely held opinion, and I said so. And when he continued to repeat it, I became exasperated, saying, 'Listen, what you and other people in Letterkenny need to face up to is that the way your town has developed over the past decade or more, it's as if God had vomited all over the landscape.'

I also got involved in trying to save historic buildings, including Blake's Corner in Ennistymon, Co. Clare, which was threatened with demolition to create a useless roundabout catering for traffic on the road to Lahinch. Among the churches in danger of being junked was St Maur's, a perfectly decent nineteenth-century building in Rush, Co. Dublin. Specious arguments were advanced to justify abandoning it, including claims that the old church was unsuited to Vatican II 'liturgical requirements'. Yet the Church got its way despite a vigorous campaign by local parishioners to save St Maur's, which had its origins in Famine times. It was subsequently converted into a functioning library by McCullough Mulvin Architects, long after the replacement church was built 200 metres away. I was somewhat more sympathetic about the 'reordering' of Carlow's Regency Gothic cathedral, mainly because it was carried out by Richard Pierce, a larger-than-life architect who I greatly admired; he had built a quite extraordinary house for himself, inspired by the Grianan of Aileach, overlooking a deep lake west of Derrygonnelly, Co. Tyrone, with not another house in sight and zero visibility from the public road. And I *always* took into account the track record of architects in judging their latest projects.

One of the many historic buildings under threat of demolition at the time was the Jubilee Hall in Blackrock College. I became aware of this after receiving a remarkable letter at the *Irish Times* from a fourteen-year-old Blackrock student, David Watchorn, seeking my help to save it. He wrote about how it had been built in French Gothic style to mark the college's 1910 jubilee; now, he warned, the plan was to replace it with a new sports hall. I was impressed that someone so young was taking an interest in such matters, so I went out to meet David and have a look at the building, taking photographs of it and of him, and going for coffee afterwards in Café Java on Blackrock's main street. He was a typically gauche teenager then, but clearly very bright, knowledgeable and unswervingly committed to the conservation cause; he had read *The Destruction of Dublin* when he was eleven or twelve, he told me.

To his delight, the article I wrote alerted past pupils of Blackrock College about what was being planned and this led to the school authorities having second thoughts about demolition. By the time I spoke at the launch of the school's Green Week a year later, they had decided to keep the Jubilee Hall and build the new sports hall elsewhere. David and I kept in touch, often by email and text messages, and I took him on a couple of walking tours of central Dublin. He had a chunkier Nokia than mine and called it Ol' Bluey. While he was at a summer camp for talented youth in DCU, I got a message from him saying, 'I have to design an art gallery, but inspiration has run dry. Help!' He was mired in a 'lazy, ugly jumble of styles' and needed a 'unifying element'. This was pretty amazing, coming from a fifteen-year-old.

I replied, 'Forget about style, it's all about function . . . Big walls are essential for a modern art gallery to work, which is why [IMMA at] the Royal Hospital doesn't.'

It always seemed to me that David would make a great architect, but he followed his twin brother Richard into medicine instead, and is now a registrar in one of the big teaching hospitals.

I can't quite recall when or where I first encountered Randal MacDonnell, but it was probably at a drinks party at the home of tweedy Michael O'Sullivan in Kildare Street, opposite the side door of the Shelbourne Hotel. O'Sullivan, who used to present *Oireachtas Report* on RTÉ television, was known among his gay friends as 'the Diva', hence the building where he occupied the *piano nobile* became 'Diva Mansions'. Randal styled himself as The MacDonnell of the Glens, Isla and Kintyre, 'Chief of the Name' and Count of the Holy Roman Empire, a hereditary title dispensed like confetti by Austrian emperors over the years. His mother was Kathleen Dolan, who was one of the continuity announcers on Teilifís Éireann in the 1960s. Randal had gained the confidence of the Guinness heir Garech de Brún, for whom he had become an indispensable factotum, whether booking the Ritz Hotel in Paris, getting a table at La Mère Zou or Les Frères Jacques – Garech's favourite restaurants in Dublin – or arranging long-haul trips to India and Singapore, where dwelt Garech's wife, Princess Purna, a daughter of the Maharajah of Morvi.

I had first met Garech in the Shelbourne's Horseshoe Bar, where his regulation tipple was a snipe of 'the Widow' (Veuve Clicquot), to talk about the OPW's wicked plan for a Wicklow National Park 'interpretative centre' not far from his home at Luggala. That battle was ultimately won by the conservation lobby, and Garech subsequently sold a large tract of his own estate to the State, as an addition to the national park, to raise funds for the restoration of the Regency Gothic former shooting lodge. It was Randal who resolved the fiendishly complex pattern of ribbing on the ceiling of its library in advance of a full reinstatement.

Randal lived by his wits, with an impressive facility for cultivating titled folk, and he also knew everything there is to know about European royalty, going back centuries. A brilliant raconteur, he would regale us all with often-hilarious stories about consorting with such characters as Noël Coward, John Gielgud, a variety of Hollywood stars, and John Charles McQuaid, even claiming that the Archbishop's last words were, 'Oh, Randal, you do go on!' Despite his pallid complexion and balding pate, he had an extraordinary gift for picking up attractive young fellows, and surprised many of his detractors by writing a very good book, *The Lost Houses of Ireland* (2002), a chronicle of more than twenty great houses peppered with witty anecdotes about the people who lived in them.

One dark night in December 2000, while Eamon was away in Germany working as a chef in Irish bars in Hanover and Berlin, I got a call from Randal to say that he had just met a beautiful young South African in the George and wanted me to meet the lad. 'You'll be amazed!' he said. And so I went there to be introduced to Thinus Calitz and his older friend Pieter Watson. Thinus (a diminutive of Marthinus) was just twenty-one then, with blondish hair and a winning smile; I thought he looked just like Matthew Broderick in the 1986 film *Ferris Bueller's Day Off* and was smitten by him, as was Pieter.

A month later, over dinner *à deux* in Cooke's Café, Pieter told me about how he had first seen Thinus two years earlier dancing on the podium of a nightclub in Cape Town and fell in love with him there and then. As he recounted the story, tears were streaming from his eyes, behind his spectacles, and running down his cheeks in rivulets which he dabbed with a linen napkin. And all because he knew deep down that Thinus, the love of his life, was not really available to him on a long-term basis, and now he was 'wary of him, like a dog used to arbitrary kicks in the ribs'. (It was Pieter who suggested that it would be a good idea to keep every text message I sent or received, as he himself did. As a result, I have them all from 2001 onwards, up to fifty or sixty messages per day at times, running to perhaps three thousand pages if printed out, filled with drama, fun, love, pain and tragedy as well as mundane everyday things – a different kind of diary.)

Unlike in the 'straight world', cross-generational friendships and relationships are relatively common among gay people. Not only are younger guys – 'twinks' in gay parlance – more attractive, but many of them also benefit from having older friends or lovers, particularly if they have just 'come out' and are still trying to find their way in the world. Those of us who have lived through it, with all the ups and downs, can give them not only the benefit of our knowledge and experience, but also a shoulder to cry on, when they need it. The original bar of Dublin's biggest gay venue, the George, is usually populated by a variety of older 'bears' or 'sugar daddies' and their younger acolytes; not for nothing did it come to be known as Jurassic Park. I had always liked younger guys, so I suppose I was purposefully seeking out their company and cultivating friendships with the brightest and the best of them, especially after turning fifty. But I never anticipated that I would be surrounded by so many young friends at my advanced age, and that's been enormously positive for me and for them, or so they've told me many times. The bonds we have established are very deep, embracing their partners and even their families, and this has enriched our lives. For Eamon and for me, it's like having an extended family that keeps on giving, even as we get older and older.

I had great fun with Thinus, even though we never became lovers. He would regularly call to the flat for a chat and we'd drink Backsberg Chenin Blanc from Vaughan Johnson's shop in Essex Street; one of its staff, the charming young actor Conrad Kemp, was also from South Africa and knew the country's wines well.

Thinus had grown up on an ostrich farm in Oudtshoorn, in the Western Cape, but preferred to say he was from Cape Town because it sounded better, and he was working as a waiter in Kingswood House, near Citywest. We would often have cocktails in the Morgan Hotel's swish cream leather bar and then have a bite to eat in or around Temple Bar. On one occasion when we dropped in to the Mermaid for dinner, before the smoking ban was introduced, one of the waitresses scanned the room and said, 'Smoking – active or passive?' I even took him to a Christmas lunch at the Royal Irish Yacht Club, Dún Laoghaire, hosted by the Very Reverend Robert MacCarthy, contrarian Dean of St Patrick's Cathedral, much to the amusement of everyone at the table. One night, we posed as 'Men in Black' in the Spy nightclub at the Powerscourt Centre, dressing up in black suits and the crispest of white shirts, just for the fun of it. Thinus and his various young lovers spent lots of time in our flat, which became a sort of emotional clearing house for young people and their feelings about life, love and the whole damned thing. What I had done, in effect, was to turn it into a 'homo orphanage', as my partner Eamon put it so colourfully after he came home from Germany that October.

Graham Egan, then a trainee counsellor in his late twenties, became a good friend; he was a great listener and had lots of useful advice to offer, especially about my brief infatuation with Thinus. Other new friends from this hectic period included Paul Moley, then a freshman economics student at Trinity College; Stephen O'Farrell, a twenty-year-old arts student in Maynooth University, who Randal had introduced to me over drinks in the Morgan; and the Reverend Dr Alan McCormack, the youthful Church of Ireland chaplain at Trinity, who added Brazilian liturgical dancers to the sung Anglican Mass in its collegiate chapel until he was reprimanded by the Archbishop for 'excesses'. Alan hosted themed parties around Christmas in his small ground-floor flat off Patrick Street – black-and-white, Roman togas, turbans or whatever. He also landed the plum job of looking after St George's Anglican Church in Venice every August while the rector was on holidays, and I joined him there for a boiling hot week one summer. His partner at the time was Eugene Downes, future director of Culture Ireland and the Kilkenny Arts Festival, who also became a good friend.

Stephen became the closest of my young friends, even though I was old enough to be his father. With zero hang-ups about being gay, his email address at the time was fagtastic69@hotmail.com, which amounted to shouting it from the rooftops. The thing about Stephen, as I told him early on, is that he seemed to have been born to spread joy in the world, and we've had a lot of laughs together over the years wherever he was living at the time – in London, Paris, Berlin and Brooklyn, as well as in Dublin. (When he won a 'green card' in a US Embassy lottery at the age of twenty-eight I was thrilled for him because I knew how much he wanted to go to New York, but I also realized that I'd miss him being around – and he felt that too. 'Hey. So. Out of all of my friends I just think that I'll miss you the most (there I said it). You've just been such a stable in my life. Love ya. Ste x,' he texted me as his plane was about to depart from Dublin Airport.)

In late 2001, the *Irish Times* was facing one of its periodic financial crises, prompting management to seek 250 redundancies, equivalent to a third of the staff then. When Pieter Watson texted me to ask what was happening, I replied, 'Fear & loathing, in a phrase, and a lot of hugger-mugger about what we should be doing.' I was to appear on the panel on RTÉ's *Questions & Answers*, with John Bowman in the chair. Inevitably, the crisis at the *Irish Times* came up, and I spoke on behalf of my colleagues. 'Truly magnificent performance for the troops,' Mark Brennock texted afterwards, and I even got a congratulatory phone call from Conor Brady, which unnerved me slightly.

By January 2002, a group of us had got together and agreed that Brady had been at the helm for too long and we needed a new editor. I had two discreet meetings with newly appointed managing director Maeve Donovan to press home this point. Whether my intervention made any difference, I have no idea. But not long afterwards, Brady agreed to go and the editor's job was publicly advertised. Donovan would have favoured economics editor Cliff Taylor as Brady's replacement, but Brady himself was on the interview board and effectively engineered the choice of Geraldine Kennedy to succeed him, as he believed she would defend editorial against commercial pressures. On the first day of the new regime, managing editor Pat O'Hara, a genial Dubliner who never once lost his temper, raised a sensitive issue: all letters to the editor used 'Sir' as the form of address, so what were we to do about that?

'Well, it'll just have to be Madam then!' the paper's first female editor declared.

Shortly before the changing of the guard, I had to deal with another sensitive matter at the paper. Robert O'Byrne, who had become known for his *Irish Times* articles on fashion, was now writing about architecture, much to my dismay and that of many architects I knew; he was encroaching on my turf, and they didn't warm to his style. So I convened a meeting of commissioning editors and put a stop to this, with the imprimatur of poet Gerry Smyth, one of Brady's four managing editors. Less than six months later, I texted Shane O'Toole, 'Robt O'B is taking the package & will be gone from the IT in two weeks.' This was a reference to the quite attractive voluntary redundancy deal being offered by *Irish Times* management in order to thin out the staff.

O'Byrne, an expert on social manners who was always impeccably dressed, moved to a gate lodge in Co. Meath and reinvented himself as an author of well-researched coffee-table books, notably *Luggala Days: The Story of a Guinness Mansion*, as well as becoming vice president of the Irish Georgian Society and trustee of the Alfred Beit Foundation. He also writes a highly regarded blog, *The Irish Aesthete*, already a substantial archive of fascinating material on historic buildings in Ireland. Coincidentally, just a few weeks after O'Byrne left the *Irish Times*, I was invited to Luggala for a party that included such cultural glitterati as film director John Boorman; poet John Montague; Paddy Moloney of The Chieftains; Louis le Brocquy and Anne Madden; and Desmond FitzGerald, Knight of Glin, and his charming Dutch-born wife Olda. With Garech de Brún presiding in one of his handmade Irish tweed three-piece suits, it was a very jolly affair, fuelled by a seemingly endless supply of 'the Widow'. What impressed me more was the magnificent setting, with the entrance gate on the high road from Roundwood to Sally Gap, leading down over blanket bog profuse with heather, descending all the way until the trees start to appear, then the lake, the deer, the little Doric temple by the white sandy beach, the simple tomb of Garech's younger brother Tara Browne, whose death was memorialized in the Beatles' 'A Day in the Life', and finally the Regency Gothic house, now restored both inside and out by its long-time custodian. 'Magical' is an understatement.

Soon there was a new crisis in the *Irish Times*, after the company's accounts revealed for the first time the salaries being paid to the managing director and the editor – a 'basic' of €323,000 per annum in each case, plus bonuses, company cars, pension entitlements, etc. And this was happening at a time when staff were being told of the need for 'rigorous cost management' to ensure that high overheads didn't 'threaten the future of the newspaper'. Furthermore, its executive directors had sought to divert attention from the scale of their emoluments, which many of us regarded as staggering, by highlighting the fact that Conor Brady was being paid an annual sum of €100,000 by the *Irish Times* for ten years, per the terms of his severance package. Not surprisingly, Brady was livid about that and held a long meeting in Liberty Hall with members of the Editorial Committee to outline his side of the story.

I regarded all this as disgraceful and was quoted as saying so in other publications, much to the chagrin of Donovan and Kennedy. Columnist John Waters decided to write about it in the paper, but his piece was pulled at the last minute by Kennedy, citing concerns about libel and accuracy. Then he was sacked for sounding off about it all on RTÉ radio – and, soon after, reinstated. Donovan and Kennedy decided to brazen it out, confident that huge revenues from property and recruitment ads, and record circulation, would continue to enrich the *Irish Times* and that they were entitled to a share of this booty; at the height of it, the 'property porn' supplement on Thursdays was so loaded with ads that it ran to sixty-four pages and had to be divided into two parts.

When Cliff Taylor was leaving to become editor of the *Sunday Business Post*, there was a drinks reception in the Mint Bar of the Westin Hotel, hosted by Donovan. At one point, she approached me, all smiles, and asked how I was getting on.

'I'm pissed off, Maeve, because too many people at the top are taking far too much money,' I said bluntly.

'Well, you didn't complain about that when the Major was doing it,' she replied.

I took this to be a reference to the fact that Major McDowell (along with Douglas Gageby and three other directors) had each made a tax-free windfall gain of £325,000 when Irish Times Ltd was turned into a trust company in 1974, and that the Major himself continued to be extravagantly remunerated even as non-executive chairman after 1997.

'We didn't know the details then. Now we do,' I said. 'And this is happening at a time when the rest of us are being paid relative buttons for what we do.'

She said, 'Ah, so it's a personal issue then,' to which I responded, 'No, it's not. It applies right across the board.'

Clearly miffed, she asked, 'Is there anything else you want to say to me?' and I said, 'No,' and turned away.

I then got together with religious affairs correspondent Patsy McGarry and political correspondent Deaglán de Bréadún to organize a petition to the Irish Times Trust complaining about the unconscionable levels of pay for the company's executive directors and seeking to have more modest rates imposed. More than eighty colleagues joined us, including Lara Marlowe, Fintan O'Toole, Kathy Sheridan, Lorna Siggins, Martyn Turner and Michael Viney.

Richard Barrett said in an email:

> Jesus. That's some list. You have them on the ropes. I think mass exodus and start a new paper gives the journos a much better salary

> and free equity than anything you're likely to get from the management . . . you have in the IT. We would be on to put up €20m or €25m for that purpose . . . But you need every single important journo to jump ship simultaneously and in the strictest secrecy. This has to be a midnight raid that stakes them through the heart so they can't respond. In case you don't know, the reason why people buy the bloody paper is you lot, not Geraldine Kennedy.

I thought Richard's proposition would be 'a tall order, given that most people with the security of a permanent job tend to be averse to risk & put up with the divil they know, for that reason'. Quite predictably, nothing came of it. But all those who signed the petition were deeply concerned that the extraordinary emoluments enjoyed by those at the top of the *Irish Times* undermined the paper's moral standing as well as making it more difficult, if not impossible, to criticize excessive pay levels elsewhere. We didn't even get an acknowledgement, let alone a reply, from Professor David McConnell, the Trinity genetics don who was chairman of the Irish Times Trust, although we did get courteous responses from two other trust members, David Begg and Noel Dorr. In the end, Donovan and Kennedy got even more extravagant sums of money during the phosphorescent phase of Ireland's economic boom, thanks to a remuneration committee chaired by McConnell. Kennedy had insisted on parity between the salaries of the editor and managing director, but Donovan got more bonuses than she did, bringing the value of her package to well over €500,000 per annum.

Of course, the country was awash with money, and Taoiseach Bertie Ahern announced his plans for an overblown national sports campus in Abbotstown, off the M50, including an 80,000-seat stadium that was instantly dubbed the 'Bertie Bowl'. I thought it was a crazy idea – not least because an estimated 40,000 people were projected to travel by car to Abbotstown on big match days, with horrific consequences for congestion on the M50 – so I put in a Freedom of Information Act request to the Department of Finance, asking for all documents relevant to the project. To my amazement, the department dispatched two Xerox boxes of stuff, which took me a couple of days to wade through.

Clearly, senior Finance officials were as sceptical as I was about a project that looked certain to cost the Exchequer at least €1 billion. What all the FoI documentation enabled me to do was to compile a devastating chronology detailing how the sports campus scheme was being developed under the leadership of Paddy Teahon, Secretary-General of the Taoiseach's department, with 'executive services' provided by Laura Magahy, who by then had set up her own consultancy. For Abbotstown, amazingly, Magahy & Company was to be remunerated based on a percentage of the *out-turn* cost; in other words, the opposite of securing value for money. Mary Harney, Tánaiste in the Fianna Fáil–Progressive Democrats coalition, was so appalled when she read our exposé that a review of the project was ordered, leading to a substantial scaling down, including – most crucially – abandoning the proposed stadium. I had met Bertie Ahern in Johannesburg, at the 2002 UN summit on sustainable development, and put it to him that the obvious solution was to redevelop Lansdowne Road, arguing that this would retain both rugby and soccer in the city centre, rather than consigning them to the M50 ring. And that, in the end, is what finally happened.

Meanwhile, Thinus was swept off his feet by a London-born accountant, Karl Facer, who was in his early thirties and already had a long-term partner, Chris Savvides. Chris, a young lighting designer at the National Theatre, and Karl were into fashionable clothes, trendy restaurants, VIP rooms in nightclubs and expensive foreign holidays. Within months, the three of them were on a cruise to New York aboard the QE2, complete with dress suits in case they were invited to dine at the captain's table, which they were, of course; Karl had arranged everything. Thinus showed me all the pictures when he came back to Dublin; what a happy-looking *ménage à trois*, I thought. Clearly, a bright life in London beckoned, and Thinus went for it.

They shared an ex-council flat at Churchill Gardens in Pimlico with a view from their balcony of the long-redundant Battersea Power Station that would be bought in November 2006 by Real Estate Opportunities plc, controlled by Treasury Holdings, for £400 million. I thought this was insane, and said so in an email to Richard Barrett, noting that previous purchasers of the power station had all come a cropper. But RB was convinced that it was worth such a large punt because of its location just two kilometres (as the crow flies) from the Palace of Westminster – although the Battersea site could only be 'opened up' by investing heavily in a new London Underground line to serve it.

James Nix, who was at the King's Inns studying for the Bar, was to become one of my best friends, even though he was less than half my age and straight. We had so many interests in common, with similarly sceptical views on how Ireland was developing during the boom years. He had grown up on a dairy farm in Meelick, Co. Clare, on the outskirts of Limerick, and brought a welcome rural counterpoint to my metropolitan perspective. One weekend I was staying there when a cow was about to give birth, so I got up extra early in the morning to watch his dad dealing with it, using a rope to pull the calf out. When I got a Lord Mayor's Award in June 2003, thanks to Dermot Lacey, James was among the eighty guests in the flat who went through nearly fifty bottles of South African 'champagne'.

Over meals in places like Gruel, Yamamori, Il Vicoletto and the long-lost Bistro on Castle Market, we talked and talked about the state of the country and what might be done about it. We did a radio series on transport, produced for RTÉ by the late Richard Hannaford, and threw ourselves into writing a book on the environmental destruction of Ireland during the boom for Gandon Editions. I wanted to call it *Direland* or simply *Shambles*, but we ended up with *Chaos at the Crossroads* and it took rather longer to get into print than either of us anticipated. If it hadn't been for Richard Barrett's offer to raise €20,000 in sponsorship by having a 'whip-round' among people he knew, the book might not have been feasible at all. Certainly, I'll never forget the whole experience of our collaboration, which was intense from start to finish.

Richard was so impressed by James that he hired him to work for Treasury Holdings, essentially focusing on the environmental sustainability of its development projects. He did that for a couple of years before returning from the 'dark side', to work for the Irish Environmental Network and An Taisce. Then he moved on to Green Budget Europe and the influential Transport and Environment think tank/lobby group, both based in Brussels, where he met Claire McCamphill, a Ballymena-born European Commission official, and they got married over there in May 2017. It was a small family wedding, to which no friends were invited; they were trying to save money to buy a home in Dublin – an example, perhaps, of how the boom could make life less fun.

Paul Moley was like a surrogate son, and would call in regularly for dinner in the flat, as a respite from his tiny bedsit in Rathmines. The youngest of five brothers, he was a native of Crossmaglen in Co. Armagh and remembered well when part of its GAA ground was encroached upon by a British Army base. His mother ran a fish-and-chip shop on the square in Cross, right opposite the IRA memorial, while his father owned the local bus company, transporting the Armagh football team to Croke Park for big matches. To support himself through college, Paul got a job as a sales assistant in Louis Vuitton's new outlet in Brown Thomas, easily racking up €1,500 on his first day.

He was somewhat reticent at first about getting involved with other guys; my advice to him was, 'Let yourself go!' as he has often reminded me since. He met a young French music teacher, but their romance didn't last more than a few months, although they remained friends afterwards. Then it was Javier Saez, a beautiful Spaniard who worked for Stewart's Hospital in west Dublin, running respite homes for mentally handicapped young people. Right from the start, I got on really well with Javier; he had been a left-wing student activist in Madrid, and was fiercely anti-religion, even more so than me. He also had buckets of empathy. We even walked hand in hand all the way down Grafton Street one Valentine's Day, without a wicked word from anyone.

Politically, things were going from bad to worse. The FF–PD coalition had been re-elected, which was a shame in itself; and then they launched their National Spatial Strategy. This designated nine 'gateways', including Dublin, and a further nine 'hubs', but Bertie Ahern let the cat out of the bag when he described it as 'a twenty-year strategy designed to enable every place in the country to reach its potential, no matter what its size or location'. In other words, there would be 'something for everyone in the audience', as per usual. Just a year later, the government thrashed its own spatial strategy by unveiling a 'decentralization' programme aimed at shifting more than ten thousand public servants out of Dublin to fifty-three locations in twenty-five counties. The staggering scale of this wheeze was known to less than a handful of ministers until Minister for Finance Charlie McCreevy unveiled it in his budget speech in December 2003. Martin Cullen, then Minister for the Environment, told me that 'there were only four of us involved: Bertie, McCreevy, Mary Harney and myself', and he chuckled with delight at the thought of such a tight little conspiracy.

On budget day, Cullen spuriously claimed that 'now we see real life being given to it [the NSS] right throughout the country. It hits all of the hubs, all of the major areas that have been identified, the major county towns.' In fact, at least forty of the fifty-three decentralization locations were neither 'gateways' nor 'hubs'. The whole thing was an elaborate political hoax. It was also an abject failure, with only 3,400 civil servants and just one department HQ – the Office of Public Works – moved out of Dublin before the whole daft programme was eventually cancelled in 2011.

I had a run-in with Mary Harney one night in Ronan Ryan's Bridge Bar restaurant beneath the railway line on Grand Canal Quay. She was leaving with her husband, former IBEC director Brian Geoghegan, and stopped to say hello to Richard Barrett, Treasury's Rob Ticknell and myself; all three of us had 'drink taken'. Reminding her of the FF–PD coalition's failure to implement a carbon tax, I said, 'Mary, you used to stand for something, but what do you stand for now?' She was appalled at being confronted in this way and, after RB told me afterwards that she had made her displeasure known to him, I wrote a letter of apology.

It was clear where Martin Cullen's priorities lay – with the building industry. Shortly after taking over from Noel Dempsey as Minister for the Environment, he set about eviscerating Part V of the 2000 Planning Act, under which up to 20 per cent of any new residential development was to be allocated for 'social and affordable' housing. 'We're going to have to do something about Part V,' Cullen told me. Why? Because the builders were 'up in arms about it', he said. I was surprised that he expressed himself so bluntly about his intentions, especially to the likes of me. Cullen made it possible for builders merely to give money to local authorities in lieu of 'social and affordable' housing obligations, meaning that instead of mixed estates, we got more social segregation.

Like Ray Burke before him, Cullen liked to bang the Sellafield drum and invited environment correspondents including Tracey Hogan, of the *Indo*, and myself to travel to Rotterdam with him on the government jet for the opening of Ireland's case against the UK under the little-known Ospar Convention, before the Permanent Court of Arbitration in The Hague; it was the first and only time I was on the jet. Inevitably, Ireland didn't win and the nuclear plant at Sellafield is still in business.

Around this time, I became aware that socialite Marie Donnelly and her husband Joe, a wealthy and wily Cork-born bookmaker and modern-art collector, had built a remarkable house in Dalkey, designed by London-based Italian minimalist Claudio Silvestrin. Its main façade looking out over the Irish Sea stretched to 90 metres (nearly 300 feet), presenting a continuous glass wall sandwiched between concrete slabs. With a planning policy presumption against new houses along the coast in this exclusive area, the Donnellys had only been able to secure permission on the basis that it was an 'art gallery', rather than their spanking new home. The 'gallery' was open to the public only occasionally, with Robert O'Byrne acting as guide.

Glenageary resident Aidan Devon told me that it had 'just four oil paintings, two drawings, a bronze sculpture and some "art" furniture in the "gallery" space – minimalist indeed'. What happened, he said, was that Dún Laoghaire–Rathdown County Council had 'allowed developers of substantial wealth and influence to abuse the planning laws'. I managed to get Marie Donnelly's mobile number and rang it to put this issue to her. 'I have no comment to make,' said the former chair of IMMA, and then she hung up. In February 2004, the Donnellys were at a reception in the Chester Beatty Library for the opening of Colm Tóibín's *Blue* exhibition, and I decided to confront them. After introducing myself to Marie Donnelly, I asked her why she had hung up on me when I rang to ask her why they had used the 'art gallery' ruse to get planning permission for their house in Dalkey. She literally recoiled at the mention of it, while Joe Donnelly barked, 'That's not true!' Then they left. (In 2012, the Donnellys sought planning permission to convert their 'art gallery' into a home, but this was rejected by the county council, largely on zoning grounds.)

In *The Destruction of Dublin*, I wrote critically of Ronnie Tallon's design for the Bank of Ireland headquarters on Lower Baggot Street, a homage to Ludwig Mies van der Rohe. Years later, I retracted this verdict and conceded that the three blocks, all clad in the same Delta manganese bronze as the Seagram Building in New York, had been cleverly inserted into the south Georgian core, with minimal impact on their surroundings. Not long afterwards, Ronnie invited me to the first of three lunches at his home in Foxrock, which he shared with his devoted wife Nora. Inspired by Mies's Farnsworth House in Illinois, it was also built on a podium and had been extended twice over the years to accommodate more rooms for their children as they were growing up and, later, a tranquil 'home office' for Ronnie himself, looking out onto Foxrock Golf Club. And, naturally, they had authentic Mies Barcelona chairs in the living room.

Shane O'Toole was with me and the guest of honour was Terence Riley, then architecture curator of New York's Museum of

Modern Art. I gave Riley a walking tour of Temple Bar and other Dublin delights, before heading off with Annie McCartney and my goddaughter Katy to Rory Guinness's thirtieth birthday party in the brewery Storehouse's Gravity Bar. John Meagher, of de Blacam and Meagher Architects, was at that very convivial gathering and introduced me to his old friend Tony Ryan, the former aircraft-leasing magnate and founder of Ryanair. I told him I'd heard glowing reports (from John, among others) of his great work on the Lyons Estate in Co. Kildare, and said I would really like to write about it for the *Irish Times*. 'Dr' Ryan said I could do that alright, but I wouldn't be allowed to name him or identify the house. Needless to say, I did not accept these ludicrous conditions.

Geraldine Kennedy had been putting her unique stamp on the paper. Preoccupied by the goings-on in Leinster House, she expanded the political staff to cover every angle, but declined to give Mark Brennock the title of political editor, as she intended to bring Stephen Collins in from the *Sunday Tribune*. So Mark applied for an attractive severance package in 2004 and then joined Murray Consultants as their new director of public affairs. He was a great loss to the *Irish Times*, and to journalism. The following February, Kennedy allowed Kevin Myers to refer to the children of single mothers as 'bastards', before apologizing. We were also faced with a 'restructuring' of work practices, on the basis of a management document, *Building on Success*, that 'reads like it was written by a nineteenth-century factory proprietor', as I noted at the time; it was all about flexibility, multi-skilling, homogenization and standardization. No wonder John Maher – the best news editor I had ever worked for – decided to jump ship, carving out a new career as a barrister and author of a textbook on our still very restrictive libel laws.

In June 2004, we had mourned the loss of Mary Holland, who had died after being afflicted of scleroderma. She was one of the finest journalists of her generation, utterly fearless in her reporting of the Troubles in Northern Ireland and giving readers a unique insight into the developing peace process. Although she came into the office only once a week, to write her opinion column, I knew

Mary quite well. Some two years before her death, I recall her sighing audibly as she sat down at her desk, so I asked her what was the problem. 'Physical decay is not a pleasant thing,' she said, without going into any details.

But what I remembered most were the sparkling Christmas parties over the years at her home in Ranelagh, with her daughter Kitty doing most of the catering; they became a model for our own year-end parties in Temple Bar, though we didn't bother with the food. All sorts of people came to that old house off Oakley Road, including Marie and Seamus Heaney, Pat and Des O'Malley, John Bowman and his wife Eimear Philbin, Colm Tóibín and Catriona Crowe, musicians like Fintan Valelly, and several journalists, including me. Nearly everyone had their party piece. Heaney would give us some of his poetry, Tóibín would always sing 'Boolavogue', Valelly would play his tin whistle or guitar and Des O'Malley would throw in the odd rhyme or recitation. One Christmas back in the eighties, while he was Minister for Industry and Commerce in Charlie Haughey's FF–PD coalition government, O'Malley asked me when I was going to look into the 'fact' that CJH had done a deal to sell his Kinsealy estate to Patrick Gallagher. It was obvious that his animus against Haughey was as strong as ever, even though he was now sitting at the Cabinet table with his arch-enemy.

10

I was on the east coast of Greenland in June 2006 having a look at melting ice and retreating glaciers, on a press trip organized by the European Environment Agency, when I got the news that Charles J. Haughey had died. At last, I would be able to write about the lunches we had in Kinsealy during his final years.

It had started with a suggestion from Malahide estate agent and developer Brian O'Farrell over dinner with Richard Barrett in Il Primo (oh, how Dieter Bergmann, its owner, loved to see rich people coming in!); Brian knew the Haughey family and was sure that CJH would talk to me about his environmental record. So in late August 2003 I wrote the former Taoiseach a letter in which I mentioned the renovation of Government Buildings, the renewal of Temple Bar, and other things he had done. A week later, I got a call on my mobile.

'Is that Frank McDonald Esquire?' said the unmistakable voice at the other end. 'Come out for lunch next Thursday and we'll talk then.'

I texted James Nix, 'At Tara St Station waiting for train to Malahide. Have booked taxi from there to Kinsealy. Wish me luck . . .'

James shot back, 'He didn't pay his taxes – seize a Charvet shirt for us.'

Il Duce was at the door as my taxi pulled up outside Abbeville. We shook hands and he led me to his study, lined with bookshelves, where I presented him with a copy of *The Construction of Dublin*, inscribed, 'For Charles Haughey, with best wishes – and thanks for Government Buildings! Frank McDonald, 11/09/03.' As we sat there chatting, he fixed me with one of his looks, saying this was 'a social event, all off the record for the moment. Let's just call it talks about talks.'

After I accepted these ground rules, he took me on a tour of the main rooms, including the large dining room with two fireplaces, each surmounted by a portrait of a Taoiseach at the dispatch box in the Dáil – the one of Seán Lemass, by Seán O'Sullivan, far superior to a rather static rendering of CJH himself, by Roderic O'Connor. He then steered me into his traditional Irish bar, designed by Sam Stephenson, and took a bottle of Montagny Premier Cru from the fridge, saying, 'I thought you'd never get here so that I could open this.'

We sat on wicker chairs, clinking glasses, before tucking into what Kenneth Williams would have called a 'cold collation' of olives, pâté from Alsace, Irish cheeses, fresh brown bread and salads of avocado, tomatoes, lettuce and scallions. He looked frailer than before, moving quite slowly. I cheered him up by telling him that my dad was still renewing his driving licence every year even though he was in his late eighties. He talked about how wonderful Inishvickillane had been during the month of August, with the best weather in thirty years and the Atlantic 'like the Mediterranean'. I said I'd never been to the Blaskets, but told him a story about having spent a weekend on nearby Skellig Michael. Sometimes, I felt like pinching myself to make sure I was really lunching with CJH at his home. It was surreal.

Inevitably, we talked about the *Irish Times*. I told him Mary Holland was ill, and he was sad to hear that as he had always admired her work. Dick Walsh, a long-time foe of Haughey as the paper's political correspondent and later political editor, had died six months earlier after being laid low for years by scoliosis. I offered my view that what had sustained Walsh for so long was his hatred for the former Taoiseach, as much as the love of his family; one of Walsh's favourite phrases was a political one from his native Co. Clare: 'Vingeance, bejaysus, vingeance!' CJH merely commented that he had heard of someone who 'carried venom in his hump'. But he had 'great respect' for the *Irish Times* Paris correspondent, Lara Marlowe. 'I often watch French TV and she clarifies things in the *Irish Times* the following morning. You could describe me as a great fan of hers.'

We talked about France, and Paris in particular, and he was most impressed that I had been there more times than I could count. He loved to stay at the Ritz, on Place Vendôme, not only because it had a good restaurant but it was 'very convenient too, with Charvet just across the street', as he said without a hint of irony. The famous restaurant Tour d'Argent, on the other hand, was 'too touristy'. We also ranged globally to talk about whether the US had 'peaked' – he felt that it had. I mentioned that Donald Rumsfeld had commissioned academic research into how and why previous empires had collapsed, and CJH noted that money would count in the end. 'You have to pay the soldiers at the front,' he said. 'That's what went wrong with the Roman Empire. The Rhine froze in 410 AD and its soldiers defected to the barbarian hordes.' He gave me a book, *The Complete Roman Army*, featuring lots of illustrations of young centurions with bare thighs; I still wonder whether he felt this might particularly appeal to me.

After I suggested we should go out to sit on the west-facing terrace, seeing as it was a sunny afternoon, he bade me open a second bottle of Montagny, and I asked if I could smoke a cigarette. 'Ah, so that's why you wanted to come out!' I mentioned the smoking ban in pubs and restaurants, which I had welcomed; he felt that there were 'too many restrictions on people's liberties', with the Gardaí, Revenue and others being given 'too many powers'. His wife Maureen joined us briefly to say hello, and expressed concern that Garda security at Abbeville was to be withdrawn the following week. Years earlier, as CJH recalled, a press photographer had tried to gain access to the estate by offering a bribe of £250 to a groundsman, only to be told that 'he could fuck off with himself'.

The Haugheys had sold Abbeville, its Gandon-designed stables and 247 acres of land to Manor Park Homes for €35 million two years earlier. 'It's too big for just the two of us,' CJH said, adding that they had an agreement with the developers that would allow him and Maureen to stay living there. He felt that Manor Park Homes were 'good people who won't mess it up' although he had no idea what they might use the house for. He himself had planted all the trees to the west of the mansion, and many others elsewhere, and said he was 'sure they'll survive', whatever happened to the estate. The view towards the lake 'won't change, I'm convinced of that', he added. All the time we were chatting outside, polishing off that second bottle of Montagny, planes were flying quite low just to the south on their final approach to Dublin Airport, and I remarked that I could always pick out Abbeville from the right-hand side of a plane whenever I was coming in to land. CJH knew a lot about helicopters because he had been on them so often travelling to and from Inishvickillane: 'Two hours from the back lawn here, or an hour and a half with the wind behind you.'

I told him I was once in a helicopter piloted by his son Ciarán, flying over the Wicklow Mountains to get a bird's-eye view of raging forest fires being doused from the air.

Our conversation was all very relaxed. But when I pressed him to do a formal interview, he appeared reluctant, saying that he got nothing but criticism 'every time I raise my head above the parapet'. He did not rule it out, however, and got his Garda driver to take me back into town, with me sitting in the front seat of the Mercedes Benz, as Haughey himself always did. His Christmas card that year, showing dolphins off the Blaskets, had a nearly indecipherable handwritten message from him: 'Man marks the earth with ruin – his control stops with the shore.' How true, I thought, especially about Ireland.

I had sent him a letter of thanks for the lunch rather belatedly, explaining that I'd been to Helsinki, Cork, Derry, Dundalk, Tangier and Carrick-on-Shannon in the intervening five weeks as well as completing the RTÉ radio series on transport in between working for the *Irish Times*. 'It should be my turn to entertain you to lunch and, if that were possible, you would be most welcome to come to my home in Temple Bar . . . But I have to warn you that there are three flights of stairs to the front door – and no lift!' I also mentioned the possibility of inviting CJH's old friend Arthur Gibney, who designed his Christmas cards every year, to join us, as I knew Arthur well and had great respect for him.

For one reason or another, that didn't happen. But I was invited back to Kinsealy for a second lunch in November 2004, having just returned from my first visit to Bucharest. I told him all about the vast palace Nicolae Ceauşescu had built and the Boulevard of Socialist Victory that stretched out for nearly three kilometres in front of it, noting that all this had required the demolition of an Olympic stadium, two monasteries, thirty churches and seven thousand homes.

He fixed me with one of those baleful looks and said, 'Mmmm, it must be great to be a dictator.'

I laughed out loud, exclaiming, 'Well, you'd know something about that!' at which point he laughed too. Sure wasn't it well known that most of his ministers were scared to death of him, and he himself had once memorably described them as 'only a crowd of gobshites'. I also reminded him of the opening of a Garda station on O'Connell Street, which he had agreed to perform on his way to Government Buildings at nine o'clock one morning. As he was leaving in the chauffeur-driven Merc, City Manager Frank Feely rushed out to tell him that there was a reception in the Gresham Hotel. Feely then got 'the look' as the Taoiseach asked him, with some emphasis, 'Have you no *job* to go to?'

There was a framed plaque on the window ledge of his Irish bar in Abbeville, inscribed with the mock Latin dictum, *Non illegitimis carborundum* (Don't let the bastards grind you down). One suspects that this was CJH's own motto. At one stage, when I again mentioned doing a proper interview, he changed his tune from the previous occasion. This time, he said – almost menacingly – 'Yeah . . . I know a lot of things.'

We didn't see each other again until January 2006, after I had sent him a copy of *Chaos at the Crossroads* with a letter saying that if he was still receiving guests, I'd be delighted to drop out to visit him. A phone call and another invitation followed soon after. 'Come out on Friday at 4.30 – that'd be a respectable hour to start drinking,' he said. When I arrived, the front door was opened by someone else and CJH emerged from his study, walking cane in his right hand, the book I had sent him in his left. We shook hands and I asked him how he was. 'Only middling,' he said. I told him that his picture was on a billboard at Portmarnock Station, in an advertisement for a DVD of the RTÉ television series about him, broadcast the previous summer. Much to my surprise, he said he hadn't watched it. I didn't believe him.

CJH was shuffling very slowly as we made our way to the bar, where he sat down in one of the wicker chairs and got me to open another bottle of Montagny. He congratulated me on the book, and said he particularly liked the title, because he saw what James Nix and I were on about. On his helicopter trips to Inishvickillane, 'you'd see forty or fifty houses stuck in fields on the outskirts of a village or town, with no relationship to the place'. He thought this was 'terrible'. But he also believed there was 'a lot of Dublin 4 intellectual snobbery' in criticizing the designs of these houses. 'There are too many pseudo-environmentalists who wouldn't know anything about the real thing,' he said.

Even though he was seriously ill with prostate cancer by this stage, his mind was good. He spent part of every day replying to letters, often from pensioners who had just qualified for free travel, which he described as the best thing he ever did, because it had 'revolutionized' the lives of older people. When I told him that the long-awaited book about Scott Tallon Walker was coming out, he recalled Ronnie Tallon complaining to him in 1980 that 'the fellows in the OPW' wanted to take down the papal cross that he had designed for Pope John Paul II's Mass in the Phoenix Park. He assured Tallon that there was no way this would happen and, of course, it didn't – because CJH simply got on to the OPW and vetoed the proposal. But he stressed that he 'never tried to influence a planning decision', having learned an 'important lesson' early in his political career, after he was first elected to the Dáil in 1957. There was a proposal to build a scout den in Donnycarney, and he wrote a letter of support. It turned out, however, that local residents were opposed to it, so his endorsement backfired. 'I thought everyone would be in favour of having a scout den, but there you are,' he said ruefully.

We talked about Dermot Desmond, who had sold him the idea of the IFSC, and how well he looked in a photograph in the *Irish Times* sitting in a winged armchair in his newly renovated Georgian house in Merrion Square. 'Very dignified,' CJH said. He had a lot of time for Desmond, remarking that Seán Lemass had once told him that he should surround himself with 'fellows who get things done'. Haughey said the IFSC was a 'great success' and had made a major contribution to the Exchequer. But Desmond never forgave me for persuading him to sit for that photograph in the winged chair, or for the article I wrote on the Merrion Square house; indeed, he made that clear to me in no uncertain terms during a brief and quite unpleasant encounter one night in Town Bar & Grill. Ironically, it was while cycling past that uber-chic 'Celtic Tiger' restaurant some six months earlier that I had to pull in to take a call from Desmond on my mobile phone. He told me he was getting a lot of grief from Dublin City Council's planners for carrying out 'unauthorized alterations' to the interior of the Merrion Square house, notably the installation of a dumb waiter serving all floors, and he wanted me to see for myself that it had all been done in the best possible taste. It was, but not in a style that I liked; the rug in the library, for example, was a tiger's pelt, complete with snarling head. I also took the view that some of the principal rooms had been materially changed by his alterations, and wrote that in the *Irish Times*. But Desmond, never a man to be bested by bureaucracy, challenged the council's planning enforcement notice and won a resounding victory in the High Court, allowing him to retain it all.

The most significant thing CJH told me at what turned out to be our last meeting was that he was 'shocked' by a new opinion poll showing that support for the FF–PD coalition government had gone up, because in his view, 'It's the worst government in the history of the State – the worst.'

Why?

'Because they can't seem to get anything right,' he said.

When I suggested that although Bertie Ahern might be good at fixing things and had more resources at his disposal than any of his predecessors, he had no real vision of the future of Ireland, CJH agreed: 'But the public don't seem to care, as long as they have money.'

As he and Maureen got older, he said, it helped that they had their children and grandchildren around them. (Each of them had their own detached house along Baskin Lane, on the southern fringe of Abbeville.) 'Even though they all have their own pursuits and aren't around all the time, it's a tradition that we all gather on the island every August.' Old friends were also very important to him and, in that context, he mentioned Arthur Gibney. Like himself, Arthur had not been well, but CJH said he'd invite the two of us to lunch next time.

'Thanks for coming out – we'll do it again,' he said. With that, the former Taoiseach slumped into the sofa in front of a plasma TV screen to watch the six o'clock news, and waved his left hand limply, leaving it to Maureen to show me out.

The lunch with Charlie Haughey and Arthur Gibney never happened because the two of them died within weeks of each other. Haughey's Tricolour-draped coffin was borne from the big barn church of Donnycarney by members of the Defence Forces and then taken by hearse in a solemn procession to St Fintan's Cemetery in Sutton, overlooking Dublin Bay. At the graveside, after three volleys were fired by Naval Service personnel, Bertie Ahern delivered a remarkable eulogy, in which he addressed CJH as 'Boss' and described him as a political leader of 'peerless acumen and commanding talent . . . a patriot to his fingertips'. Given all we now knew about Haughey and how he had greedily corrupted the highest office in the land, this was totally over the top, even for a funeral oration. So one can only imagine Ahern's reaction when he opened the *Irish Times* the following day to read my piece, which began with this bald statement, 'Charlie Haughey believed that the present Fianna Fáil–Progressive Democrats Coalition is "the worst Government in the history of the State – the worst", because "they can't seem to get anything right" and had no real vision of the future of Ireland.' CJH was biting Bertie back from the grave.

On RTÉ's *The Week in Politics*, future Fianna Fáil leader Micheál Martin said he didn't believe that Haughey had ever uttered such words. Ah, but he did, Micheál, he really did; I was not making it up. Vincent Browne, another long-time critic of *El Diablo*, had also been lunching in Kinsealy, and wrote a lurid account of their meetings for *Village* magazine. The most memorable bit was Browne's recollection of his last encounter with CJH, when the former Taoiseach asked him to 'give me a hug' as he left Abbeville, and his own admission that he had cried all the way down the avenue afterwards. What CJH had been doing, in effect, was making peace with some of his old enemies.

(I went back to Abbeville in May 2012, when the estate was put up for sale by Savills on behalf of debt-laden Manor Park Homes, and found it quite desolate. The photographs that used to line the main staircase were gone, as was nearly all the furniture; and Haughey's study, where he held so many confidential meetings, was bare of books. But at least I got a chance to go upstairs to see the west-facing master bedroom, which still had a king-sized bed, and a large en-suite bathroom with a sunken travertine bath as its centrepiece. A year later, the entire property was acquired by a Japanese hotel chain, Toyoko Inn, for €5.2 million – a fraction of what Manor Park Homes had paid for it in 2003.)

Life goes on. 'William Jacob McDonald was born half an hour ago in Liverpool,' a text message from my brother Liam announced in July 2006; just like that, he had become a grandfather. I read it twice or three times, thinking, on becoming a 'grand-uncle' for the first time, Jeez, I've just been catapulted into the previous generation! But I immediately accepted my lot, sending a congratulatory message to my nephew Murraigh and his partner Lyndsey 'from Grand-uncle Frank'. Fifteen months later, their second son Thomas was born, and we were all delighted by that too; it even cheered up my mother in her wheelchair.

A new addition to my circle of young friends was John Beattie, a Presbyterian from Co. Tyrone working in Dublin as a building conservation surveyor, whose dedication I admired enormously. He had become Paul Moley's best friend, despite the fact that they were on opposite sides of Northern Ireland's sectarian divide; being in Dublin was a great leveller, in that sense. It was with John that I saw *Brokeback Mountain*, the most emotional gay film ever for me. Later on, John, Paul and myself went to Paris for a weekend, and I can still remember John's awestruck reaction to his first sight of the sun streaming in through the soaring stained-glass windows of the Sainte-Chapelle; it hits me every time I see it. (John was laid off by Carrig Conservation when the recession hit and went back up north to train as a thatcher in the Ulster American Folk Park near Omagh; he became quite an expert at this ancient skill, but was still glad to resume his old job in Dublin once the Irish economy recovered.) I also got to know the incredibly talented Ronan Healy, a friend of Stephen O'Farrell's; he runs Catapult, Ireland's most creative event design and management company, with offices in Dublin and New York.

Eamon had been working as a chef in restaurants such as the Expresso Bar on St Mary's Road, and Bailey Court in Howth, as well as in the Arts Club, before he enrolled in the Trinity Access Programme for mature students at Pearse College in 2006. He did really well, revelling in the academic life, and got an offer from Dublin Institute of Technology to do electronic engineering in Kevin Street College, returning to a field that had grabbed his imagination when he first used a soldering iron in secondary school. Even though all his new classmates were less than half his age, he threw himself into it and got great results. As soon as he had embarked on the course, I was fantasizing about seeing him in an academic gown, stripe and mortar board on his graduation.

But it was not to be. His father, who had also worked for Telecom Éireann, was taken ill and admitted to Tallaght Hospital for a lengthy period, leaving his ailing mother at home, so the family had to organize a rota to look after her. Eamon also had a mole near the bridge of his nose, which was diagnosed as malignant and had to be surgically removed. As a result of these setbacks, he dropped out of second year in Kevin Street and never returned. I didn't want him to give up, and neither did he, so he eventually applied for admission to Trinity College as a mature student. After being interviewed there, he got a letter of acceptance to do a degree in earth sciences. But Eamon did not enjoy the Trinity course as much as he had the DIT one. His parents' health was also deteriorating and, between one thing and another, including the onset of deeply irritating tinnitus, he didn't feel up to sitting the exams either in June or September. So that was that, sadly.

I was quite stunned when the president of DIT, Professor Brian Norton, sent me a letter in August 2006 asking if I would accept an honorary DPhil. Of course I said yes, I'd be very honoured to get it; though it occurred to me that with the DIT planning to relocate its diffuse operations to a single huge campus in Grangegorman, perhaps they wanted to keep me onside. The conferring ceremony was held in St Patrick's Cathedral, and I had to dress up in a scarlet academic gown and black floppy hat for the occasion. I was delighted that all my family, including my mother, could attend; for my parents, in particular, it was overdue compensation for my churlishness in leaving UCD without bothering to wait for the graduation ceremony. As Tom Dunne, head of the DIT's School of Surveying & Construction Management, read out a long citation of my activities as a journalist and author, I had the out-of-body experience of being at my own funeral, especially because of the ecclesiastical setting. But we put an end to such morbid thoughts by throwing a big party in the flat, and I made it clear to everyone that there was no way I would be following the example of Michael Smurfit or Tony Ryan by calling myself 'Dr'. I was also delighted to attend Paul Moley's graduation from Trinity College and lunch afterwards with his family at Fallon & Byrne's, where his father warmly thanked me (and Eamon) for looking after him during his student years. 'Thank you for being my friend since my very first year in Dublin . . .' Paul said in a text message later.

In Paris the following February, the dazzling lights of the Tour Eiffel were turned off for an hour to mark publication by the UN's Intergovernmental Panel on Climate Change of its latest scientific assessment of global warming. It made grim reading, spelling out the risks for humanity and the planet we inhabit with much greater certainty. I consoled myself by taking Maeve Jennings, my old friend from Temple Bar Properties who's a dead ringer for Jackie Kennedy, to lunch in Brasserie Georges, on top of the Centre Pompidou, and she then took me to dinner at the chic Baccarat Cristal Room, festooned with chandeliers, in the suffocatingly *riche* 16th arrondissement. We got to talking about the property boom at home and the relentless increase in house prices – which was happening mainly because the FF–PD government had failed to implement key measures proposed by Dr Peter Bacon in his three reports on this phenomenon from the late 1990s. And Morgan Kelly, professor of economics at UCD, had already issued his verdict that the property market was heading for a crash, in an *Irish Times* opinion column, published in late December 2006, that debunked fanciful notions that there would be a 'soft landing'. Maeve got a sheet of paper from one of the waiters, and we worked out that residential prices in Dublin, per square metre, were now higher than they were in Paris. Not surprisingly, this glaring anomaly was totally unsustainable – for how could values at the periphery be higher than they were at the centre? After all the haute cuisine, we needed a nightcap and headed for the Hotel George V, now part of the Four Seasons group, where we drank Bas-Armagnac until 3 a.m.

The madness of what was happening in the Dublin property market came home to me when I went to see a stunning contemporary house in Dalkey with the architect Tom dePaor, who had designed it for a professional couple and their two young children. The couple had decided to put it on the market after living there for barely twelve months because they were dazzled by the prospect of making a killing; the 'guide price' was a staggering €6 million. God help the purchasers, I thought, if Morgan Kelly was right. Which he was, with knobs on.

Through the good offices of Roddy Guiney, head of Ogilvy-WHPR, I managed to get four tickets at face value for the historic Ireland v England Six Nations rugby match at Croke Park in February 2007. I brought Liam and his two younger sons, Jamie and Arran, who had come over from Somerset to cheer for Ireland. On our way to Croker, we had to go through a Garda security cordon at the junction of Jones's Road and North Circular Road, where there was an elderly man with a wizened face holding up an A4 sheet with the hand-scrawled message, 'Rugby and soccer out of Croke Park.'

As we passed him, I said, 'Ah, go on,' to which he responded by spitting out, 'Remember Bloody Sunday!'

I said, 'Let's just get over it.'

And that's what we all did, that day. As we took our seats in the Hogan Stand, the Garda and Army No. 1 bands emerged from the corner of the Canal End, marching diagonally across the pitch to take up their position. Everyone knew they had come to play 'God Save the Queen' as well as our own national anthem and 'Ireland's Call'. And there was President Mary McAleese, who never once let us down, walking out onto the red carpet to greet the teams. The atmosphere in the stadium was electric and at the same time apprehensive, because nobody among the 80,000-plus crowd knew what might happen; I feared that republican dissidents would throw smoke bombs onto the pitch or cause some other commotion. But nothing happened, not even a vocal protest, as the England fans sang their national anthem with gusto and the rest of us remained respectfully silent until we could sing our own with even greater fervour. Then we went on to hammer England by 43 to 13. The stadium itself was also a triumph, turning out just as architect Des McMahon had imagined when he designed it in the 1990s for a more forward-looking GAA.

With this famous victory under our belt, I felt quite chuffed about going to London for the installation of former Trinity chaplain

Alan McCormack as Priest-in-Charge of St Botolph-without-Bishopsgate. This early eighteenth-century church, with its beautiful steeple and neoclassical portico, was one of the casualties of an IRA truck-bombing of the financial district in 1993, which blew out its stained-glass windows. But because it was supported by two of the ancient (and often very rich) 'worshipful companies' of the City of London, all the damage had since been made good. I brought Thinus Calitz to the ceremony, and we sat in the front row of the gallery above more men in frocks than either of us had ever seen, with the formidably tall and burly Bishop of London, the Most Reverend Richard Chartres, presiding over it all. Not only were there clergy in full canonicals, but also members of the two worshipful companies that sponsor the church, all kitted out in their rival regalia.

With his booming voice, the Bishop began the proceedings by saying, 'It's most unusual on these occasions to start with a letter from the Prime Minister – in this case, the Prime Minister of Ireland.' There was a ripple of laughter through the congregation, but not in a disrespectful way. I think they were all just pleasantly surprised. The letter began, 'Dear Alan,' and the Bishop recited its contents, which were along the lines of how Alan had been such a great chaplain in Trinity that he was bound to do very well in London too. 'And it's signed, "Bertie, Taoiseach",' the Bishop told us all. Everyone must have thought how unusual it would be to get such a letter from their own Prime Minister, who always seems so remote, so 'up there', as to be unapproachable. What they didn't appreciate was that, Ireland being such a small society, their new Priest-in-Charge could simply rustle it up. Which, indeed, is what he had done.

Afterwards, at a reception in the Great Eastern Hotel, Alan introduced us to the Master of the Worshipful Company of Bowyers, and I asked him what exactly they did.

'We made the bows and arrows for Agincourt!' he said, almost shocked that I didn't know about their key role in the Hundred Years War.

'And are you still making bows and arrows?' I asked.

'Not at all. I'm a solicitor in the City.'

A large number of guests were then invited to a buffet supper at Alan's home, beside St Vedast's Church, very close to St Paul's Cathedral, of which he was also Rector. The house, built by one of his 1960s predecessors, who doubled as ballet correspondent of the *The Times*, was designed for entertainment, with a long reception room overlooking a medieval courtyard from three French windows, all with wrought-iron balconies.

Many of the guests were gay, and both Thinus and I were invited to an after-party at Westminster Abbey – not in the 'Royal Peculiar' abbey itself, but in an early eighteenth-century house in the grounds, accessed through a discreet gate on the right-hand side of its west front. It was one of those louche gatherings of gay clerics, some of them quite elderly and others much younger, draping themselves on big old sofas and drinking champagne or port, or whatever. But there was a limit to how much conviviality I could take, so I made my excuses and left at around 2 a.m., walking through the musty stone-vaulted cloisters that I imagined would have been known to Archbishop Thomas Becket and King Henry II, his nemesis.

In May 2007, Fianna Fáil was re-elected for a third time in ten years.

'What a disastrous day!' Tara campaigner Muireann Ní Bhrolcháin texted as soon as the tallymen had done their sums.

'Yeah, just confirms my worst fears that we're a selfish people,' I replied. My belief was that the electorate had voted as they did because they feared that the boom would come to an end if they didn't. The only crumb of consolation was that the Green Party would be in government for the first time, although it was an open question whether it would have any influence in the development of public policy. James Nix had stood as a Green candidate in Limerick West, racking up a more impressive performance than most of his party colleagues in other rural constituencies, although he still lost his deposit. I was in Cork as the results were coming

With solicitor Nick Robinson and the Reverend Professor F. X. Martin, who led the public campaign against the construction of the Civic Offices on Dublin's Wood Quay, on the tenth anniversary of the campaign in 1989.

On Hardwicke Street, in front of St George's Church, in 1989. My dear friend Caroline Walsh gave me a framed copy of this picture by Paddy Whelan for my sixtieth birthday with this caption: *'Friend of My Youth. Happy 60th Birthday Frank from Caroline. This is you when you were 39 on the beat in Dublin. How come you have only got more handsome in the intervening years? La jeunesse may be behind us now – but we have la sagesse instead. Lots of love from myself and James.'* Caroline, the *Irish Times*'s literary editor, died tragically in December 2011.

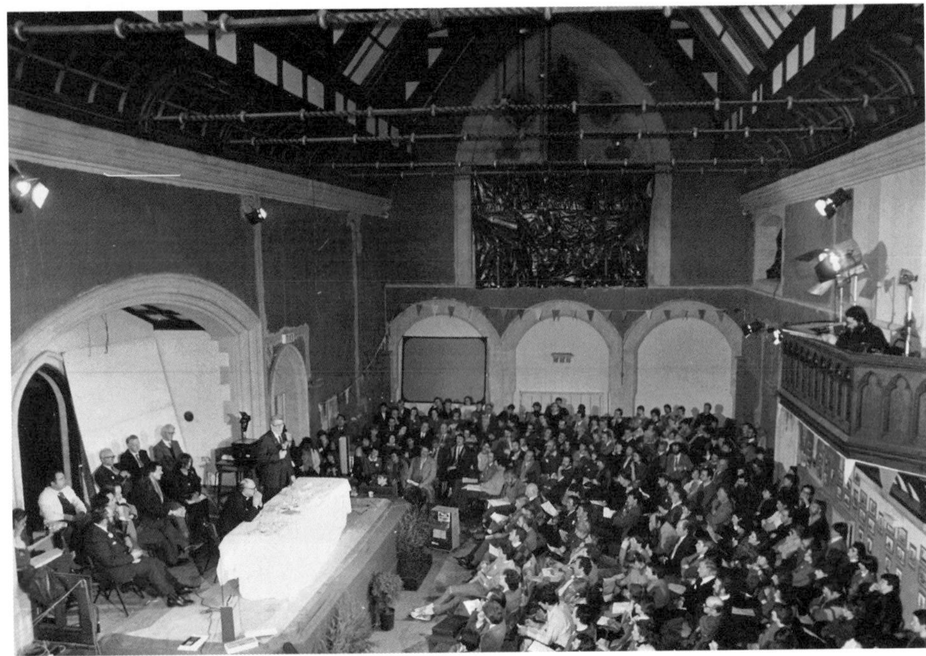

Taoiseach Garret Fitzgerald addresses the Dublin Crisis Conference at the Synod Hall, Christ Church Place, in February 1986. After the publication of *The Destruction of Dublin* inevitably I became an activist.

Left: With architect Sam Stephenson, outside the Central Bank in Dame Street – which he had designed – in 1989.

Below: In full flight, making the opening speech at the Dublin Crisis Conference.

Interviewing Taoiseach Charlie Haughey in 1982 about Dublin Corporation's plan to turn Patrick Street, New Street and Lower Clanbrassil Street into a dual carriageway. In his final years I had a number of lunches with CJH in his Gandon-designed mansion, Abbeville.

At the wreath-laying ceremony at the War Memorial Park in Islandbridge, during Queen Elizabeth's historic visit to Ireland, I took this cheeky picture of her with President Mary McAleese (though we had been instructed that there was to be 'no personal photography').

My long-time friend Annie McCartney at the 1993 Neil Young concert in Slane.

Friend Stephen O'Farrell on his thirtieth birthday in Craft restaurant, New York City, in May 2012.

John Beattie from Tyrone and Paul Moley from south Armagh – the best of friends though coming from different traditions.

Javier Saez and Grania Willis in Ibiza at Richard Barrett's 'Feck the Recession' party in 2009.

Partners Denis Ryan and Diego Gautama in Bucharest, shortly after they first met in 2015.

McDonald on how cycle tracks will surely abound in Utopia

I moustache you a question, but I'm shaving it for later

'I became a journalist because I didn't want to rely on newspapers for info'

THE IRISH TIMES

A Special Edition

Frank by name... Frank by nature... Frankly my dear...

Replacement of hanging baskets with hanging developers high on priority list

The politics of the volatile Dublin region is set to face a major earthquake with the news that scourge of developers Frank McDonald is to contest the first election for a directly elected mayor.

Following his retirement from active – well, semi-active – journalism, Mr McDonald is preparing to launch a new party to campaign for his election as mayor.

"The author of *The Destruction of Dublin* will become the saviour of Dublin," campaign manager Ian Lumley said.

The news was welcomed by veteran political strategist Frank Dunlop who promised him a 22nd preference vote – "No better man. Iconic ... well, since Liam Lawlor anyway."

Mr McDonald, who is currently in Lima, has, most unusually, refused to comment, but it is understood that the party, yet to be named officially, is temporarily being known as *Dublin Rerouted*.

Under consideration for its main campaign slogan is are, *No more hot air ... Vote McDonald*.

The new party's Secretary General-elect James Nix has drawn up a manifesto including many of the lifelong policies of Mr McDonald whose input has been limited by his existing commitments to cover the Venice Biennale, attend a rainforest conference near Cairns and chair a session of a beach life seminar in Rio de Janeiro.

He has, however, committed to being in Dublin on a regular basis if he is elected.

Among the demands in the manifesto are: the replacement of hanging baskets with hanging developers and climate change deniers; passport controls on Temple Bar, Dublin's "designated party zone", to exclude stag parties; a restoration of the Kingstown tram; the conversion of city centre roads to cycleways; a ban on cars within two miles of the Spire; recognition of the state of Palestine; and the reopening of Jammet's.

Mr McDonald, who last night was believed to be en route from Taiwan to San Francisco for a conference on the impact of climate change on vineyards in the Napa Valley, is also determined to make human rights central to his mayoralty.

Delivering an after-dinner speech in Noma in Copenhagen last month, he quoted Danish urbanist Jan Gehl on the tyranny of car-mad planners running Dublin.

"They have allowed traffic planners to exert undue influence, with silly ideas like every time a pedestrian approaches a crossing, they have to 'apply' to cross the street when it should be a human right."

Stepping off in Bonn the following day, Mr McDonald denied he might face hostility from voters in Dun Laoghaire over his "brave" support for the new library and said every borough should have one.

"Anyway I'm appointing Eoin Keegan as my deputy – Dun Laoghaire voters can Geraldine Kennedy off."

Mr McDonald is expected to launch his campaign with a personal appearance – connecting flights permitting, and lunch being over in time – at a crowded event in Merrion Square on Friday, January 30th.

He has denied that several large brown envelopes will be distributed to allow the attendance to contribute to his campaign and old age comforts.

"This is a digital age", he said enigmatically.

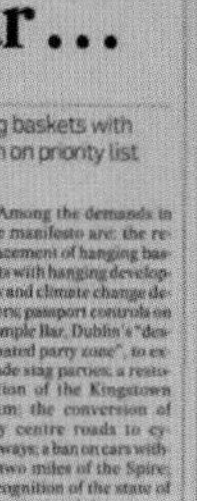

Frank McDonald is preparing to launch a new party to campaign for his election as mayor.

Journalist who was one of a kind – thankfully

A leading international media training institute is to send a team to Dublin to study the "out of sight" journalism methods pioneered in Ireland by Frank McDonald.

Journalists in more than 500 media companies in nearly 100 countries have indicated an interest in learning more about McDonald's modus operandi in order to convince their employers to introduce it for them.

"If what I have heard is true, his approach to the practice of journalism is really quite remarkable and I doubt if any other journalist anywhere in the world has pulled it off the way he did for the last 20 years," said one Washington reporter.

McDonald lived closer to the offices of The Irish Times than any other member of the editorial staff, but visited the premises less often than the paper's Beijing Correspondent.

He only failed to eliminate visits altogether owing to the company's failure to put in place more efficient arrangements for dealing with administrative matters relating to expenses, days off, holidays and foreign travel.

Frank and friends take a break from clearing out his desk at The Irish Times offices. They initially went to the D'Olier Street offices before being told the newspaper was now twice as far away from Frank's house.

As a young man, he followed a similar career path to many other journalists – he came to work in the office on the days he was rostered and remained most days until the end of his shift.

On many days, he wrote several stories, even taking on some tasks demanded by the news desk.

"Entirely unremarkable – just another hard-working, award-winning reporter who knocked out copy that hardly needed a word changed and wrote with passion and authority. Just like most people in The Irish Times newsroom then and now," recalls one veteran editor.

But McDonald, more than any other reporter, was determined to overcome the structural weaknesses of the employment regime laid down by house agreements, the Editor's office, the News Desk, the HR department and various "nervous Nellies" in positions of authority.

His phone rang far too often for one man – even one who wrote so informatively on world affairs – to bear. "It would keep ringing, so much so that I'd eventually give in and answer it. And then there would nearly always be someone on the other end who wanted to talk. It was an unsustainable situation," he said at the time.

Back then in the 20th century, letters used to arrive in newspaper offices. Opening the ones addressed to him was a burden almost on the same scale as answering the wretched telephone.

So he declared, a long time ago, that everything must change utterly. He would do what he wanted, when he wanted, where he wanted (at home or abroad), how he wanted – if he wanted to do it at all.

It was a simple and triumphant formula – which journalists the world over wish to understand more fully so as to embrace it themselves.

Weather

It'll get steadily warmer and warmer until it's far too late to do anything about it. And then, well, it'll be all your fault for not listening to me, won't it?

THE IRISH TIMES

Home News

With Frank's departure, The Irish Times will never be the same again. A source in the newspaper said Mr McDonald was an expert at separating the wheat from the chaff. "Without fail, he only submitted the chaff to be printed."

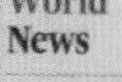

World News

Benjamin Netanyahu has said Frank brought new meaning to the saying, 'if you don't read the newspaper, you are uninformed – if you do read the newspaper, you are misinformed'. The IDF said they'll miss Frank, but then there's nothing new in that.

Gardaí have arrested Frank McDonald for stealing from hundreds of construction sites in Temple Bar.

A friend said they didn't want to believe it, but when they went to see him at his home all the signs were there.

Books & stuff

Dublin City Council has released a long statement congratulating Frank on his retirement and thanking him for all the kind words he wrote about the council down the years. It also said it believes Mr McDonald has another book in him and that that's "an excellent place for it".

Business + Unrelated

In his retirement, Frank is expected to finally look at the real environmental issues facing people today, such as:
- Why is the shortest distance between two points always under construction?
- What do you call a building after its built?
- and why is marble taken for granite?

Plus + Finally

The very best of luck Frank in your retirement from everyone at The Irish Times!

Home: 1-8 Environment: 9-15 World: 16 Arts&Ideas: 17 Opinion: Yes Letters: Many Crosswords 18

A retirement present from the *Irish Times*, the traditional mock front page.

A Christmas family gathering in the Botanic Gardens in 2006. *Front*: nephew Murraigh and his baby son, William; Liam; Edel; Mam; nephew Seánie. *Back*: niece Jane; Murraigh's wife, Lindsay; niece Kate; nephew Arran; Edel's husband, Paul Maher; Denis; myself; Dad; niece Nessa; Liam's first wife, Maura; and nephew (and godson) Jamie. Jamie and Arran are Liam's sons with his second wife, Karen Stoner.

In robes for my conferral with an honorary DPhil from the Dublin Institute of Technology, being interviewed by my *Irish Times* colleague Olivia Kelly.

My godson Alex, then nearly fourteen, son of my great friends Mark Brennock and Yetti Redmond, at the marriage equality vote count and celebration at Dublin Castle in May 2015.

On the Dublin Bus wedding bus on the way to our wedding reception at the National Botanic Gardens on 3 June 2016 – complete with plastic flowers!

The McDonalds in birth order – me, Liam, Edel and Denis – at the wedding reception.

Eamon and me in the National Botanic Gardens on our wedding day, photographed by architect John Meagher in front of the Teak House.

through, speaking at a National Sculpture Factory symposium, *desIRE*, which focused on designing new homes for contemporary Ireland, along with Shane O'Toole and others.

In the course of a spirited discussion, I complained that not one of the lucrative property-based tax incentives introduced since 1986 was conditional on quality being delivered. Responding to criticism from architect Alan Mee that we were being too negative, I said, 'We have all, to some extent, retreated into ourselves. We are actually well on the road to the realization of the Thatcherite vision of there being no such thing as society.' And while I acknowledged that such a message was bleak and depressing, the transcript records me as adding, 'That's what I think, and I'm entitled to feckin' say it!'

In mid-2007, Geraldine Kennedy became fascinated by how the property developers were getting along, so she commissioned Kathy Sheridan and me to do a major series on the big players, such as Liam Carroll, Seán Mulryan, Bernard McNamara, the Cosgrave brothers, Seán Dunne and Treasury Holdings. I made contact with Richard Barrett, who was taking a break in Sicily in the midst of an international tour to raise several hundred million euro for Treasury's investment vehicles, so I flew out to meet him in Palermo. During long conversations over lunch or dinner in various restaurants, he told me what Treasury was doing, what others were at and gave me some useful insights into the overall state of play.

Seán Dunne was about to lodge a planning application for the Ballsbridge hotel sites he had bought for up to €60 million *per acre*, and I was offered an 'exclusive' briefing at his Merrion Square headquarters by architect Ulrik Raysse, a partner in Copenhagen-based Henning Larsen Architects. Also dancing in attendance on the 'Baron of Ballsbridge' that day was then Gate Theatre director Michael Colgan, who had been retained as cultural adviser on the project; according to him, Ballsbridge was a 'cultural desert' that needed to be livened up with 'a bit of burlesque'. The standout element of Dunne's scheme was a thirty-seven-storey 'diamond-cut' glazed tower, aligned on the axis of Pembroke Road, and this was to be flanked by a dense concentration of buildings ranging in height from ten to eighteen storeys. I was aghast at the arrogance of such a monumental scheme in a very sensitive part of Dublin, but restrained myself from expressing this opinion. (Incredibly, I discovered that then City Architect Jim Barrett, who I knew well, had suggested the addition of five floors to the originally planned thirty-two-storey tower, in the interest of improving its 'slenderness ratio'.) Dunne himself wasn't at the presentation, but popped in right afterwards.

'So . . . what do you think?' he asked, in a superficially charming but menacing manner.

'Well, let's put it this way,' I said. 'It's very challenging.'

In fact, I didn't think it would fly at all. Even though senior city planner Kieran Rose gave the overall scheme an enthusiastic endorsement in his report, permission was eventually refused on height and density grounds by An Bord Pleanála, then chaired by the conscientious John O'Connor. Dunne later went bankrupt both in the US and Ireland.

An Bord Pleanála could still be swayed by big-name 'starchitects', such as Norman (Lord) Foster, although I was dubious about his audacious plan to redevelop the Clarence Hotel, right from the start. The Clarence and adjoining buildings – all protected structures – were to be demolished, apart from their front façades, and the whole lot raised to a uniform height of eight storeys, with a 'skycatcher' atrium topped by a flying-saucer-type bar and restaurant on the roof; my friend Richard Conway likened it to Tolkien's Eye of Sauron. I stood on Ormond Quay, diagonally opposite the Clarence, imagining its visual impact on the riverscape, and didn't like what I saw in my mind's eye.

The scheme was being driven by Paddy McKillen and Derek Quinlan in partnership with U2's Bono and the Edge, as co-owners of the five-star hotel. Bono himself phoned one day in an effort to convert me, saying that what the Foster scheme needed was a 'champion'. I agreed to meet him and the Edge for lunch in the Clarence to talk about it all, but was laid low by a chest infection and couldn't make it on the day, so I left a message to say so. Imagine my surprise when a waiter in a long black apron turned up at my door carrying a flask of hot whiskey on a silver salver, with a card saying, 'Get well soon, Frank. Bono & The Edge.' I appreciated the gesture, but didn't change my view.

Shane O'Toole came to the rescue, with some reservations, in the *Sunday Times*. He had gone to London to interview Norman Foster, who flew in from tax exile in Geneva to meet him at the offices of Foster & Partners and talk about the scheme, which the starchitect himself described as 'a boutique hotel that expresses itself on the skyline'. McKillen's spokeswoman Breda Keena invited me to stay at the Connaught Hotel in Mayfair, where McKillen was spending £70 million on a restoration and a new bedroom block. A standard room would be fine, I made clear in advance, but when I checked in they gave me a suite with a bottle of champagne on ice in the living room and a huge bed that must have been seven feet wide in the equally large bedroom, with a lavish marble bathroom in between. Thinus called in for a few glasses of champagne and we went to the swish Wolseley restaurant on Piccadilly, where Joan Collins and three friends were at the table next to us.

McKillen reckoned (rightly) that I would be impressed with the restoration work on the Connaught, and (wrongly) that I would see it as a harbinger of what he and the U2 lads would do with the Clarence. Unlike the Connaught, which is also a protected structure, the Clarence was to be junked, in effect. Yet the scheme was approved by An Bord Pleanála despite a strong recommendation from Kevin Moore, the senior planning inspector who dealt with the case, to reject what he described as a 'conceptually brilliant but contextually illiterate' design. But by the time planning permission was granted, in July 2008, it was too late; the property bubble had burst and the redevelopment plan no longer made sense.

Penguin Ireland had commissioned Kathy Sheridan and me to write a book on the strength of our series of articles on the big developers, and Ballina-born Professor John Naughton had offered me a Press Fellowship at Wolfson College in Cambridge for a full term, with the choice of going there either in January or in April. I rang Geraldine Kennedy to tell her the good news, and she said it was a great honour for me and for the *Irish Times*, adding, 'I suppose I'll have to let you go.' Since my old friend Paul Brown of the *Guardian* was already there as a Wolfson Press Fellow, I decided to go for the Lent term and simply headed off, without any further communication with G. K. I had accumulated enough time off to cover it, so it was no skin off her nose whether I went earlier rather than later, or so I thought. And I wanted to get stuck in to the book, using Cambridge as my bolthole, while Kathy took sabbatical leave to work on it at her home near Sallins, Co. Kildare, with the two of us communicating by email, phone calls and the occasional meeting until we had broken the back of what became *The Builders*.

Our most memorable meeting was with Seán Mulryan, the mega-developer from Co. Roscommon, who had made a big splash in London's Docklands, earning a well-deserved reputation for delivering quality schemes. A chauffeur-driven car picked us up from King's Cross, but we'd have been a lot quicker taking the Tube to Ballymore's HQ near Canary Wharf. Mulryan was appalled to discover that Kathy had booked in to a nearby Holiday Inn and insisted that she switch to a much smarter hotel in the area, built by Ballymore – at no charge, naturally.

After doing a tour of some of Ballymore Properties' schemes, we went out on the town with Mulryan and David Brophy, who had recently joined Ballymore as chief operating officer from Smurfit-Kappa. The venue was Harry's Bar, an expensive salmon-pink restaurant in Mayfair, where 'Mr Mulryan' was greeted deferentially by the Filipina maîtresse d'. At another table, future BHS 'undertaker' Philip Green was having a tête-à-tête with Stuart Rose, then head of Marks & Spencer; it's that kind of place. Kathy sent me a text message the following morning: 'Just woke up in my SUITE the size of the Ritz with a pounding headache from wine that probably cost the price of a decent mortgage, hallucinating about a big developer who longs to be Castro and save the planet. Can't remember when last so upended. May have to lie down in darkened room for week or so . . .'

It turned out that Geraldine Kennedy was livid about me going to Cambridge when I did, judging from a curt email I got from her several weeks later, saying she 'heard from the news desk that you had just taken off without my authorisation. Do I take it that you are now finished with Cambridge and back to work?'

I explained that I had had no option because both Kathy and myself had been under pressure to produce a first draft of our book by 15 April and it was all on my own time because I had accumulated so much leave; but I did apologize for 'not having the courtesy' of letting her know in advance.

She followed this up with a formal 'human resources'-style letter saying, 'I find your conduct in relation to this matter unacceptable and an abuse of the goodwill shown to you,' and finishing up with a warning that, if I failed to follow the correct procedures, 'any such absence will be viewed as unauthorised, which will lead to disciplinary action'. When I wrote a feature for the education pages on Cambridge University and how it was planning to commemorate its eighth centenary, any reference to the fact that I was there as a Wolfson Press Fellow was unaccountably omitted.

Caroline Walsh, who was now the paper's literary editor, had commissioned Morgan Kelly to do a review of *The Builders*, and it was all ready to go when GK ordered her to pull it on the basis that the paper – having published an extract from the book – had 'given it enough publicity'. Caroline was devastated, as Kelly's review was leading one of her book pages; it was 'the lowest moment I ever had in *Irish Times*', she told me. Kathy and I were disappointed, naturally, but carried on regardless, appearing together on *The Late Late Show* with Pat Kenny. *The Builders* sold like hot cakes. The fact that Lehman Brothers had collapsed the previous month, and our book told the story from boom to bust, gave it a zeitgeist quality that pushed it right up the bestseller lists in the run-up to Christmas. 'Eat your heart out, Cruella!' I texted Stephen O'Farrell.

In fairness, Geraldine was having a tough time. Despite her enormous pay package, she found herself waging a constant battle, ably assisted by deputy editor Paul O'Neill, to prevent Donovan from diluting the traditional primacy of editorial, without which there would be no 'product' at all. Given the rapidly changing media landscape, Donovan not unreasonably sought to transform the *Irish Times* into a multimedia organization, in which the paper would be a core element. After all, the *Guardian* had already done that, so why not the *Irish Times*? Thus, the entire proceeds of the sale in January 2007 of the buildings on D'Olier Street and Fleet Street – nearly €30 million – were ploughed into the purchase of property website myhome.ie, which cost the company €40 million up front. The consortium of estate agents that owned it (Sherry FitzGerald, the Gunne Group and Douglas Newman Good) must have laughed all the way to the bank. I thought it was madness, as the website's revenue stream was based on property transactions; if the bubble burst, these would reduce to a trickle.

Donovan also engineered the acquisition of other 'assets', such as a 50 per cent stake in the *Gloss* magazine, plus shares in radio stations such as 4FM, the *Metro* free-sheet, the Gazette Group of local Dublin papers, and other questionable boom-time investments that led to write-downs of €26 million in 2008 alone. Her biggest play was to bid for the Leinster Leader Group of regional papers, which would have cost the *Irish Times* well over €100 million at the time – most of it to be financed by bank debt. In the end, mercifully, Irish Times Ltd was the underbidder to Thomas Crosbie Holdings; the newspaper group's value soon plummeted to a mere €25 million.

'Do you know something? I said a prayer the previous night that we wouldn't get it,' Geraldine told me several years later. And she was absolutely right: that one last fling on the merry-go-round could have sunk the *Irish Times*. No wonder the journalists who depended on it for a living called on the board and the Irish Times Trust to review the company's 'flawed investment and diversification strategy'.

I was in King's College Chapel in Cambridge when my Nokia pinged receipt of a text message from barrister Teri Dungan in Dublin, telling me she was listening to Nuala O'Faolain talking to

Marian Finucane on RTÉ radio about her impending death from metastatic cancer. Nuala had two brain tumours that had been diagnosed just six weeks earlier and was also found to have cancer in her liver and her lungs. All I could do was cycle back to my room in Wolfson to listen to a podcast of her searing interview on my laptop.

'Beauty means nothing to me any more,' she said at one point. 'I tried to read Proust again recently, but it has gone, the magic has gone. It amazed me how quickly my life turned black.' I cried as I listened to Nuala talking like that and remembered calling to her home in Ranelagh not long after her 'accidental memoir', *Are You Somebody?*, was published to great acclaim. I was raving about the book, but she was still racked by self-doubt, saying, 'I can't really write.' I said, 'That's nonsense, Nuala!' and then opened my copy of it and read aloud her lyrical evocation of winter in Oxford in the 1960s, saying I couldn't have written anything like that. I also recalled Stephen O'Farrell and myself arranging to meet her in the magnificent New York City Public Library on Fifth Avenue. 'I'll be in the four hundreds,' she said. And that's where we found her, sitting at a desk towards the back of its immensely long reading room. She had just had her front teeth crowned and was all smiles as we escorted her out, down the big stone staircase, to a little narrow café across the street, where we talked with great animation about all that was happening in our respective lives.

Listening to her talking to Marian, I remembered us walking around Berlin, on her first visit to a city I already knew well. We saw Daniel Libeskind's Jewish Museum while it was still under construction, going in without let or hindrance from anybody, down long sloping corridors to the tall triangular room with its single chink of light and the pivoted steel door that clunked as it shut behind us. It was all very moving, much more so in its raw state than later, when the museum was filled with exhibits. I also brought Nuala to Bebelplatz, off Unter den Linden, to see a memorial to the burning of books by the Nazis in 1933. 'Where is it?' she asked, peering across the seemingly endless expanse of cobbles.

'You'll soon see,' I said. We walked to the middle of the square where there's a glazed cut-out in the stone paving, and looked down into a well-lit room of empty white bookshelves, designed by Israeli artist Micha Ullman. Nuala gasped in amazement at how utterly appropriate it was to commemorate the burning of books with bare shelves.

Less than a month after pouring her heart out to Marian Finucane, Nuala was dead. A huge crowd filled Kirwan's Funeral Home in Fairview, where she was laid out in an open coffin. I could see her bald head from a distance, but couldn't bring myself to go closer; I wanted to remember her in one of her summer print frocks sailing down Aungier Street on her bicycle. It was very hard that she was gone, but at least we gave her a great send-off from Fairview Church on a remarkably sunny day in Dublin.

After nearly a decade of being helpless in a wheelchair, my dear mother died peacefully at St Mary's Hospital in the Phoenix Park on 16 January 2009 with my brother Denis by her bedside. We all rushed out there as soon as we heard the news. Mam was lying rigid on the bed, her mouth still open after taking her last breath an hour or so earlier, and Dad was visibly upset at seeing her lifeless body for the first time. After noting that they had been together for more than sixty years, he led a decade of the Rosary as I held his hand, trying as best we could to come to terms with her death. But it was a release for her from the indignities and pain she had suffered since the stroke nine years earlier. I remembered what Paul Moley had said in a text message the previous September about the loss of a loved one: 'Remember your father fell in love with your mother, and spent the best part of his life with her. It must scare him to think of not having her. It's the same with my Dad.'

After Mam's body was embalmed, we took her home, where she lay in an open coffin in the front bedroom for what became an informal Irish wake. Various relatives and friends called that night, in advance of the funeral at Aughrim Street Church the following day, and we gathered as Dad said the prayers the two of them used to say every night before bed. Even for someone as agnostic as me, it was an emotional experience just to be there as incantations to Padre Pio and others were recited. In the morning, the undertakers arrived and there was that emotional moment when the coffin is finally closed before being carried out into the hearse. Some of us travelled in a funeral limousine, but many others walked behind the hearse as we made our way slowly down Glenbeigh Road and onto Blackhorse Avenue. At the junction with North Circular Road, all the traffic miraculously stopped to allow our funeral procession to pass unimpeded onto Aughrim Street, where there were people gathered outside as Liam, Denis, myself and three of Liam's sons shouldered Mam's coffin into the church she had known so well.

The fact that Mass was concelebrated by our first cousin, Father Niall Coghlan, who Mam adored, and the parish priest, Monsignor Dermot Clarke, who was also very good to her, made the whole ceremony more personal. It fell to me to deliver the eulogy, recalling what she did for us while we were growing up – all the baking, the knitting, the hours spent at her Singer sewing machine, the swimming lessons, the picnics, and the endless gardening later on at their holiday home in Co. Wexford, with drills of potatoes, onions, broad beans and lettuce behind the suspended and trailing sweet pea; it was no surprise that her stall was one of the star attractions at the annual field day in Ballygarrett, where she sold little yoghurt pots of propagated plants for charity and was always able to give advice on how and where they should be planted. I also spoke about how devoted our parents were to each other and how the last thing Dad expected at his age was that 'he would become what's known as a "principal carer", looking after Mam day after day . . . Our hearts go out to Dad on this very difficult day.'

I ended by thanking everyone for coming to her funeral and, with my voice finally breaking, invited them all to join with us in giving our mother a well-deserved round of applause for a life so well lived. It was bitterly cold in Glasnevin Cemetery's crematorium chapel as we finally parted with Mam, but we warmed ourselves up with a buffet for fifty or more at Denis's home in

Cremore Road, for which Eamon and Brian Yore did the catering. Some weeks later, Liam collected the urn containing her ashes and these were planted with an Irish cultivar of silver birch (selected by Edel and her husband Paul) in the oldest part of the cemetery; we all thought that she would really like the idea of helping to grow that beautiful tree, with its speckled white bark.

Liam and I took Dad on several rail tours in the years that followed; it was in the genes, of course, and he enjoyed the trips as much as we did. The most memorable was an outing to the Ulster Folk and Transport Museum, in Cultra, Co. Down, not least because it was Dad's first time to visit Northern Ireland, in his nineties. The museum's centrepiece, much to Dad's satisfaction, is Ireland's greatest-ever steam locomotive, the Medb, which was built at the Great Southern and Western Railways' Inchicore Works in 1939 and still holds the speed record for Irish railways; rather shamefully, it ended its working life hauling wagonloads of beet from Wellington Bridge in Co. Wexford to the sugar factory in Carlow. But here it was in all its glory, standing on a turntable in Cultra, where it was clearly valued.

When Dad queried why it wasn't in a railway museum south of the border, I pointed out that we didn't have one, so we were quite fortunate that the Medb was being looked after so well 'up North'. He got a kick out of sitting in an early Third Class railway carriage, with no windows at all, as if that was his lot. On another rail tour, I steered him into the First Class carriage on the Cork train at Heuston Station, having seen that the rest of the train was packed. He had a free travel pass for himself and a companion, so all I had to do was to pay the supplement.

'Are we travelling First Class?' Dad asked me, in a tone of annoyance. When I confessed that we were, he shook his head sadly and said, 'The only time I ever travelled First Class on a train in Ireland was in 1928, with your uncle Paddy, from Rathnew to Wicklow.' As an army officer, Paddy had the perk of travelling First Class on trains, and he thought it would be a nice treat for his nephew, then just twelve years old, who would usually have walked the two miles to the CBS school in Wicklow and back again. When I gave him a book on the Dublin South Eastern Railway, he was delighted, remarking that it even had a photograph of the old station house, in its elevated position at Rathnew, 'including the gable window from where I first saw the sea in 1922' – when he was six. And when the line between Waterford and Rosslare Harbour was due to close, we took one of the last trains through south Co. Wexford, crossing the Barrow Estuary on a rusting box-girder railway bridge.

Once the global 'credit crunch' began to make itself felt, everything changed in the Irish property market. Developers found it more and more difficult to raise money for their projects, and architects suddenly found that schemes they had designed were being pigeonholed. Richard Barrett made light of it at first, even suggesting – tongue in cheek – the idea of setting up a 'vulture fund' to acquire distressed residential blocks in Manhattan and sell them on at inflated prices when the market recovered. I said it ought to have some sort of patriotic name, like the American Eagle Fund, to conceal its real purpose, which was to profit from the misery of others. I also resisted his suggestion that I remortgage the flat in Temple Bar to finance a buy-to-let investment.

'I don't have the money,' I told him.

'Sure the banks would give you the money,' he countered.

'No, no,' I insisted. 'There's just no way I would get into debt at this stage of my life.' I suppose I still had a memory of growing up in the era of thrift.

A couple I know well who had been investing heavily in property – 'Section 23' apartments, half-shares in office blocks, Quinlan Private syndicates, etc. – lost everything. At the peak of the bubble, they had been invited to Quinlan's offices in Ballsbridge to be told the glad news that they were worth €35 million, with the suggestion that they needed to get more 'leverage' to become even richer. Just fifteen months later, they were 'worth' *minus* €15 million. Some time later, the husband who had lost so much ran into Derek Quinlan in a Dublin pub, and told him what had happened, in case he didn't know. 'Well, it's been tough for all of us,' was all the Pied Piper had to say.

There was 'D&G' at the *Irish Times* too – 'doom & gloom, not Dolce & Gabbana', as Caroline Walsh noted. As the recession began to bite, management was seeking a 10 per cent pay cut across the board, a return to working five days per week (as opposed to the long-established nine-day fortnight) and reduced holiday entitlements. By then, the paper had relocated to a rented seven-storey office block on Tara Street, with Dublin City Council as its landlord. Our sanitized new accommodation resembled an untidy insurance claims-processing office, complete with swipe-card turnstiles inside the entrance. Ironically, this barrier was presided over by a fine little bust of Dick Walsh, for whom such corporate trappings would have been anathema. Even regular contributors who were not strictly employees, such as art critic Aidan Dunne or film critic Donald Clarke, had to get a member of the staff to sign them in.

Paul Moley had found a new French boyfriend, Patrick Arnaud, a lovely twenty-two-year-old law student from Nancy, with his own studio apartment (courtesy of his granny) on Boulevard du Montparnasse in Paris. Patrick would have given anything to get a job in Dublin, but there was little chance of that happening as the recession took hold, so the pair of them did a lot of flying back and forth to be with each other; by then, Paul himself had got a secure job in the Central Bank of Ireland. I might also have ended up in Paris, standing in for Lara Marlowe while she was in Washington covering Barack Obama's first term as US President. The proposition was put to me by the paper's new foreign editor, Denis Staunton, over dinner with Mark Brennock in Il Vicoletto on Crow Street one night in July 2009. 'Frankie goes to Paris . . . I can see it in lights!' Denis said.

I was completely taken aback. But I felt I couldn't ignore his insistence that I should apply for the Paris post, and began taking lessons to improve my French as well as reading books such as *The Secret Life of France* by Lucy Wadham, an Anglo-Saxon by name and nature. Her thesis about the difference between the two neighbouring countries was that the English were devoted to truth whereas the French valued beauty. She had just finished up in Oxford University when she went to Paris for the first time and fell in love with a charming French guy called Laurent. They got married and, in time, had four children, all fluently bilingual in French and English. Noticing that many of Laurent's French friends were having affairs, she asked him what would he say if she was cheating on him.

'I'd hope you wouldn't be stupid enough to let me find out,' he said.

'But wouldn't you want to know the truth?' she asked.

'The truth is overrated,' he said.

The interview for the Paris job went very well, I felt, almost a *promenade du gâteau*. Asked about being taken out of my comfort zone, I recalled being commissioned by features editor Conor Goodman to participate in a Modified Motors rally near Mitchelstown, Co. Cork. My piece was accompanied by a big photograph of me sitting on the bonnet of one of the souped-up cars with two scantily clad showgirls; it provoked more comment than nearly anything I had ever done for the *Irish Times*. It took Geraldine Kennedy more than two weeks to make up her mind between Ruadhán Mac Cormaic and me for the Paris job. I tried to forget about it all by going with Grania Willis, former equestrian correspondent of the *Irish Times*, to a 'Feck the Recession' party hosted by Richard Barrett over a wonderful weekend in Ibiza. Finally, on 2 October, I got word from managing editor Willy Clingan that Madam had given the post to Ruadhán.

When I texted friends to let them know, Stephen O'Farrell was philosophical: 'I guess Dublin needs you more . . . Well, fair fucks to you for trying. And bring on the next adventure . . .'

It was disappointing, but far from devastating, and probably the right decision in hindsight. After all, I was already an old dog, set in my ways, whereas Ruadhán was lean and hungry, and still relatively young. He did very well in France and went on to become the *Irish Times* legal affairs correspondent as well as writing a groundbreaking book on Ireland's Supreme Court.

I was delighted when Mark Brennock and his wife Yetti asked me to become godfather to their adopted Russian son Alex, in advance of his First Communion, and I promised to send him a postcard from everywhere I went, at least until he was eighteen. They already had a lovely daughter, Maggie Rose, and had decided to adopt in 2002 after being told by medical experts that they couldn't have any more children of their own.

I'll never forget the text message they sent to all their friends then, because it read like a birth notice: 'Brennock/Redmond: to Mark & Yetti in Voronezh, Russia. A little boy, Alexander Vladimir. Home Tuesday.' They had gone to an orphanage in Voronezh, 460 kilometres south-west of Moscow, and looked at all the babies in their cots before choosing one of them to be their son. Alex was eleven months old at the time. After I texted asking how he was, Mark wrote back, 'He's fine. In crummy orphanage yesterday afternoon. Asleep in linen sheets in suite in Moscow Marriott today. Funny old world etc.'

I enjoyed seeing him grow from a toddler to an impish kid who would write notes like, 'Poo, poo. You are poo!' and give them to me with a giggle when I'd call to their home in Ranelagh. On a snowy Christmas Day, when he was seven, we had a great snowball fight in the Botanic Gardens with his younger sister Anna, who had been adopted from another Russian orphanage. When Alex was ten, Mark, Eamon and I took him to Paris for a long weekend, and I managed to rent the stern of a converted river barge moored in the Seine near the Tour Eiffel. I had told Alex that Paris was much better than London and, even at the end of our first day, as we watched Line No. 6 metro trains trundling across the Pont de Bir-Hakeim, my young godson enthusiastically agreed, 'Yeah, it's *so* much better!'

One day, he told me he had asked his dad about the Pantheon.

'Yeah, it's in Paris,' Mark replied.

'Ah, but the original one is in Rome,' Alex pointed out.

And then, turning to me, he asked *sotto voce* if I knew what was written on the front. 'It says *fecit*!' he said, grinning from ear to ear.

As the economic recession deepened, there was not much sign of austerity in Ranelagh. Alex was developing an awareness of brands, concluding that Mercedes-Benz were the only cars worth having, Ray-Ban had the best sunglasses, and four-star hotels were preferable to budget alternatives because there was a better chance they'd have a swimming pool. Exasperated by Alex's interest in bling, I told him he was living in a bubble and that we really needed to take a tour of the poorer parts of Dublin to see how the other half lived.

'But I'm quite happy in my bubble,' he declared.

We have yet to take that tour, opting instead for Dublin Bay Cruises and suchlike.

When Alex was about to enter secondary school in Sandford Park, I sent him a letter of encouragement which concluded:

> *You're bright, beautiful, engaging, good fun and great company. It's a privilege and delight to be your godfather . . . You're a real star, and there will be some who may resent that because they know they'll never be as good as you are. But don't let anyone bully you, ever. Tell your Mum and Dad, tell the teachers, tell me, tell everyone! We won't let anyone grind you down. You may not know too many of the other boys (and girls!) in your class at Sandford Park, but some of them will become your best friends, I'm sure. You will brighten up their lives, as they will yours. It'll be one great, long-running adventure;-))) And here you are taking your first steps on the next stage of your life. Our hearts go with you, as always.*
>
> *Love, Frank*

A couple of days later, Alex sent me a text message, which simply said, 'I loved your letter.' Eamon has an equally positive relationship with his godson Sidney, the son of costumier Veerle Dehaene and musician Ken Edge, so much so that they also made him godfather to their daughter Alice, who is totally devoted to him. I suppose they're like surrogate children for the two of us, really. We took Veerle and Sid (then twelve years old) to Iceland for a long weekend, to mark Eamon's sixtieth birthday, and had a wonderful time in Reykjavik, visiting the award-winning Harpa concert hall, eating out in local restaurants, taking a tour bus through the snow-laden landscape to see the spectacular Gullfoss waterfall as well as the snorting eruptions of Geysir and Strokkur, and an expensive dip in the warm waters of Blue Lagoon on the way back to Keflavik Airport.

II

Turning sixty, as I did in January 2010, was a real shocker. Twenty is welcome, thirty is a bit iffy, forty is officially middle-aged, fifty is more of the same, but sixty marks the start of the slippery slope that leads in one direction only – towards the tomb. It didn't help that I had fallen flat on my back along an icy footpath in Leixlip, having rolled out of Caroline Stephenson's Ryevale House with Shane O'Toole after a very convivial dinner party. The stab of pain I felt immediately was from a cracked lower right rib, and it only got worse after the anaesthetic effect of all the wine I had drunk had worn off. As a result, I was unable to attend the funeral of Michael Dwyer, the renowned *Irish Times* film critic who had died from lung cancer at Our Lady's Hospice in Harold's Cross on New Year's Day, and to sympathize with his long-term partner, RTÉ Radio One newsreader Brian Jennings. I could barely breathe without causing pain, never mind laugh, so I was tortured by a slew of hilariously salacious text messages about the Northern politician Iris Robinson and her nineteen-year-old boyfriend, Kirk McCambley.

'It is a secret,' my friend the diplomat Brendan Ward texted, 'but you will probably wish to know that Paul [Moley] and John Beattie are negotiating to have Kirk McCambley leap out of the cake in a spangled orange jock strap with an iris behind his ear.'

On a more serious note, I nearly hit the roof over an *Irish Times* editorial on the weather that January, with 'Global cooling' as its ridiculous title. 'So much for all of that guff about global warming! Are world leaders having the wrong debate? We are experiencing the most prolonged period of icy weather in 40 years and feeling every bit of it . . .' Its title and opening lines presaged Donald Trump's silly tweets, in which he repeatedly confused climate with day-to-day weather. I'd like to think it was a feeble attempt at humour, rather than the paper's considered view, especially as the *Irish Times* had sent me to so many UN climate summits all over the world.

When the big day dawned I looked at myself in our new bathroom mirror and saw – shock, horror! – that my right cheek had ballooned outwards, making me 'look like a lopsided chipmunk', as I texted close friends. Jeez! I suspected a dental abscess. 'Is there any way you can get this down by this evening?' I asked my doctor, Niall Joyce. Not being a miracle worker, all he could do was to give me a prescription for some heavy-duty antibiotics with a caution that it could take a week for the abscess to clear. As I said to Kathy Sheridan, 'I wouldn't mind if it was a boil on my bum, or even a cold sore or two, but it's the high visibility of my facial asymmetry that's real torture.'

But I was quite overwhelmed by all the goodwill and messages from friends, both young and old. Most memorable of all was an email from Javier Saez, headed 'Frank's Super Sweet Sixtieth!!' in which he wrote:

> You know better than anyone the endless amount of wonderful moments that build up your life. I would sign up to experience a quarter of what you have already experienced . . . I hope that you continue to surprise others but more so that you continue to surprise yourself. The list of treasures to be discovered is endless, and the things that will add richness to your life are ahead of you. Look after yourself and look after the rest of us . . . 60 is a very special big birthday.
>
> Kisses and hugs, I love you very much,
> Javier

I was so touched by what he wrote that I almost cried; as I told him in a text message, 'It was amazing and really wonderful. I'm so glad you are my friend, and I love you too. Xx.' Platonic love really does exist, you can take my word for it.

On the night of the party, 150-plus friends and hangers-on packed the Ormond Wine Bar for champagne and canapés, going on till all hours. Mark Brennock, Annie McCartney and Stephen O'Farrell delivered witty speeches, with some slightly embarrassing disclosures regarding the dim and distant past, and I replied to them all, with a big surprise for Eamon at the end – that I hoped we would tie the knot as soon as Civil Partnership legislation was passed. There were 'oohs' and 'aahs', drowned out by a big round of applause, and some tears. Eamon was delighted. After all these years, we thought, what I had proposed would actually be possible now . . . in Ireland.

Things were changing at the *Irish Times*. Maeve Donovan was finally gone as managing director, which was good news. Her severance package, it transpired, amounted to €1.1 million, plus continuing payments of €50,000 per annum. Geraldine Kennedy's contract as editor was due to expire in May 2011, and there was uncertainty about whether it would be renewed. A gang of us got together in Il Vicoletto to chew the cud, as it were. All were 'old hands' – Jack Fagan, Orna Mulcahy, Patsey Murphy, Kathy Sheridan, Denis Staunton and Caroline Walsh. I gave them Prosecco in the flat before we headed around the corner for our conspiratorial get-together.

Metaphorically, to paraphrase Flann O'Brien, everything under the sun was discussed, from the price of tea to the speed of light through mahogany, and there was general agreement that we needed a new editor. There was also a lot of chuckling about the appearance on Twitter of a spoof account in the name of Madam Editor, which so uncannily captured Geraldine's tone and preoccupations that it must have been the work of an *Irish Times* insider, though the author's identity has never been established – irritating errors were being made on an almost daily basis. 'Kevin, how is it possible that Lord Mount Charles is referred to twice on p. 2 today as "Sir Henry"?' I texted news editor Kevin O'Sullivan. 'Bruce Williamson must be turning in his grave! A corr, surely.'

But no correction appeared, as the supposed 'paper of record' no longer admitted such infelicities unless an aggrieved person made a complaint. On the other hand, where else would you find such incisive and witty cartoons as Martyn Turner's or quality writing as Frank McNally's 'An Irishman's Diary'? I sent Frank a text saying a diary he had done on accents was 'a masterpiece – just in case no one said so'. Even his response was a classic: 'You're too kind, but the encouragement is appreciated. Especially since I've just scoured the papers and I'm now sitting here, staring at a blank screen, yet again, wondering what in the nama jazus I'm going to fill tomorrow's diary with . . .'

One day I casually walked into Hodges Figgis and spotted a new book by John Waters on the bestseller shelves: *Feckers: 50 People Who Fecked Up Ireland*. The blurb promised a lot. 'Which 50 people turned Ireland into the fecked-up country she is today? Bono? Haughey? Louis Walsh? de Valera? It's time to name and shame the great, the good and the gobshites . . .' All the usual suspects were there all right – and so was I! Waters's argument was that my campaign against Bungalow Blitz in the countryside had herded people into suburban housing estates on the edges of provincial towns and, since too many of these had been built, I was also to blame for the phenomenon of 'ghost estates'. This was so ludicrous that I didn't even bother to make contact with my erstwhile colleague to point out that there were nearly half a million 'one-off' houses in rural areas, many of which had been built long after the *Irish Times* took a stand against this uniquely Irish form of suburbanization more than twenty years earlier.

I also had reason to celebrate, as the Royal Institute of the Architects of Ireland had made me an Honorary Member on the proposal of my old friend Seán Ó Laoire, the institute's outgoing president. Just like the honorary DPhil from DIT, it took me by surprise, as did a RIBA Honorary Fellowship in 2011. But I was nonetheless delighted by this gong, particularly as I had written some unflattering things about RIAI members over the years. Tragically, Seán's long-established practice went into liquidation the following month.

Developers were also on the ropes, of course, including happy-go-lucky Mick Wallace TD. Mick and I were on *Tonight with Vincent*

Browne together talking about the bust when Ireland's interrogator-in-chief asked him how much he owed to the banks. 'Oh, about forty to forty-five million,' Mick replied.

Afterwards, sharing a taxi into the city from TV3's studios in Ballymount, I asked him what was the craziest thing he had done during the bubble era.

'Well, I bought this site on Upper Dominick Street that was a fifth of an acre, and paid €4.8 million for it,' he said.

'But could you not see at the time that it was a mad price?' I asked.

'Not really, because that's what all the so-called experts said it was worth – you know, estate agents, chartered surveyors, etc.'

Ah, yes, I thought, the same people who wrongly predicted a 'soft landing' for the property market before the bubble finally burst. But Wallace's debt mountain was a relative hillock compared to others. Bernard McNamara had gone bust for €1.3 billion, Liam Carroll for €1.4 billion and Treasury Holdings for a whopping €2.7 billion – to name but three. What spared Richard Barrett much grief was that, unlike Johnny Ronan, he had declined to give personal guarantees to any of the bankers who loaned him money to acquire assets. He always read the small print, going through every loan agreement in fine detail, and if there was any mention of a personal guarantee, he would simply point out that he never gave one – putting it up to the bankers to decide 'whether they wanted the business, or not', as he told me. And given that Treasury was riding high at the time, the bankers and their lawyers would drop the offending paragraph. That explains why his assets never ended up in NAMA, as Johnny's did.

Whenever I told anyone I was living in the Temple Bar, their response was the same: 'How do you put up with the noise?' But we didn't take it lying down. Temple Bar Music Centre (now the Button Factory) was an early offender, but by objecting to the renewal of its music and singing licence, we managed to get Paddy Dunning to upgrade the main entrance by installing a secondary set of heavy timber doors to minimize the nuisance. Nonetheless, I had to make numerous complaints about regular blasts of noise from the venue over the years, mainly due to poor management by guys running gigs there.

More serious was the persistent and outrageous abuse of the neighbourhood by the Mezz Bar and Nightclub at the River House Hotel, on Eustace Street. Over a period of time, I wrote seven letters of complaint to its proprietor, Frank Conway, without once getting a reply. It came to a head one night when noise from the Mezz close to 2 a.m. was so intolerable that I went there to find a crowd of drunken revellers milling around the entrance, with heavy bass booming all over the street. I asked to speak to the manager. A Czech woman called Vera, who was in her early thirties, came out and identified herself as such. I told her that I lived just around the corner and couldn't sleep because of the near-deafening noise.

She smirked and said, 'It's a nightclub. What do you expect?'

I flipped, fearing that our flat would become uninhabitable if this almost nightly racket continued, and put my hands on either side of her head, shaking it briefly. I was pursued by bouncers, pinned against a wall in Curved Street and then frogmarched back to the Mezz, where I immediately apologized to the bar manager. Nobody called the gardaí, but I duly reported the incident to Frank Conway. Some time later, in what I interpreted as an attempt to intimidate me, a solicitor's letter on behalf of the bar manager arrived, claiming that she had suffered injury as a result of the incident – 'whiplash' was mentioned – and threatening to sue for damages. But after our exemplary solicitor, Eoghan McKenna, wrote back to say that we would be vigorously defending any court action, I heard no more about it.

Eoghan managed to prove that the Mezz had been trading without a publican's licence for at least two years, and this resulted in Circuit Court proceedings, with an outcome that was far from favourable to Conway. The court granted a licence, subject to very strict conditions, which included no late-night 'special exemptions', no live music and measures to contain noise within the premises. Profits plummeted at the River House Hotel, and Conway sought to have the restrictions lifted, hiring Michael McDowell SC to represent him. It transpired that the 'hotel' was making five times as much revenue from the bar and nightclub as it did from rooms; and Conway claimed to have invested €80,000 in soundproofing the premises.

I had to give evidence in the case, based on a book of letters and emails stretching back ten years or more, and this inevitably included reference to the incident involving Vera, the bar manager. Circuit Court President Judge Matthew Deery had a copy and so did McDowell, although he had told me that he would not be making an issue of it. As I was going through all the stuff, I was acutely conscious of having sworn to tell 'the truth, the whole truth and nothing but the truth', so I felt that I couldn't simply gloss over references to the incident. I decided to come clean about what happened.

'I hit her – I very much regret that – and I apologized,' I told the judge.

Freelance court reporter Ray Managh now had his opening paragraph served up on a plate, and the tabloids had a story. Managh's report was so one-sided that *Irish Times* news editor Kevin O'Sullivan rang me to see if there was more to it. I was able to tell him that, in granting the licence, Judge Deery accepted that the manner in which the Mezz was run had been a 'central problem' for residents over the years and had given 'serious concern' to the gardaí. The judge also described my complaints about noise from the Mezz as 'well-voiced and well-grounded', saying that the rights of Temple Bar residents 'have to be respected'. He also commended me for being 'scrupulously honest' in the evidence I gave in court.

It wasn't just the bars: we were having terrible problems with a group of bongo-drummers – all of whom happened to be young foreign nationals. Four or five of them would regularly congregate on East Essex Street, in front of the Temple Bar Pharmacy, creating the most appalling racket. Coming up to 2 a.m. one night, I went down there and spoke to one of them, telling him that there were people living in the immediate vicinity and they probably couldn't sleep as a result of all the noise.

'You should move,' the young fellow told me. He also said that Dublin was 'the best place in Europe for busking'.

'Why so?' I asked.

'Because we get no trouble from the police,' he replied.

I raised this at one of those generally meaningless Temple Bar Forum consultative meetings, chaired by a Dublin City Council official, and the Garda representative – Inspector Dan Flavin – took it seriously.

'What can you do?' I asked.

'Well, we can give them a warning under the Public Order Act and, if they ignore that, we can arrest them,' he replied.

Within weeks, the bongo-drummers had moved on and were no longer causing sleepless nights for residents of Temple Bar. I had also raised the issue of graffiti vandalism, and someone recommended a proprietary spray to deal with it. So I got the stuff and was carefully applying it to a 'tag' on the front of our building when I felt a hand on my shoulder. I turned around and who was it but Inspector Flavin, about to make an arrest. As he recognized me, and I him, we both laughed at the irony. Sadly, Dan disappeared off the radar not long after that encounter; he had been shifted to Newcastle West in Co. Limerick, despite the fact that – in my experience – he was the most effective Garda officer we ever had in dealing with the day-to-day (and night-to-night) problems faced by Temple Bar's two thousand residents. Indeed, it is unlikely that the phenomenon of heavily amplified busking would have got so out of hand in the area had he remained in Dublin. And so, a five-piece rock band could happily set themselves up on East Essex Street, with massive amplifiers blasting the area at levels of 100 decibels or more, while gardaí on the beat would saunter past without thinking that this was anything out of the ordinary; for several years, indeed, it became the 'new normal'.

*

When the Civil Partnership Bill had passed into Irish law in July 2010, Eamon and I had a discussion about when, or whether, we would avail ourselves of it. Eamon took the view that it was only marginally more prestigious than a dog licence and that we should hold out for the real thing – marriage – and I agreed with him. But we were delighted to be invited to the wedding party for Graham Egan and the love of his life, Alan Bigley, a partner in PWC, who weren't prepared to wait any longer.

In September 2010 I heard our hapless Taoiseach, Brian Cowen, interviewed live on *Morning Ireland*: he sounded drunk or hungover. Two months later, he had no alternative but to surrender Ireland's sovereignty to the EU/ECB/IMF troika, a truly shameful episode in the country's history. Cowen and his predecessor, Bertie Ahern, had helped to inflate the bubble by retaining a broad range of property-based tax incentives long after they should have been scrapped. 'Biffo' became a public pariah, so much so that when he performed the official opening of Dundalk Institute of Technology's renovation of the iconic P. J. Carroll cigarette factory, all classes were suspended and students barred from the building in case they might throw eggs at him.

Cowen resigned as Fianna Fáil leader in advance of the 2011 election, knowing he'd drag the party down; but even under the new leader, Micheál Martin, the election was carnage for FF. The Green Party, too, paid a big price for its role as the junior partner in government; leader John Gormley lost his seat in Dublin South East, garnering just 6 per cent of the poll. I used to meet Gormley quite regularly while he was Minister for the Environment and, on each occasion, he seemed more shell-shocked, reeling from the horror of Ireland's debt burden. Months before the election I had told Pat Rabbitte that what Labour needed to do was to force Fianna Fáil into coalition with Fine Gael to implement an austerity programme, while the party of James Connolly could lead the opposition. But nothing would do the old Labour stalwarts but to get their bums on seats around the Cabinet table, even at the risk of being decimated at the next general election, just as the Greens were in 2011.

While the new Fine Gael–Labour coalition was being formed, I sent a text to Ruairi Quinn: 'Ruairi, anything you can do to keep Phil Hogan out of the Custom House would be good for the environment. He thinks John Gormley's proposed probe of planning irregularities in six local authorities was "mostly spurious", which isn't true, and he's advised by Conor Skehan, a climate change sceptic . . .' I didn't get a reply from Quinn, and Hogan became Minister for the Environment.

As the new government took office, with Enda Kenny as Taoiseach, Ireland was going down the tubes. We, the people, were saddled with €65 billion in bank debt and the public finances were in a parlous state, now that all the revenue from property-related taxes had dried up. I told Kathy Sheridan in a text that I had 'never been more depressed' about the state of the country. 'It's so small really and we simply can't afford to pay off the mind-boggling debt racked up by those chancers.'

Vanity Fair ran a lengthy and at times hilarious article on the Irish crash by Michael Lewis. Referring to bogus assurances given on *Prime Time* by then Financial Regulator Patrick Neary, with his 'insecure little moustache', just two weeks after the collapse of Lehman Brothers, he wrote, 'Now the Irish people finally caught a glimpse of the guy meant to be safeguarding them: the crazy uncle had been sprung from the family cellar . . .'

Lewis then quoted this absolute gem from plain-speaking economist Colm McCarthy: 'What happened was that everyone had the idea that somewhere in Ireland there was a little wise old man who was in charge of the money, and this was the first time they'd ever seen this little man. And then they saw him and said, *Who the fuck was that??? Is that the fucking guy who is in charge of the money???* That's when everyone panicked.'

I was not among the crowd of fifty thousand who came to hear Barack Obama deliver a speech in College Green later that month, for two reasons. Firstly, I blamed him for doing a back-room deal with China, India, Brazil and South Africa that led to the collapse of the Copenhagen climate summit in December 2009. And secondly, just weeks before Obama landed in Ireland, his Treasury Secretary, Tim Geithner, had made it clear in a G8 conference call that there could be no question of 'burning' the Irish banks' bondholders, even those who held unsecured debt; that cost us billions. I could hear the roar of the crowd as Obama delivered his empty rhetoric down the street.

'Speech seemed inspiring on telly. But reading the words, it is just awful platitudinous guff,' Mark Brennock texted.

'Indeed yes,' I replied. 'He's a fraud.'

Queen Elizabeth II was much more impressive in the exemplary way she carried herself, shortly thereafter, during the first State visit by a British monarch to Southern Ireland since her grandfather, King George V, was welcomed in 1911 – exactly a century earlier. I was glued to the television watching the Queen and Prince Philip's arrival at Casement Aerodrome, Baldonnel, then the scenes at Áras an Uachtaráin where they were greeted warmly by President Mary McAleese and her husband Martin, and most especially the very moving ceremony at the Garden of Remembrance when she laid a wreath beneath Oisín Kelly's symbolic *Children of Lir* sculpture, then stepped back and graciously bowed her head. It was one of those rare moments when you could really feel the weight of history being lifted by a single gesture, even as the Garda riot squad was containing a violent demonstration by republican dissidents on Dorset Street; they were accurately described as 'hatchet-faced hoodies' by one of the tabloid papers.

I'll also never forget Olivia O'Leary, in her speech at the British Embassy's concert in the Convention Centre, recalling the reaction of one excited schoolgirl as she watched the royal motorcade making its way through Mountjoy Square to the hallowed ground of Croke Park: 'It's the Queen. Oh my God, it's the *actual* Queen.'

That came after the State Dinner at Dublin Castle, from where Ireland was ruled for centuries by Britain, when the guest of honour opened her speech in Irish, saying, *'A Uachtaráin agus a chairde'* (President and friends). I knew that the content of the Queen's speech that night had been worked and reworked over and over again, with contributions from Irish historians and literary figures such as Diarmaid Ferriter, Seamus Heaney and Colm Tóibín; which of them came up with the great line, 'With the benefit of historical hindsight we can all see things which we would wish had been done differently or not at all,' I cannot say.

I managed to wangle an invitation to the wreath-laying ceremony at the War Memorial Park in Islandbridge. Ignoring instructions to the guests that there was to be 'no personal photography', I took my Lumix camera with me, and sat through the event alongside some jovial fellows from Belfast who might, or might not, have been veterans of the Ulster Volunteer Force. As the Queen and the President were leaving, McAleese spotted Kevin Myers behind a barrier and said, 'This is the journalist who kept the flame of this place alive for so many years. He fought the good battle and, like so many good battles, it was worth fighting.'

Myers, who regularly wrote about the valour of the Royal Dublin Fusiliers in the Great War, was almost dumbstruck at being singled out. And when the Queen nodded approvingly in his direction, he bowed his head and blurted out, 'Your Majesty.' Whereupon I whipped out my Lumix and took a picture of the two heads of state, with the British monarch looking straight at me, 'as much as to say you cheeky bugger', as my friend Joe Smith in Cambridge commented after I emailed it to him.

At the *Irish Times*, the reign of Geraldine Kennedy was coming to an end after it became clear that her contract would not be renewed, and all sorts of people were lining themselves up to succeed her. I met Kevin O'Sullivan for coffee in Mac Turcaill's pub on the corner of Townsend Street to talk about it all and was quite astonished when he told me that he was going to throw his hat in the ring, as I thought he was too decent and simply not ruthless enough to occupy the editor's chair. What he did have, however, was a good working relationship with Liam Kavanagh, the new managing director, who had obviously decided that Kevin was the type of guy he could get along with; he and Kevin even played golf together.

Geraldine, for her part, had got her stray eye fixed.

'So what do you think?' she said to me after I popped in to see her.

'About what?' I said.

'About my eye. I had it fixed!' she replied.

'I think that's fantastic,' I said. 'But why didn't you have it done years ago?'

She said anything could have gone wrong with an eye operation in the past and she might have lost her sight altogether.

'So what prompted you to get it done at this stage?' I asked.

'Well,' she said, 'I had this builder in doing a bit of work on the house and he said he used to have an eye like mine, but he got it fixed and so should I. So I did.'

That sums up Geraldine to a tee: direct and to the point.

By the end of May, a broad field had been narrowed down to five contenders – Geraldine's deputy, Paul O'Neill; news editor Kevin O'Sullivan; London editor Mark Hennessy; foreign editor Denis Staunton; and features editor Hugh Linehan. After a second round of interviews, there were just two left – O'Sullivan and Staunton. I was in Istanbul for a long weekend with Paul Moley, staying in a flat near Istiklal Caddesi, when the news came through. 'Kevin O'Sullivan editor of Oirish Times,' Richard Barrett texted me out of the blue and I rushed to an internet café to read all about it.

I learned soon afterwards that there had been a large gathering in the newsroom for Geraldine's announcement about who was to succeed her. Like a reality TV host, she kept everyone on tenterhooks until the last minute, delivering a valedictory address that highlighted the importance of standing up for journalism against commercial pressures; she had even admitted on radio that she felt 'uncomfortable' about the fact that the property supplement bankrolled the paper during the boom years. There was intense and prolonged applause when she finally revealed that the new editor was to be Kevin O'Sullivan, and he immediately gave Denis Staunton a big hug.

About a week later, I met Kevin for a drink in the Westin Hotel and reported to Derek Scally that it was 'all very positive and encouraging!' at least in those very early days of the new regime. Other long-time colleagues were equally enthusiastic, including Patsey Murphy, halfway out the door herself, who texted: 'My god the atmosphere has changed utterly . . .'

In the late autumn of 2011, Caroline Walsh was being treated for a thyroid condition, although I had no idea how serious it was. Patsey texted me in December, 'Was thinking of you just this morning walking around Chicago. So many great buildings . . . Am also thinking of our pal Caroline all the time.' I was a bit unnerved by her reference to Caroline, and rang my dear old friend to see how she was, but only got the opportunity to leave a message.

'Many thanks for lovely voicemail Frank – yes I am in poor shape unfortunately but always always lovely to hear from you xxxx C,' she texted back.

'Thanks Caroline. I'm sorry to hear that. Where are you and would you be up to une petite visite par moi? ;-) x,' I replied.

'I'm at home now – hope to see you in time – meanwhile all love as always xxxxx,' she said.

'And the same to you dear Caroline. Please keep me posted and I will pop in as soon as possible. Xx,' I wrote, to which she responded: 'Xxxxxx.'

Little did I realize that this would be our last communication. Less than a week later, on 22 December, I got a phone call from Denis Staunton telling me that Caroline had been rescued from the sea off the West Pier in Dún Laoghaire and had died later at St Vincent's Hospital. I was in a state of shock, crying my eyes out, and immediately texted James Ryan, her husband of nearly thirty years. Mark Brennock and I called out to the house on Ashfield Avenue in Ranelagh, where their son Matt and daughter Alice sat down with us and recounted what had happened.

Caroline had begun to suffer from psychosis (which, they later learned, was a rare, but recognized, manifestation of thyroid malfunction). She had been admitted to St John of God's Hospital in Stillorgan for two weeks. When her condition improved, she was discharged. Then, in the midst of Christmas preparations, she went missing from home. She had taken the family car and, now in the grip of what would be identified as a 'thyroid storm', driven from one coastal location to another, finally ending up in Dún Laoghaire, where she got out of the car and went for the water. Over an hour later, with family and their friends now assembled at the pier, Caroline, who had been located in the course of a helicopter search, was taken from the cold waters of the harbour and rushed by ambulance to St Vincent's Hospital, still alive but unconscious. Following two hours of intensive efforts at resuscitation, her death was announced to James, Matt and Alice, who had been anxiously waiting in a nearby room with friends and relatives.

The funeral was on Christmas Eve, and University Church on St Stephen's Green was filled to overflowing with mourners, all of them as shocked and almost as bereft as her family, and awestruck by the ability of James, Alice and Matt to deliver eulogies for the wife and mother they had just lost so tragically. At our Christmas party in Temple Bar four days later, we remembered Caroline with heartfelt speeches by Deaglán de Bréadún, Catriona Crowe, Colm Tóibín and myself.

Less than two weeks into the New Year, we were mourning the loss of fearless RTÉ television producer Mary Raftery, who had died after a courageous battle with cancer. I had known Mary since she was a bright young journalist with *In Dublin* magazine in the 1980s, always with a singular mission to chip away at the once-solid edifices of Church and State to reveal unpleasant truths about how they operated over the years. The highlight of her very moving humanist funeral, held in the Great Hall of the Royal Hospital, Kilmainham, came when the wicker basket containing her remains was carried into the courtyard by six of her closest friends, all of them women. I also remembered the last conversation I had with Mary, at one of Colm Tóibín's parties in Pembroke Street, about eighteen months earlier, when she told me how Geraldine Kennedy had dispensed with her weekly opinion column in the *Irish Times*, for reasons best known to Geraldine herself.

In between the two funerals, our despondent mood was lifted by invitations to the annual New Year's Day party hosted by Paul McGuinness and Kathy Gilfillan at Avonmore House, near Annamoe, Co. Wicklow, culminating in a spectacular fireworks display that must have cost €40,000; it also served to separate the wheat from the chaff, with the select few being invited back in for dinner, while the rest of us were directed to the car park. I could never think about Kathy without remembering her contemptuous put-down of Mother Teresa of Calcutta when she came to Dublin in 1993 to receive the Freedom of the City. At a dinner party in the architect Paul Keogh's house in Rathmines, smoking a long thin cigarette, she exclaimed, 'Mother Teresa is a lesson to us all about the horrors of not using face cream!'

But I also knew, as a member of the Irish Georgian Society's Conservation Awards jury, that Kathy was the anonymous sponsor who had kept that show on the road for several years, enabling us to travel around the country – North and South – to visit short-listed projects in the sparkling company of people like architectural historian Eddie McParland; Royal Society of Ulster Architects director Frank McCloskey; former director of the Irish Architectural Archive David Griffin; and Desmond FitzGerald, the 29th and last Knight of Glin, who sadly died from cancer in September 2011. Less than two years later, one of my great mentors, Kevin B. Nowlan, died at the age of ninety-one; he had taught me Irish history at UCD, and was chairman of the Dublin Civic Group, which fought many a battle to protect the city's architectural heritage.

Paul Moley lost his mother Rose in April 2012; she had been diagnosed with Alzheimer's disease several years earlier and died in a nursing home near Crossmaglen. There was a proper Irish wake, and Eamon and myself travelled up for it. I don't think I've ever seen so many people in and around a house. A neighbour opened a field to serve as a temporary car park while two local men in hi-viz jackets directed all the traffic. Paul's mother was laid out on the bed in her clothes, as if she was taking a nap, while relatives, friends and neighbours paid their respects, and others made soup and sandwiches in the kitchen. A couple of months earlier, Paul had been thrilled to meet Seamus Heaney and his wife Marie in San Lorenzo's restaurant on South Great George's Street. The two of us were having dinner there, and they were at another table, so we joined them for a drink afterwards. Although Seamus was looking more frail following his stroke six years earlier, he was in good form that night and neither of us imagined that he would be gone just eighteen months later.

An Bord Pleanála's decision in February 2012 to refuse permission for the proposed National Children's Hospital on the Mater site, because of its excessive height and bulk, rocked the political establishment. The vast building, designed by O'Connell Mahon Architects, was to be sixteen storeys high, extending more than 150 metres along Eccles Street, and would have been seen on the skyline from O'Connell Street. The most visible part of the project – its over-sailing ward block – would be equivalent in scale to *eight* Liberty Halls side by side, and twice as deep.

After a lengthy oral hearing the previous autumn, I wrote an opinion piece saying that the appeals board would be doing Dublin a favour by rejecting this monstrous scheme, but I was as surprised as anyone when it fell at the last fence. Devastating photomontages had shown its visual impact, yet Minister for Health James Reilly, his Department, the Health Service Executive, and Dublin City Council's planners had stuck by the original plan, seemingly unable to get their heads around the salient fact that the reason why the building was so imposing was that the site allocated for it was too small.

Harry Crosbie, chairman of the National Paediatric Hospital Development Board (and recent recipient of an OBE, having organized a concert in the Queen's honour at the Convention Centre), wrote an *Irish Times* opinion piece pitching a tweaked scheme for the Mater site even after Reilly ordered a review of all options. I wrote a riposte, but it never appeared in the paper. It seemed to me that it was quite inappropriate for Crosbie to be taking sides at that late stage. When the government eventually opted for St James's Hospital as the preferred location, I felt strongly that Crosbie, having rooted so hard for the Mater site, was now on a sticky wicket. So I texted him suggesting that he should be considering his position.

He rang me immediately and we had an argument on the phone, after which I sent him this: 'Really Harry, you should resign. That's what a person in England who found himself in a similarly untenable position would do. And for good reason too.'

He was clearly displeased about that, replying, 'It is inappropriate that you address me in this way. I am making a complaint.'

I wrote back, 'It is not inappropriate at all, unless the OBE has gone to your head. The facts are that you ran with a plan that was firmly rejected by ABP – ignoring early warning signs – and then publicly backed Mater's latest scheme, which has been rejected by the Govt in favour of St James's.'

I heard no more about it, although I did mend fences with Harry later on, after he and his board had been replaced by a new team to progress the €1 billion project.

A much better scheme, designed by Gerry Cahill Architects, was put forward by Dr Chris Fitzpatrick, then Master of the Coombe Hospital, for the former Player Wills site on South Circular Road and adjoining lands, but it was pipped at the post. Gerry, one of my closest friends, was in and out of hospital because his dear wife Florence was seriously ill from cancer, and died in May 2012. Indeed, Chris himself believed that 'the experience of Florence's illness had a profound effect on Gerry's work on the children's hospital in terms of light, space and the importance of a healing environment'.

I can't count the number of sketches Gerry has given me over the years – not of buildings but still-life renderings of wine glasses and bottles on our dining table in Temple Bar, or in some restaurant, sketched in pen-and-ink on A4 sheets of paper in memory of another convivial evening; he was always an artist manqué. After Florence's death, and the collapse of his once-thriving architectural practice under the burden of debt, Gerry and I got into the habit of dining out in Nico's on Dame Street – probably Dublin's oldest restaurant, dating from 1962; we still enjoyed its unique ambience, even after a radical but sympathetic renovation was carried out in 2008. When Gerry found love anew with Una McQuillan, a vivacious Belfast-born architect who had worked with him on the children's hospital project, I was absolutely delighted for them, particularly at their wedding on a glorious summer day in Dublin.

Things were also going from bad to worse in Temple Bar, and not just because An Bord Pleanála had betrayed us all by granting permission for a McDonald's burger joint where Fitzer's restaurant used to be on Temple Bar Square. Derry-born Dermot McLaughlin, previously traditional music officer with the Arts Council, had taken over from New Yorker Tammy Dillon as chief executive of Temple Bar Cultural Trust in 2003, and almost immediately launched a new management plan for the area. Drawn up by Seán Harrington Architects, this ill-fated scheme contained all sorts of goodies, including a helium balloon tethered to the Civic Offices' amphitheatre, new art spaces in temporary buildings beneath the Central Bank's huge undercroft and a 'rainscreen' for films and other events in Meeting House Square, which was the only element that developed any traction. Installed in 2012, it consists of four very large upturned umbrellas supported on pylons that double as drains, with clunky galvanized steel plates over the channels running between them.

There was a round of 'consultations with stakeholders', run by McLaughlin's deputy, Dara Connolly, at which I expressed concern about potential noise pollution from loud music gigs on the square. Then, without letting us know, TBCT slipped in a planning application for the project that generated not a single letter of objection, and permission was swiftly granted by Dublin City Council. It also transpired that TBCT had obtained a music and singing licence for Meeting House Square – again, with no objections, as nobody knew about it – that would permit events to be run there till 2.30 a.m., with a nightclub-like noise level of 96 decibels. In this scenario, even its own acoustic consultant admitted that heavy bass would leak out all over the place. Although TBCT had supported us in objecting to the Mezz Bar and Nightclub, it was now running much noisier gigs in the square, and the company anticipated that up to thirty 'commercial hires' per year would be needed to repay its investment in the rainscreen – estimated to cost €2.5 million.

As I told McLaughlin in a text message complaining about yet another noisy gig, 'It sends out the message that Temple Bar is merely an entertainment zone, and to hell with the residents. You should be ashamed of yourselves, but I suppose that's expecting too much.'

By then, I had given up on him. Under his leadership, TBCT ruthlessly pursued a policy of sweating the assets it owned or controlled. That's why nearly half the public space in Temple Bar Square was effectively privatized, carved up between the restaurants, bars and cafés around it, and why a brace of telecommunications antennae appeared on the roof of FilmBase (formerly Arthouse), on Curved Street; in both cases, the rental revenue proved irresistible to McLaughlin and his cohorts. TBCT was also involved in disputes with several of the area's cultural organizations over the rent they were paying, or not paying in some cases. To avoid potential compensation claims from passers-by who might slip or fall, McLaughlin had the smooth limestone surfaces of Curved Street and paths through Meeting House Square roughened up by a concrete grinder. A crude steel handrail was added to the stepped entry into the square, for 'health and safety' reasons, even though it already had a built-in stone handrail. Worse still, Portland stone bases of the two modernist buildings on Curved Street – the Button Factory and FilmBase – were painted over in magnolia, ostensibly to make it easier to deal with the plague of graffiti 'tagging'. I asked my friend Niall McCullough, architect of the Button Factory building, to take a look at TBCT's handiwork.

'Jesus, Frank,' he texted later. 'I see what you mean. Magnolia. Dematerialised. Cheapened at one blow. Triumph of style over substance.'

McLaughlin soon came a cropper. Dublin City Council's internal audit department, headed by Gerry Macken, carried out a detailed audit of TBCT, and uncovered a litany of corporate governance failures. McLaughlin had been seconded to a role as project director for Derry UK City of Culture, taking leave of absence from Temple Bar, so he was away when I got my hands on a copy of the damning report in March 2013. Board minutes showing that loans and overdraft facilities for the Meeting House Square rainscreen were approved by its directors didn't exist, even though 'certified extracts', purportedly from the minutes, had been provided to Ulster Bank. The report also found that TBCT's strategy/business plan for 2010 and 2011 had not been approved by the board, that proper financial accounting procedures were not in place and that company credit cards were being used for personal expenditure. Architect Seán Harrington was paid some of his fees for the rainscreen in a very unconventional way – by getting the rights to hold ten events of his own in Meeting House Square, valued at €1,500 a pop.

Documents had also been shredded, although reference to this was removed from the audit report at TBCT's request. All this (and more) was detailed by me in the *Irish Times*, much to the annoyance of the company's new chairman, former diplomat Daithí Ó Ceallaigh, who complained that 'details . . . of a highly confidential nature' about what was happening at board meetings were appearing in the paper. In the eye of a storm, McLaughlin resigned from his temporary post in Derry and announced that he would be returning to his job in Temple Bar. But acting chief executive Ray Yeates, DCC's Arts Officer, nailed that by writing to McLaughlin as follows: 'Given the difficulties the company is now facing in dealing with all of the issues arising at present, the board have asked that you do not attend at the offices of TBCT . . .'

The board then decided that Temple Bar Cultural Trust should be wound up; one of its directors – artist, activist, independent city councillor and Letterfrack survivor Mannix Flynn – publicly branded it as 'a wreck'. McLaughlin threatened legal action and got his job back, but only briefly. After it was revealed that he had offered three senior staff redundancy packages, each worth €100,000 or more, he was suspended by the board – then firmly in the hands of DCC – pending an investigation. Under the threat of further legal action, TBCT negotiated a severance package with him, and McLaughlin finally departed to pursue a new career as an arts consultant.

My younger friends were doing well, despite all the challenges of living with austerity. Richard Conway, a former editor of *Plan* magazine, won a scholarship to do a year-long master's degree in journalism at Columbia University after I wrote a glowing recommendation for him, and then got a job with *Time* magazine running its online content. Javier Saez had already done a higher diploma in psychology at UCD and was now doing a master's degree course in humanistic psychotherapy on a 'semi-presential' basis with the Galene Institute of Psychotherapy in Madrid – studying at home in Mulhuddart, watching lectures on Skype and attending residential seminars at the institute from time to time – a bit like the Open University, really. And Stephen O'Farrell was over the moon about a big break in New York City. 'Great news!' he texted me. 'I was just offered a new permanent position in Carnegie Hall! In Development! . . . I finally get full benefits, which is fabulous, especially over here. And I'll be meeting all the rich donors in New York!! 1,000 people applied for the position, if not more! Haha.' He also met and fell in love with Greg van der Veer, a young documentary film director from Vermont, who sold funky T-shirts on Brooklyn Bridge when he wasn't making movies.

My godson Alex was settling in to Sandford Park School, but kept pestering me to replace my trusted Nokia 6310, a classic of its type, with a smartphone. He piled on the pressure, teasing me with a text, asking, 'Are you still on your Nokia blokia? ;-).' I finally relented and managed to get a free iPhone 4S from the *Irish Times*, even though I had no idea at all how to use it and told Alex that he would need to give me an iPhone tutorial, which he duly did after I said that 'life is too short to read the effin' manual'.

12

I was on an Aer Lingus plane en route to Ibiza in September 2013 when a story I read in the paper so irritated me that I signed up for Twitter to sound off. 'Wasn't it just great that the *Irish Times* let us know, via its news pages, that Fairy Liquid really does last twice as long as its nearest rival,' I tweeted. The story, by consumer affairs correspondent Conor Pope, was four hundred words long, and apparently based on a quasi-scientific study that someone or other had done. Oh dear, I thought, the 'paper of record' is really going down the tubes if such a 'finding' is regarded as worthy of its news pages.

It also irked me that the *Irish Times* was allowing such abuses of the English language as 'from the get-go' (what's wrong with 'from the start'?), or letting a fashion tipster write such twaddle as, 'Shirting: Think of normcore evolved. Peacocking is so passé, so ditch the bling and do as the fash-pack does and sport a classic crisp shirt instead.' Ugh! Or abandoning the correct use of accents in words such as café or façade, as well as using the wrong photographs, failing repeatedly to identify architects even while showing computer-generated images of their projects, and making so many errors that are simply not corrected, except quietly in online versions. Some subeditor changed my 'principal sewage treatment plant' to read 'principle . . .'

One of my biggest cribs about how the *Irish Times* was being run had to do with the emergence of a new cadre of ruthless middle managers on the editorial side of the house who thought it was perfectly all right to hack to bits stuff I'd written, without any consultation. And if this was happening to me, as an assistant editor, how much worse must it be for freelancers or young journalists on short-term contracts? The residential property supplement on Thursdays became even more fawning and market-driven than it was in the 'property porn' era. The paper as a whole was becoming increasingly commercialized, with more and more 'sponsored content' both in print and online, and clickbait-driven editorial decisions about what to run or not to run.

In October 2013, at the launch of Fergal MacCabe's book *Friends' Houses* at the National Yacht Club in Dún Laoghaire, I ran into Conor Brady.

'How are you getting on?' he asked.

'Struggling through the tide of trivia,' I replied.

In his typically erudite way, he asked me if I knew the origin of the word 'trivia', and I had to confess that I didn't.

'It derives from the three roads that led into ancient Rome,' he explained. 'When Roman armies were coming back from conquering new territories, these bright boys would go out along the roads, talk to the commanding officers about their exploits and then rush back into Rome to tell people about it. They were the first journalists, in effect.'

I was suitably enlightened, and said, 'OK, not trivia. Just drivel.'

Brady, by then a member of the Garda Síochána Ombudsman Commission, told me something else I thought was quite unnerving. After the presentation of an elaborate picture of himself by James Hanley RHA, commissioned by the *Irish Times*, he wouldn't even have a glass of wine, just sparkling water. He had been on his way home to Monkstown the previous week when his car was stopped at a Garda checkpoint on Stillorgan Road and he was promptly breathalysed; fortunately, he hadn't taken any drink that night.

'Do you think you were deliberately targeted by the gardaí?' I asked him.

'Of course,' he replied. 'They know our number plates.'

In May 2014, just eight months before I was due to 'retire' on reaching the age of sixty-five, I got a call from Frank McGovern, the Environmental Protection Agency's chief scientist, telling me that Professor Thomas Stocker, co-chair of the UN's Intergovernmental Panel on Climate Change, was coming to Dublin to give a public lecture and asking if I would do an interview with him for the *Irish Times*. Naturally, given the importance of his post and what he might say, I agreed, so the three of us met for a light lunch in the Westin Hotel's atrium, and I flagged it to both the news desk and foreign desk in advance.

Stocker was every bit as impressive as I had expected, talking about how climate scientists such as Michael Mann were being 'vilified' by so-called sceptics on Twitter and other forums; some had even received death threats for daring to speak out about the dangers faced by humanity in a warming world. He told me he would be flying home to Zurich the following morning and said he'd pick up a copy of the paper at Dublin Airport. But the story I wrote about our interview didn't appear, and I emailed Kevin O'Sullivan to complain. Five hours later, having received no response, I sent him another email, marked 'URGENT!' telling him that it was 'a matter of acute personal embarrassment and distress to me that stuff I write as Environment Editor of the *Irish Times* is not carried either in the paper (where space is admittedly limited) or online (where it's not) . . . This is just the latest in a long line of such happenings, which I believe cumulatively undermines my position. Accordingly, I wish to resign as the paper's Environment Editor, effective immediately. Yours sincerely, Frank.'

A few minutes later, Kevin rang me, sounding rather sheepish. I gave out yards to him, saying I never had any difficulty getting stuff into the paper while Geraldine Kennedy was editor – it had all happened on his watch. I also reminded him that I would be retiring from my staff position in January 2015 and said, 'I am fucked if I am going to be treated like this in the few months I have left working for the *Irish Times*.' He assured me that it wouldn't happen again and, if it did, I should go straight to him to have any problem sorted out. I took Kevin at his word and consented to remain on as environment editor for the duration.

The year had started badly with the untimely death (from a brain tumour) of Seán Flynn, education editor of the *Irish Times*, which left us all reeling. His funeral Mass was held at the church on Home

Farm Road, where my parents were married, and no one who was there will ever forget the heartfelt tributes paid to him by his young sons. Bertie Ahern was among the large attendance, but all I did was to nod in his direction when he recognized me; I couldn't bring myself to shake hands with him. Less than two months later, my South African friend Pieter Watson also died prematurely, from cancer, at the age of forty-eight. I knew that he had been unwell for quite some time, but I was still shocked to get a text message from Thinus Calitz in London, telling me the sad news. (Not long afterwards, Thinus met and fell in love with Sheldon Halvorsen, a cute South African in his early twenties, and they got married there before settling in London.) Then, in June, Gordon Colleary died from prostate cancer at the age of seventy-three, in East Sussex, and I was honoured to be asked by the family to write his obituary for the *Irish Times*. Less than a week later, the great Ronnie Tallon died at the age of eighty-eight, three years after he received the RIAI's James Gandon Medal for lifetime achievement as 'one of the most influential architects of the last century'. Sadly, I was unable to attend his funeral, but got Shane O'Toole to write his obituary for the *Irish Times*.

I had my own brush with mortality when I started getting tightness in my chest, accompanied by shortness of breath, and an angiogram showed that I needed a stent in my left circumflex artery, expertly inserted by Dr Niall Mahon at the Mater Private, with VHI picking up the bill. I was a bit unnerved by the procedure, especially when the risks included heart attack and/or death. Admittedly remote, but nonetheless . . .

'Must take up Vape!' I wrote to Paul Moley in a text message.

'Yes, you must focus! We want you to enjoy your retirement, not keel over,' he replied.

My father, then in his late nineties, was still going into town by bus on an almost daily basis to attend Mass in the Carmelite church on Clarendon Street, usually popping into Marks & Spencer afterwards for some provisions, or to the Franciscan church (Adam & Eve's) on Merchants Quay, which was convenient to the post office where he collected his pension. But one day he suffered a fall, gashing his forehead on a footpath not far from our family home. Helped to his feet by passers-by, he was taken by ambulance to the Mater's accident and emergency department where the wound was dressed and he was then released. It looked awful, but I found it encouraging that even at his age his body was still able to heal itself, and the gash was nearly undetectable just a few weeks later. A more serious setback followed, as he needed to be taken into the Mater with a chest infection, and spent three miserable weeks there. Dad struggled to accept being in hospital and would regularly refer to the doctors, nurses and other staff as 'the people in this establishment'. What annoyed him was that he had to live by their regime, rather than his own.

One day, when I called in to see him while he was having his tea, he looked at me fiercely and snarled, 'You're all traitors!'

I was taken aback, and asked him why.

'Because you've got me incarcerated in this place.' I explained that we were trying to organize a home care package, so that he could be released as soon as possible. And when we managed to make arrangements with Home Instead, he was let out to return to 9 Glenmore Road. He was still able to read at that point, and would go through the *Irish Times* from cover to cover every day; but soon his eyesight began to fail as a result of macular degeneration, and he would complain that the print in the paper was too small, or too grey. Worse still, as he lost his central vision while retaining some on the periphery, he started seeing things that weren't there, such as fellows in the back garden, and this added to his overall anxiety.

The rota of Home Instead carers was also something that took a while for him to get used to, but we thought it was essential in case he might have another fall without anybody knowing. We took turns to visit him on a daily basis, every evening between five and seven o'clock. On 24 December 2016 he hit his one hundredth birthday, and was delighted to get a letter from President Michael D. Higgins, with a cheque for €2,540 – the euro equivalent of the old £2,000. All he wanted to mark the milestone was a Mass in

Aughrim Street church, followed by a reception for family, friends and relatives in the sacristy, with tea, buns and a big iced cake topped by lit candles that he happily blew out. By then, he had become a vegetarian, having read an article in *Far East*, the Columban Missionaries' magazine, about how eating meat was killing the planet.

Normally, retirements of staff members are marked by speeches in the newsroom, but I did my own thing, as usual, organizing a big party for a hundred and fifty or so at the Irish Architectural Archive on Merrion Square. There were speeches by Kevin O'Sullivan, former Dublin City Manager John Fitzgerald, former Gill & Macmillan publishing director Fergal Tobin, Shane O'Toole, James Nix and Richard Barrett, with Catriona Crowe cracking the whip as emcee. Fergal described *The Destruction of Dublin*, which he had had the guts to publish, as 'a game-changer . . . because it changed the nature of the public discourse about how this city is governed'. Shane was even more generous, saying that 'nobody in history has written more words about Irish architecture and few have had such a positive impact on the discipline. That's not bad for an old hack, a mere scribbler . . .' James did an 'A to Z' on it, while Richard's speech was wickedly witty in getting his own back at me for attacking developers like himself over the years; he got a lot of laughs. And Kevin said that my body of work for the *Irish Times* would 'stand for centuries as a chapter in the definitive history of Dublin', even suggesting that a street should be named after me.

I was quite overwhelmed, because it had been a very tough week, with two deaths that affected me deeply: my first cousin Eamonn Coghlan, who was eight years younger than me, had had a fatal heart attack while on holiday in Lanzarote; and my good friend Graham Egan, then just over forty, was found dead by his partner Alan at their home in Dublin 6. In my own remarks, I noted that the newspaper was now referred to, in management-speak, as the 'print platform', and expressed my fear that we were 'the last generation that will be able to claim direct succession from Gutenberg'.

I also reiterated my long-held view that the primary purpose of journalism was – and is, or should be – 'to find out what the hell is going on and tell people about it'.

As for how I had managed to conceal my advanced age for so long, I told everyone that it wasn't L'Oréal, but the fact that I had so many young friends who kept me youthful, as well as the love and support of Eamon, whom Catriona described as 'one of the very best human beings I've had the privilege to meet'. Nearly eighty of them joined us in Temple Bar for a Vietnamese buffet in Pho Ta, behind the Central Bank, and the hard core came back to the flat afterwards. As is the tradition in newspapers, Kevin had presented me with a framed mock *Irish Times* front page, featuring a Martyn Turner cartoon of me with my travel bag as the main illustration, and a 'lead story' about how I would be a candidate for Mayor of Dublin, but 'last night was believed to be en route from Taiwan to San Francisco for a conference on the impact of climate change on vineyards in the Napa Valley'.

My slogan on the night, with an art poster projected onto a screen above all of the speakers, was 'Rip It Up and Start Again', and what I meant was that I intended to go on writing as well as having the luxury of being able to say 'No' if I wasn't in the mood to do this or that. I was concerned that a new environment correspondent should be appointed quickly, especially with the Paris climate summit looming, not to mention any number of environmental, planning and architectural issues arising at home; but months passed and the job remained vacant. It seemed inexplicable that the environment was being neglected by what was once the 'paper of record'; this didn't go down at all well with a whole constituency of readers who expected that issues of concern to them would be covered on a consistent basis. At least I got Kevin O'Sullivan to agree that I would be among those representing the paper and its website in Paris at the climate summit in December 2015, having covered so many of them over the years since 1995. (It was not until he surprised everyone by resigning as editor in April 2017, to be succeeded by Paul O'Neill, that the gap was filled with an announcement that he himself would be taking over as the paper's agriculture, environment and science editor.)

When Leo Varadkar, then Minister for Health, came out as gay in an RTÉ radio interview with Marian Finucane on 18 January 2015, I was enormously encouraged not only by what he said, but also by the overwhelmingly positive public reaction, which boded well for the outcome of the marriage equality referendum five months later – though in the event I wasn't confident of a good result until the final few days. Javier Saez had thrown himself into the campaign, canvassing in Blanchardstown, close to where he lives, and he was really uplifted by the almost universal goodwill the Yes campaigners were getting on the doorsteps.

We had him over for dinner on the night before the vote, and he texted me later saying, 'Fecking delighted I shared some moments with you guys last night, eyes on Ireland, cannot wait for a celebration tomorrow when the streets melt like cupcakes. Big fat YES and X x x o o O.'

I was also moved to tears by the number of Irish emigrants who had responded to the #hometovote campaign by flying in from all sorts of places or taking the boat from Holyhead. I'll never forget the sight of a group of young fellows, possibly all gay, who posted selfies of themselves on Twitter posing with a 'Home to Vote' banner as their Stena ferry steamed into Dublin Port with just hours to go until the poll closed. 'Young people of Ireland, I love you!' I remember tweeting that evening. I could feel it in my bones then that the proposition would be carried by a wide margin.

The count was being coordinated at Dublin Castle, and a huge crowd of Yes campaigners had congregated in the Upper Castle Yard, so after hearing the racket from our roof terrace, I asked my godson Alex to come into town from Ranelagh to soak up the atmosphere. Naturally, he diverted me into Brown Thomas to look at the latest range of Ray-Ban sunglasses until I put the skids under him and we finally headed for the Castle. There we found a joyous crowd celebrating as the results came in and Ireland became the first country in the world to adopt same-sex marriage by a popular vote – 62 per cent to 38 per cent. The explosion of joy in the city centre that night really did make streets – and hearts – 'melt like cupcakes'.

Within our own family, we had been celebrating the births, in relatively quick succession, of my niece Nessa's daughter Elsie (in July 2011) and son Roshan (in January 2013). Their dad, London-born Indian management consultant Umesh Mistry, explained that Roshan means 'splendid, shining light' in Sanskrit. They also livened up our Christmas Day at Edel and Paul's home in the Botanic Gardens. Elsie and Roshan were both baptized in Aughrim Street Church, as well as having Hindu naming ceremonies at the Hare Krishna Temple in London, where they live in Pinner. Stephen O'Farrell, who had been living in New York for a few years, flew in with his American partner Greg for a week, with the news that Greg's parents had offered to let them take over the family firm, a small chain of 'Christmas stores' in the north of New Hampshire, and that Stephen would be giving up his job at Carnegie Hall to throw himself into the business. His friends and colleagues thought he was crazy to leave a good career in New York to move to the wilds of New Hampshire, but they all wished him well. We entertained Stephen and Greg with a road trip to Glencree, lunching at Hunter's Hotel near Rathnew on a gloriously sunny spring day and then visiting Luggala, where Garech de Brún gave us a tour of the house. We all imagined that we could catch a whiff of Michael Jackson, who had stayed there quietly for two months in 2005. It was the last time I saw Garech. In March 2018, while having dinner in a London restaurant with his old friend, Nicholas (Lord) Gormanston, he had a heart attack, keeled over and died. It was the way he would have wanted to go, having a jolly old time.

In a determined effort to make our neighbourhood more civilized, a group of us got together in 2014 to form Temple Bar Residents, with an agenda that included the need for a more proactive approach to noise control, cleansing and graffiti removal, brighter street lighting, more tree-planting and a rolling programme to repair or re-lay street setts throughout the area. We called on Dublin City Council to set up a new Temple Bar Forum representing the residents, cultural institutions and businesses in the area as well as DCC and the Garda. We had also come to realize that the council is hamstrung by a bureaucratic silo mentality and called for the establishment of a multidisciplinary team drawn from the arts, planning, city architect, environmental health, roads and cleansing departments to coordinate its work in Temple Bar.

Assistant DCC chief executive Brendan Kenny warmly welcomed our initiative, saying there was 'not a single thing' in our programme that he would disagree with, and he pledged to work with us. But there was no real movement after we met him and the council's chief executive, Owen Keegan. The same was true of An Garda Síochána. We met senior Garda officers in Pearse Street to discuss a whole range of issues, with a major focus on noise pollution. Superintendent Joe Gannon even said that 'quietening down Temple Bar should be our legacy', but there was no real follow-up that we could see. When proposed busking by-laws were published, we made a strong submission calling for amplified performers to be banned from Temple Bar and other residential areas, but this was initially ignored because councillors were under such pressure from the busking lobby. So were we. A leading member of the lobby joined our association, claiming to live in the area, and the website was hacked, by whom we don't know.

When it came to a review six months later of how the by-laws were operating in practice, DCC management had changed its tune and now supported a city-wide ban on the use of amplifiers. Officials were also conscious of the fact that tenants would soon be moving into Crampton Buildings, after DCC itself had renovated the complex, and they needed to be protected against gratuitous noise in the immediate vicinity – notably from Temple Bar Square. So when the issue came before the city council itself, I made a point of attending the meeting and suggested to Ciarán Cuffe that the prohibited zone for amplified busking in our neighbourhood should be extended to include Temple Bar Square, which it duly was by the very narrow margin of 26 votes to 25. Thus, from 1 August 2016, it's been illegal for amplified buskers to play in or around the square, though some of them still do from time to time for the sheer hell of it.

I wrote to the management of the Bad Ass Café, asking for the removal of its external loudspeakers from the open lobby on Crown Alley and from Temple Bar Square itself. Pointing out that there were people living in the immediate vicinity, I asked, 'Can't you see that inflicting generated noise on them at all hours of the day and night is an abuse of the neighbourhood?' I got no reply.

In the good old days, the Bad Ass was a Temple Bar institution, dating from 1983. Kids loved the spring-loaded pulley and wire that waiters used to whizz orders to the kitchen. After new owners took over the restaurant in 2011, the pulley equipment was thrown into a skip, the old industrial-style interior was replaced by a 'traditional Irish pub' and this had all been done without planning permission, even though the Bad Ass is a protected structure. Dublin City Council issued a warning letter about the unauthorized works and change of use, but it took eighteen months before the new owners lodged a planning application seeking permission to retain the radical alterations.

Naturally, I exercised my right to object, noting that Temple Bar 'is awash with pubs. The last thing it needs is another one, particularly an architectural changeling of the type proposed.' Four weeks later, I got an email from prolific pub architect Frank Kenny – younger brother of broadcaster Pat Kenny – pressing me to meet him and Constance Cassidy SC, Ireland's leading expert on our labyrinthine licensing laws (and *chatelaine* of Lissadell, in Co. Sligo, and the lesser-known Morristown Lattin, in Co. Kildare). Over coffee in the Octagon Bar of the Clarence Hotel, I was assured by Kenny that the Bad Ass would revert to its earlier industrial-style interior, and he even produced sample sketches showing how this would be done. Cassidy also assured me – repeatedly – that it would operate as a restaurant, not as a pub, and said the proprietors had merely sought a full licence so that they could serve, say, a pint of Guinness to patrons with their meals, rather than 'imported wine'. On foot of these assurances, I did not pursue an appeal to An Bord Pleanála.

Although the appeals board granted retention permission to the licence-holder, Benqueues Ltd, its ruling made clear that 'no permission is granted for a change of use to this Protected Structure from its primary use as a restaurant to that of a public house' and that 'any use of the bar area for the sale and consumption of alcohol shall be strictly ancillary to the principal use of the premises as a restaurant'. Yet Benqueues carried on regardless, serving pint after pint to its patrons as well as blasting the neighbourhood with noise on a nightly basis. It was clear to me, as it would be to anyone who checked out the Bad Ass, that it had become a pub rather than a restaurant – defined in the Dublin city plan as 'a building where the primary function is for the sale of food, meals/refreshment for consumption on the premises'.

Feeling betrayed by Kenny and Cassidy, I sent a letter to Jim Keogan, then executive manager in charge of DCC's planning department: 'You know the old expression, "If it looks like a duck, quacks like a duck and walks like a duck, it's a duck,"' I wrote, urging him to take enforcement action against the proprietors for their 'absolutely flagrant breach' of An Bord Pleanála's planning permission, 'otherwise, we run the risk of other restaurants in Temple Bar (of which there are more than eighty) being surreptitiously turned into pubs in the way this premises was.' In 2014, Temple Bar Residents supported an objection by Temple Bar Company (which represents traders in the area, including publicans) to the Bad Ass licence on the basis that it was trading as a pub, rather than a restaurant. This was resisted by Constance Cassidy, who had managed in court to have a large volume of evidence excluded in advance of a full hearing of the case. As a result, we had no option but to withdraw our objections in February 2015 and settle for a weak and largely meaningless agreement, under which Benqueues said it would 'comply' with the terms of An Bord Pleanála's permission as well as engage acoustic expert Karl Searson to 'calibrate' the external loudspeakers, but without specifying any decibel levels.

Five months later, however, I was present in court when Benqueues was prosecuted by Dublin City Council, on foot of an enforcement notice for being in breach of the terms of its planning permission. There, I heard Cassidy tell the judge that the Bad Ass was a 'licensed restaurant, as certified by the Circuit Court'. DCC's case was based on minimal evidence – a statement by Planning Enforcement Officer Paddy Keogh that he had been served a pint in the Bad Ass without having to order food – because council officials had spurned offers from both Temple Bar Residents and Temple Bar Company to back it up with chapter-and-verse on how the premises was being run. Cassidy and planning law barrister Michael O'Donnell, who was also representing the Bad Ass, took a 'case stated' to the High Court, based on 'discrepancies' between the terms of its planning permission and the wording of the enforcement notice. Judge Michael Twomey ruled that selling alcohol without a meal was not sufficient in itself to prove that the use of the premises had been changed from a restaurant to a pub, and costs amounting to some €300,000 were awarded against DCC.

I wrote to Constance Cassidy, complaining that the assurances from her clients that she had repeatedly given to me had turned out to be unreliable and that her presentation of Benqueues's defence of its position – albeit within the court rules – resulted in a 'denial of justice'.

She wrote back from the Law Library, saying she had 'always tried to conduct myself in a just and professional way' while acting on the instructions of her clients, as barristers do.

Cassidy and I later faced off in the Licensing Court in March 2017, after I had objected to the renewal of music and singing licences for the Bad Ass, the Quays Bar and the Old Storehouse. I told Judge Michael P. Coghlan that I was withdrawing my objection to the Old Storehouse's licence after its owner, John Patchell, had contacted me, offering to reduce the volume of its external loudspeaker to a reasonable level. In the case of the Quays Bar, owned by Louis Fitzgerald, An Bord Pleanála's 1997 planning permission contained a specific condition that 'the public bar shall not be used for amplified music [and] there shall be no outdoor broadcasting of music from the premises'. I produced a series of emails dating back to 2011 in which I had complained about its doors being left open, with a heavily amped singer/guitarist playing right inside, at up to 100 decibels; imagine the impact of that on the health and well-being of bar staff. I also recalled giving a walking tour of Temple Bar, as part of Open House Weekend in 2015, when I asked one of the bouncers on duty to close the doors and he declined to do so, saying, 'No, it's too warm inside. Plus, we own this premises and we can do what we like.'

Judge Coghlan, who had previously described Temple Bar as 'Dublin's designated party zone' until I wrote to him pointing out that it had only been designated as the city's 'cultural quarter', granted renewal of the licence, but ordered that spring-loaded doors must be fitted to the Quays Bar to minimize the level of noise break-out. After hearing all my evidence about the Bad Ass's shenanigans over the previous five years, backed up by short videos and photographs that showed it really was 'the most abusive licensed premises in Temple Bar', as I had described it in court, the judge warned its owners that they would be 'in trouble' if there was any repetition.

Temple Bar Residents also got involved in opposing the growing plague of short-term holiday lets in the area. A two-bedroom apartment in Crown Alley, directly opposite the Bad Ass, was advertised for sale at the extravagant price of €425,000; its unique selling point was that the owner had made €79,300 in 2015 via Airbnb. We made a 'Section 5' reference to Dublin City Council, asking for a determination that this was a change of use requiring planning permission. We won that determination, though a DCC spokesman said its ruling applied only in the Crown Alley case, and not generally; in other words, every illegal conversion of an 'entire home' to short-term holiday lets would have to be fought by ordinary citizens on a case-by-case basis. The owner, Michael Melinn, appealed to An Bord Pleanála, but it ruled in October 2016 that the 'fully commercial nature of the activity' of renting out an apartment for short lets 'constitutes a material change of use' that required planning permission. At the time, we estimated that more than two thousand 'entire homes' were being short-let via Airbnb alone – plus many others through agencies such as Booking.com, the Key Collection or Handel's Hotel on Fishamble Street, which gained control of a brace of apartments in Temple Bar.

And all this was happening while Dublin was in the throes of a housing emergency, with the local authorities spending €25 million in 2015 on entirely unsuitable hotel or B&B accommodation for homeless families. Then Minister for Housing and Planning Simon Coveney promised to take action in an effort to recover lost housing stock, but all he did was to send a circular to local authorities and engage in a 'dialogue' with Airbnb, whose European headquarters are located in Dublin, on the introduction of a 'voluntary code', rather than statutory regulations. In adopting this eunuch-in-a-harem approach, Coveney told the *Irish Independent* that Airbnb had been a very positive thing for many homeowners and visitors to Ireland. 'I wouldn't like to undermine that, particularly in a country that relies on so many people coming and going for weekend breaks and so on,' he said weakly.

By contrast, effective action was being taken by other cities, notably Berlin, where the authorities introduced stringent regulations in May 2016 to recover up to twelve thousand homes that landlords had turned over to more profitable holiday lets. We banned them in our building, and so did other sensible management companies. Even so, the number of homes in Dublin being short-let through Airbnb alone continued to increase by leaps and bounds, amounting to more than four thousand at the time of writing. (In Temple Bar, it is now a plague, as more and more full-time residents in rented apartments are replaced by tourists keen to experience its 'vibrant nightlife'. Some of the publicans would probably like to see this trend continuing until *all* the apartments are taken over by Airbnb and its ilk, and then it could become a strictly 'party zone', with no permanent residents left to complain about the racket.)

But Dublin is a city of talk, not a city of action. It is a *slovenly* city. Nothing much happens, really, even when it comes to implementing official policies. Take the 2013 *Design Manual for Urban Roads and Streets*, issued jointly by the Department of the Environment and the Department of Transport in 2013. It appeared to herald an enlightened new era for street design, abandoning the old devotion to fast-moving 'distributor' roads and dreadful sheep-pen railings to corral pedestrians at major junctions. The advice it gave to local authorities was to get rid of guardrails, provide more zebra crossings, 'de-clutter' streets by removing excessive road signage and permit commercial buildings to flank distributor roads in the suburbs. But the 165-page guidance manual made no impact on the thinking or practices of road engineers, largely due to a get-out clause that says designers had no 'immunity from legal obligations'. Transfixed by the fear of being sued if accidents could be attributed to some failure by them, the engineers are still applying old thinking – as shown by the needless guardrails erected in 2015 on a traffic island at the north-east corner of St Stephen's Green, right opposite Edward Delaney's statue of Wolfe Tone, and the ever-growing profusion of signage on city-centre streets, which made nonsense of a pledge to 'de-clutter' them in Dublin City Council's 2011 public realm strategy.

Council officials sought to evade commissioning an environmental impact assessment of plans for a European-style pedestrian plaza on College Green, even after some of its downsides became evident – notably a proposal to transform Parliament Street into a two-way bus corridor, carrying up to seventeen hundred buses per day. Their strategy was to proceed with this radical scheme under the Roads and Traffic Acts, under which the approval of elected councillors would not even be needed. College Green would be closed to east–west traffic, including cars, buses and taxis, so that it could be transformed into a pedestrian plaza, traversed by a two-way cycle route, with the new Luas line running on its eastern edge. But opposition to the plan built up such a head of steam that the officials had to concede on an EIA.

Solicitor and former Dublin GAA football captain Tony Hanahoe, who owns the Sunlight Chambers building on the corner of Essex Quay, warned that it would have a 'disastrous impact' on Parliament Street, with the risk that noxious diesel emissions from buses 'would close every restaurant' along its length. If buses in Dublin were hybrid or electric vehicles, rather than diesel-powered, there wouldn't be a problem with emissions. But the National Transport Authority vetoed plans by Dublin Bus to lease three hybrid vehicles for trial runs on the basis that this would be too costly. London Transport, by contrast, introduced hybrid buses in 2007 and currently has more than fifteen hundred, amounting to 20 per cent of the city's bus fleet. In 2013, it began trials of electric-only buses with zero exhaust emissions, as well as hydrogen-fuelled vehicles emitting only water vapour. Our own government's *National Mitigation Plan* to reduce the carbon emissions causing climate change contains no commitment on fuel conversion here, other than saying that, by 2050, 'the technological ambition is for the nation's car fleet, along with some of our public transport buses and rail lines, to be low/near zero emissions'. And that's it.

Few senior officials of Dublin City Council actually live in the inner city. When Naas-based Dick Gleeson retired as Dublin Planning Officer in 2015, one of his colleagues made an affectionately barbed speech to a gathering at the Wood Quay Venue. Declan Wallace, then principal officer in the council's planning department, recalled how Gleeson would talk about the city in 'flowery, often metaphoric terms', referring to 'breathing' urban spaces, 'conversations' between buildings, 'permeability' in the public realm and other such language; this, Wallace noted, became known as 'Dick-speak'. There was a great gulf between the high ideals Gleeson espoused and day-to-day decisions on development control made by his more prosaic colleagues that so often resulted in mediocre buildings and poor public spaces. The perceived need to promote 'development', in a generic sense, has nearly always trumped sensitive planning in Dublin. And that's still the case today, sadly, with the city's legacy of twentieth-century architecture under threat, largely because of the council's failure to add more than a handful of modernist buildings to its Register of Protected Structures.

I could go on and on about the dysfunctionality of how we are governed, both locally and nationally. About the putrescent decay of our political system that has turned Dáil Éireann into a glorified county council, and the refusal of any of the parties in Leinster House to do anything to change it. Or the abject failure of successive governments, going back to the 1960s, to achieve anything that might resemble 'balanced regional development', by allowing Dublin to grow like Topsy, at the expense of Cork and Limerick in particular. Or the madness of spending €550 million on a full-scale motorway between Gort and Tuam, in Co. Galway, catering for such low levels of traffic that it's expected to reach a mere quarter of its design capacity by 2030. Or the continuing crazed pursuit of major road schemes in Galway City, when it really needs a functioning public transport network. Or the thrashing of Dublin's principal streets by Luas Cross City, with 129 thick steel poles between St Stephen's Green and Parnell Square, as well as miscellaneous gatherings of utility boxes on the footpaths.

Or the knee-jerk response to flood emergencies, with a favouritism for hard engineering solutions such as the devastating scheme proposed for Cork City by the OPW, and the nonsense of threading flood defences through the trees on City Quay in Dublin. Or the continuing availability of free car parking for public servants in and around the places where they work, such as the shameless serried ranks of privately owned cars outside Pearse Street Garda station in Dublin city centre. Or the yawning gap between the sing-a-long rhetoric of ministers on climate change and their refusal to adopt serious policies to reduce Ireland's greenhouse gas emissions, especially in the agricultural sector. Or the omnishambles created by Phil Hogan in hastily setting up Irish Water only to see it undone (after he had departed to Brussels as Ireland's latest EU Commissioner) by ruthlessly populist left-wing politicians who don't believe that even households using excessive amounts of water should have to pay for it. Or the disgraceful actions of NAMA in selling off prime assets to vulture funds, none of which had any intention of developing the sites that fell into their laps so cheaply.

In June 2015, a month after the same-sex marriage referendum was passed, Eamon and I were in Prague, where we had a lovely dinner on the terrace of an elegant restaurant called U Zlaté Studně, in Malá Strana, with panoramic views over the historic core. Afterwards, on Charles Bridge, I proposed to Eamon, or at least I tried to.

'We've been together a very long time, through thick and thin . . .' I began.

Then he said, 'Where's this leading?' which interrupted the little speech I had in my head, so I just asked him if he'd marry me, and he said, 'Yes, of course I will!' and we gave each other a big hug.

We fixed 3 June 2016 as the date, although neither of us realized that it would be such a nightmare to organize. We had been offered an incomparable venue for the reception – the upper floor of the National Botanic Gardens' Visitor Centre, with a great view of its curvilinear glasshouses – but it came with a limit of only one hundred and twenty guests, for 'health and safety' reasons.

'How many limos will you have?' my godson Alex asked me.

'None,' I replied.

Instead, we hired the Dublin Bus wedding bus to take people from the registry office in Grand Canal Street to Glasnevin. If it hadn't been for Alex's mum, Yetti Redmond, offering to help out with the arrangements, as she had just taken a career break from RTÉ, we would have been in a right pickle. She was able to get RTÉ's head of design, Marcella Power, to advise on decorating the big room where we would have dinner, as well as thinking of things that would never have crossed our minds, such as providing nice soap and scented candles for the toilets. Veerle Dehaene, the mother of Eamon's two godchildren, sorted us out with (non-matching) blue suits from Louis Copeland; she was also one of our witnesses, along with Mark Brennock, with registrar Louise Dodrill presiding.

At the wedding ceremony, Ailbhe Reddy played her guitar while the guests arrived to take their seats, and we also had some recorded music – Handel's 'Ombra Mai Fu', Bizet's famous duet from *The Pearl Fishers* and Puccini's 'Nessun Dorma'. We had a short script acknowledging that it was 'thanks to the generosity of our fellow citizens' that we were finally able to get married in Ireland, just over a year after the referendum had been passed, 'so let's get on with it, and with the rest of our lives together'. Five-year-olds Alice (Veerle's daughter) and Elsie (Nessa's daughter) brought small bouquets of flowers to the table, and little Roshan bore the palladium rings. Because the National Botanic Gardens doesn't actually do weddings, the invitations had to be issued under the name of its curator, my brother-in-law Paul Maher, to a 'special celebration for Frank & Eamon' starting with champagne and canapés in the Teak House, followed by a guided tour by Paul himself of Richard Turner's Curvilinear Range, and then a buffet dinner in the Visitor Centre.

Our old friend Bernadette Madden was the official photographer and presented us with a great selection of pictures later, in an album covered in one of her handmade batiks. It was a gloriously sunny day, and a very emotional one, too, not least because both of us were in our sixties and we had been together for so long.

'It was the best day of my life,' Eamon said afterwards, and I wholeheartedly agreed.

Needless to say, the reprobates came back to the flat for more, and we didn't get to bed until after 4 a.m. Then we spent an idyllic week in Cannes as guests of Conal and Vera O'Sullivan, our nearest and dearest neighbours in Temple Bar.

Kids are back on Glenmore Road, where I grew up, as its houses are once again occupied by a new generation of young parents; they are very lucky to be living there, just two miles from the city centre, rather than out in the boondocks, like so many others. But now, of course, the road is occupied by cars, mostly half-parked on the footpaths, so people must walk on the street – a reversal of the way things were meant to be. As I get older, the past seems strangely less rather than more distant. The Great Famine seemed so far away when we were children, but not now. And one of the real perks of being a pensioner is the free travel card that I carry, entitling me to get on any bus, tram or train and be conveyed to wherever I'm going without having to pay a cent. On Dublin Bus services, I've long noted that foreign nationals account for a disproportionately large number of bus users; people from Poland, China, Nigeria, Spain or wherever see nothing peculiar about using public transport, while the Irish drive around triumphantly in newly registered cars.

I was honoured, as a '1916 relative', to get an invitation to watch the military parade commemorating the Easter Rising's centenary from a reviewing stand right opposite the GPO in O'Connell Street. There, I spotted a Union Jack among the flags of many nations being carried right past the cradle of the Irish Republic, and nobody batted an eyelid, which showed how far we had come. Sitting beside me was a grandson of Michael Mallin, who had been executed by the British as a leading figure in the Irish Citizen Army, in place of Constance Markievicz, the 'Rebel Countess'. As we watched all the troops, tanks and armoured cars going past, and the Air Corps jets trailing tricoloured smoke in the sky, he turned to me and said, 'Well, this should frighten the shite out of the unionists anyway!', laughing at the thought of it. So did I. But not being a nationalist, still less a republican (in the Irish sense), I felt that we've moved beyond belligerent territorial claims to make way for a new Ireland based on mutual recognition and constitutional consent. Hopefully, this will survive the madness of Brexit.

Eamon and I took a road trip across Northern Ireland in August 2017, travelling from the Lakes of Fermanagh to the Glens of Antrim with our young friend Denis Ryan and his partner, Diego Gautama, a Brazilian care worker who helped to look after the painter Louis le Brocquy in his latter years. Superficially, it looked normal, apart from all the flags, or *flegs* as they call them up there. Whether red-white-and-blue or green-white-and-orange, there were so many of them flying, even in tatters, that we felt alienated by the lot of them. Denis, who's a brilliant scenario writer for video games, was doing all the driving and as we skirted around Ballymena en route to

Carnlough, on the Antrim coast, he recalled an unpleasant memory of something that happened there when he was eight years old. In the autumn of 1994, after the IRA ceasefire, his parents took him and his three older brothers on a first family trip up North from West Cork. On the outskirts of Ballymena, they stopped for petrol, and Denis went into the shop with one of his brothers to get some sweets. Hearing their lilting Cork accents as they tried to pay for them, the woman behind the counter said, 'Get the fuck out of my shop!' The depth of bigotry that lay behind saying something like that to two little boys, just because they were from the southern end of this island, is almost unimaginable to most of us. Yet it still exists, two decades later.

Three days after my sixty-eighth birthday, Dad died. It was not unexpected, but still a shock to us all when it finally happened. For months, he had been in failing health, both mentally and physically, and getting increasingly irritated by his lot. He could barely walk any more and spent most of the time sitting in an outsize adjustable chair that dominated the living room, smoking his pipe like an old trooper.

'There's not much point in saying it's bad for your health, seeing as you're nearly a hundred and one years old,' I said to him one evening, after bringing another two packets of his favourite Irish Dew tobacco from Kapp & Peterson's. He just laughed, as I filled the bowl of his pipe and lit it for him. Dad's mind was going, making him more forgetful and confused, even about whether the house on Glenmore Road that he had lived in for seventy years was really his home; the comings and goings of carers, even though he got on quite well with most of them, made it seem like a different place.

When it came to his one hundred and first birthday, he was a bit bemused to get another letter from the President, with a silver medal in a presentation case to mark his great age. In truth, he didn't see the point of going on, especially as he had lost his wife of sixty years a decade earlier, and would have wished to depart this world sooner than he did.

'Why am I being kept down here, on the ground?' he asked me one night. He wanted to be in Heaven, with her. A bout of sickness in January turned out to be the final straw. We had all decided that there would be no question of calling an ambulance to take him to A&E in the Mater, because we knew he would want to die at home, rather than on a hospital trolley. In the early hours of 27 January, he vomited in bed and inhaled some of it into his lungs, which proved fatal.

'Where am I going? Where am I going?' were his last words, as if he was being pulled by some unseen force into another world. After his funeral Mass in Aughrim Street Church, celebrated by our first cousin Father Niall Coghlan, we got Ken Edge to play 'Boolavogue' on his saxophone as Dad's coffin was shouldered out; he was, after all, a Wexfordman through and through. Then we buried him beside Mam's silver birch in the oldest part of Glasnevin Cemetery.

They deserved to be together, even in death. After Dad had departed, we rooted through drawers in the old family home and found numerous black-and-white photographs of our parents when they were going out together in the 1940s. One of the most charming was a picture of them nonchalantly cycling two-abreast down Lower O'Connell Street in 1944; it was taken by Arthur Fields, the legendary 'Man on the Bridge', who specialized in snapping people as they passed, then giving them his card so that they could buy prints later.

More poignant was Edel's discovery of a box that Mam had kept in the bottom of their wardrobe containing letters Dad had written to her in the 1940s during their courtship. It was very affecting for Edel, and for me, to leaf through those old letters and read how much he was in love with our mother. What he wrote to her was so private and personal, so tender and touching, that it revealed to us an entirely different side of his character; though always so reticent, he was clearly an incurable romantic, bursting with love for her. Of course, we knew that they loved each other dearly, but here it was all recorded, and so eloquently too, in his always legible handwriting.

I've been reading *Being Mortal*, by an Indian-American surgeon, Atul Gawande. It's a book about the modern experience of mortality – 'about what it's like to be creatures who age and die, how medicine has changed the experience and how it hasn't', and how 'things fall apart' as we get older. I know this myself, of course. My hearing is not as good as it used to be, I now wear varifocal spectacles for reading and long-distance vision, and I've got sciatica in my left leg that requires monthly visits to a young chiropractor, David Sweeney, who tweaks my spine to relieve the pressure. I've lost several of my upper teeth, including one in the front, so I have to wear a dental plate contoured to fit the roof of my mouth. I'm also prone to chest infections, due to underlying bronchitis. More seriously, I now have not just one but two stents in my left circumflex artery, to keep it open so that I don't suffer a potentially fatal heart attack. And I can feel my joints creaking, which is an unpleasant reminder that I'm a lot older than I would want to be.

I also worry about which of us, Eamon and myself, will survive the other's death, and how he or I will cope with that. Or whether one or other of us will be afflicted by Alzheimer's disease, like Eamon's mother, or even mild dementia, like both of our fathers, forgetting faces as well as names. We don't have any financial worries, as the flat in Temple Bar is long since paid for, and I feel embarrassed about the state pension money that flows electronically into my bank account week after week, especially when younger people are living on the edge, with short-term contracts and extortionate rents, such that many of them will never have the security of owning a place to call home.

What will be left of me in the end? The books, I suppose, and the *Irish Times* and *Irish Press* archives of all the stories I wrote over more than forty years as a working journalist, if anyone bothers to look them up. But, like my father, I am an incurable romantic, which is why I find this line from William Trevor so affecting: 'Only love matters in the bits and pieces of a person's life.' Or the inscription on the tomb of Philip Larkin in Westminster Abbey: 'What will survive of us is love.' I like to think that it's true.

Acknowledgements

It was a long interview with John Murray on his morning RTÉ radio programme just after I 'retired' from the *Irish Times* in January 2015 that prompted Michael McLoughlin, MD of Penguin Ireland, to call me with the suggestion that I should write a memoir – and he wanted it to be as 'frank' as possible. In doing so, I have reconstructed what it was like to grow up in the Ireland of my childhood and youth, how I coped with being 'queer' then and what I did about it.

As for my working life as a journalist, inevitably I couldn't include all of it in one volume; much of my foreign travels to more than seventy countries, all adventures of one sort or another, will have to wait for another book – a 'follier-upper', in Dublin slang.

I am enormously indebted to Shane O'Toole as well as Aoife and Tony Reddy for reading the entire text in instalments while it was being written, and to Mark Brennock, who suggested the theme of the foreword. I am also very grateful to Catriona Crowe, Deaglán de Bréadún, Patrick Guinness, Annie McCartney, Patsy McGarry, Stephen O'Farrell, Andrew O'Rorke, Andy Pollak, Denis Ryan, Javier Saez, Derek Scally, Joe Smith and Ronnie Storrs for their encouragement as I put together the bits and pieces of my life, and to Carol Coulter, who reminded me of events that I might otherwise have forgotten.

Other former colleagues in the Irish Times, notably Shay Kenny and Irene Stevenson, helped me to find photographs and other archive material. Thanks to the *Irish Times* picture desk for permission to use the following pictures in the insets: first inset – page 8, bottom right and second inset 2 – page 1 (both pictures); page 2 (all three pictures); page 3 (top); page 6 (bottom left). Bernadette Madden took the picture of my family on page 6 of the second inset (top picture). Thanks to Seán Kearns for unearthing his Soil Vent Pipe cartoon strips from the RIAI Journal. Thanks to staff at the National Library of Ireland for helping me to negotiate the new-fangled devices for reading and printing microfilm files. The Philip Larkin line on page 276 is from 'The Arundel Tomb' (*The Whitsun Weddings*). The William Trevor line on the same page is from his novella *Reading Turgenev.*

Having worked together on *The Builders,* I want to record my heartfelt sympathy to Kathy Sheridan, over the untimely death of her dear husband Pat Geraghty in October 2017, and to their daughters Sarah and Mary-Kate.

Thanks to everyone at Penguin Ireland, particularly Brendan Barrington, who did much of the 'heavy lifting'; Michael McLoughlin, who rescued the book at a crucial moment; and the always sympathetic Patricia Deevy, who finished it off.

I cannot forget my sister Edel and brothers Liam and Denis and I'm very grateful to them for their indulgence while I was working on the book. Most of all, I want to thank Eamon for all his love and support over the years, which is why it is dedicated to him as well as to the memory of my parents, to whom I owe so much.

Index